8-31-99

DISCARDED

Robin Hood

Robin Hood

*A Cinematic History of the
English Outlaw and His
Scottish Counterparts*

by

Scott Allen Nollen

McFarland & Company, Inc., Publishers
Jefferson, North Carolina, and London

ALSO BY SCOTT ALLEN NOLLEN
AND FROM MCFARLAND

The Boys:
The Cinematic World of Laurel and Hardy (1989)

Boris Karloff:
A Critical Account of His Screen, Stage, Radio,
Television and Recording Work (1991)

Robert Louis Stevenson:
Life, Literature and the Silver Screen (1994)

Sir Arthur Conan Doyle at the Cinema:
A Critical Study of the Film Adaptations (1996)

Frontispiece: **Errol Flynn as the screen's most memorable outlaw of Sherwood in Warner Bros.' classic** *The Adventures of Robin Hood* **(1938).**

Library of Congress Cataloguing-in-Publication Data

Nollen, Scott Allen, 1963–
    Robin Hood : a cinematic history of the English outlaw and his
Scottish counterparts / by Scott Allen Nollen
      p.   cm.
    Filmography: p.
    Includes bibliographical references and index.
    ISBN 0-7864-0643-7 (library binding : 50# alkaline paper) ∞
    1. Robin Hood (Legendary character) in motion pictures.
    2. Outlaws in motion pictures.   Title.
    PN1995.9.R65N66   1999
    791.43'651—dc21   99-26060
                                                    CIP

British Library Cataloguing-in-Publication data are available

Manufactured in the United States of America

McFarland & Company, Inc., Publishers
  Box 611, Jefferson, North Carolina 28640
   www.mcfarlandpub.com

David Pegg (*right*) and the author

For
my fine English friend,
the remarkable
David Pegg,
whose phenomenal musicianship inspired a
young American lad a quarter-century ago.

Thanks for "Sir Patrick Spens," "To Althea in Prison," "Reynard the Fox," "Wat Tyler" (especially), "Merry Sherwood Rangers," and "Red and Gold" (extra especially), great rebel songs all!

Contents

Preface

Robin Hood was the first hero I ever had. Although I did not see Errol Flynn in *The Adventures of Robin Hood* until I was 17, I was familiar with the legend by the time I was in grammar school. At that time, the part of town I lived in had not yet become overrun with housing development, and there was a large wooded area only a block away that my good friend, Todd ("Dane") Jacobsen, and I referred to as "Sherwood Forest." But Todd, who later became a diehard Errol Flynn fanatic (to the point where he sporadically sported a 1930s-style mustache), always got the plum role of Robin. He was built and tempered for it—and one hell of a tree climber—while I was relegated to playing the faithful sidekick, Little John. The woods I visit now (within a crow's flight) still whisper "Sherwood" to me on occasion (although, as an adult of artistic persuasions, I am more suited to the character of Will Scarlet, while Dane is still "Errol Hood").

This book is perhaps the only volume on cinema ever to cover nearly a millennium, the years 1066–1998. It is not simply a work of film history, but rather a history book including an exhaustive analysis of a specific cinematic subgenre: motion pictures based on the legends of Robin Hood. I have placed a great deal of detail into a chronological narrative, a prospect that seemed daunting at the outset but fell together quite naturally after I had written the first few chapters. Beginning with the period most associated with Robin Hood—the Norman conquest and occupation of England—I have presented an historical background (drawing on the tradition both in England and Scotland) and a survey of ballads, plays and literature to give the reader a firm grasp of the subject before plunging him into a century's worth of cinematic adaptations.

By using this comprehensive approach, I allow the reader to refer

1

to information in earlier chapters whenever encountering a specific historical reference in the later chapters on the films. For example, should the reader wonder why Prince John (Claude Rains) mentions Castle Durnstein in *The Adventures of Robin Hood*, there is no need to seek out an encyclopedia or weighty English history; the reader can merely turn back to the first chapter. The chronological structure also presents a survey of nearly 1000 years in a clear, straightforward manner, rather than inserting all sorts of historical material haphazardly into thematic analyses of the films, therefore creating untold confusion for the reader.

Although I agree with historians Maurice Keen and Stephen Knight that the "real" Robin Hood will probably never be discovered, and that examining the legend is more important than attempting to track down an elusive historical outlaw (something the great medieval historian, Sir J. C. Holt, has attempted to do), I have devoted adequate space to describing the exploits of actual outlaws and contenders for the Robin Hood mantle. (And it is from the works of the three aforementioned historians that I gratefully obtained most of my information.) Unlike my predecessors, I have dedicated a fair amount of space to examining the Scottish candidates, something that will come as no surprise to those familiar with my Scotiaphilia.

Interestingly, I had planned to include material on Scotland's two "Robin Hoods," Sir William Wallace and Rob Roy MacGregor (with a nod to King Robert the Bruce), *before* I knew of the imminent release of two 1995 films—Mel Gibson's *Braveheart* and *Rob Roy*, starring Liam Neeson. I was more than delighted when both proved to be quite excellent, and I greatly expanded my coverage of Wallace and Rob Roy (both being personal heroes) as well as adding a chapter devoted to the two films. Incredibly, this project also afforded me the opportunity of writing about one of my modern heroes, Frank Sinatra: another rebel, to be sure, who made Robin a 1920s (tough yet compassionate) gangster in the 1964 satire *Robin and the Seven Hoods*.

For the proper period atmosphere and essential emotional fuel for long writing sessions, I would like to thank the following musicians: the lutenists Jakob Lindberg, Ronn McFarlane and Paul O'Dette; the vocalist Julianne Baird; and the early music ensemble the Dowland Consort. It seemed hugely appropriate to have music of the Middle Ages and Renaissance emerging from the CD-ROM of my IBM computer as I wrote about how the history of these periods has been married to the modern art of the cinema. For welcome background to my extensive proofreading, I thank my old English and Scottish standbys: the Albion Band, Fairport Convention (*The Cropredy Box* is playing as I complete this preface—thanks, Peggy!), Gryphon, Jethro Tull, Steeleye Span, Andy M. Stewart (whom I *finally* met during the writing of this) and the Tannahill Weavers, as well as the composers of the *Rob Roy* and *Braveheart* scores—Carter Burwell and James Horner, respectively.

For interest, suggestions, encouragement, telling me they were "too busy," or actual help (*real* research materials), I would like to thank Bart Aikens, Seamus Carney, Sean Connery, Sir James Holt, Ernest Mehew, Nicholas Meyer, and the University of Iowa Main Library.

A special acknowledgment is due two individuals who have book-ended my Robin Hood experience: John Jensen, a longtime friend who co-wrote a Robin Hood song with me back in 1988; and Dragi Filipovich, a Serbian transplanted to Australia, who became an invaluable "research assistant" during the last few arrow flights of this project. Thanks, lads!

I am also grateful to my wonderful wife, Cory Ann Nollen, who, prior to marrying me, never had watched a Robin Hood movie with a broadsword in her hand.

Writing this volume has been a unique, pleasurable experience, and I truly believe that it is the first of its particular kind. It is history for film buffs, totally reflective of how I became interested in history in the first place: by watching pseudo-historical adventure films!

Scott Allen Nollen
near "Nollen Castle"
April 1999

Part I

Robin Hood in History

One

Sad Stories of the Death of Kings (1066–1276)

Christmas 1065 was not a happy one for Edward the Confessor. On the eve of his savior's birthday, he had been stricken with another of the cerebral hemorrhages that had laid him low since the previous month. A few days later, this last of the native English kings lay dying on a bed in the West Minster, the abbey on Thorney Island two miles up the Thames from London. Pious Edward considered this house of God the most important accomplishment of his reign, and now he suffered knowing that his illness had prevented him from attending its holy consecration.

So like a king, Edward was not alone as the New Year arrived. The abbey was thronged with members of his household, soldiers, clergymen and high officials of the realm. At his bedside the Queen sat with his feet in her lap, trying to drive the cold winter away. Among those standing close by were Stigand, the Archbishop of Canterbury; Robert FitzWimark, a Breton-Norman friend; and Harold Godwineson, senior earl of England and Edward's closest adviser.

On January 4, 1066, Edward fell unconscious. Attempting to keep him awake, his faithful subjects hoped that the heirless king would name his choice for a successor. A *witena gemot*, or "parliament of the wise," had assembled to make the decision, as Saxon law did not provide formal rules of succession. Restlessly tossing upon his bed, Edward named no kingly favorite but recounted a nightmare in which he had met two long-dead Norman monks who prophesied that, one year and a day after his death, a vengeful God would send devils to cleanse his unholy land with fire and sword.

Prior to drawing his final breath during the wee hours of January 5, Edward commended the protection of the kingdom to Harold

Godwineson. Completing their deliberations, the members of the witena gemot agreed that he was the most obvious candidate to maintain governmental stability. Brother of the queen, Harold was tall and handsome, a capable administrator and formidable soldier who always had been willing to march and fight, often going days without food or sleep in the service of the king. Edward's favorite ambassador, he routinely traveled abroad on important diplomatic missions.

Edward, who had ruled England by consent instead of brute force, was laid to rest in the West Minster the morning after his death; and Harold, who stood by him until the very end, was crowned only a few hours later by Ealdred, the Archbishop of York. Across the channel, in a country no larger than an English earldom, the news of the coronation was not greeted with the enthusiasm displayed by the Anglo-Saxons. Here, William, Duke of Normandy, known as "William the Bastard" because of one of his father's indiscretions, was outraged at a false promise made to him by the late king.

William, who had inherited the duchy of Normandy in 1035 at the age of eight, was not a man to be slighted. In 1047, while still a vassal of the King of France, he had transformed anarchy into national prosperity by defeating an army of rebellious barons and redirecting their innate aggression toward surrounding territories. As ruler of Normandy, a country with no written laws, William, who from youth had lived a warrior's life, enforced his own decrees with an iron hand. In 1051, on a visit to England, he had met with Edward, coming away with the belief that the king had promised him the succession. Such an impression on William's part was not difficult to understand, for Edward, whose mother, Emma, was Norman, had lived in Normandy for 25 years prior to his English coronation in 1042.

Norman chroniclers claimed that Harold, during a voyage across the channel in 1064, fell into William's hands and subsequently served gallantly during a Norman campaign in Brittany. Swearing fealty to William, he was knighted and sent back to England to act as the Duke's advocate—a plan abandoned when he failed to persuade the witena gemot that the Norman should succeed Edward.

Regardless of the facts, William, believing that he had been robbed of the throne, chose to do what no other northern European had ever done: set sail with a chivalric army to conquer another land. Descended from Vikings who had settled in northwest France, the Normans had maintained the adventurous spirit of their ancestors, never losing the urge to subjugate neighboring peoples.

Across the channel, for eight nights beginning April 18, 1066, the English, who had begun to catch wind of the Norman plans, were terrified by a heavenly event many interpreted as a portent of doom: an astronomical phenomenon later known as Halley's Comet. In a terrestrial parallel to the comet's heavenly path, William sought out God's representative on Earth, Pope Alexander II, who approved what subsequently was deemed a holy crusade. Volunteers flocked to William's banner, hoping to gain either the spoils of war or the glory of God, and the fate of England was soon to be decided by the fire and sword that so invaded the dreams of Edward the Confessor.

By mid–August 1066 Harold's forces, bored and worried about their families, had manned the Isle of Wight for over two months without catching sight of an invading force. Waiting for a favorable south wind, William had not been able to sail. Meanwhile, unbeknownst to Harold, his exiled brother, Tostig Godwineson, in an attempt to recapture his forfeited earldom, had persuaded the ferocious Viking leader, King Harald Hardrada of Norway, to invade England from the north.

On August 12 Hardrada and his fleet of berserkers sailed for Scotland. On September 8, Harold's English army left the Isle of Wight, assured that William, although not an experienced seaman, would not be rash enough to sail after the autumnal equinox (September 14 on the calendar used in 1066): historically no sailor in his right mind had ever braved a winter sea in the channel.

On September 19, only a few days after Harold reached London, Hardrada's Vikings landed in Northumbria. Although the Norsemen won some early victories at Scarborough and York, Harold's forces, which marched north on September 20, decimated them at Stamford Bridge, killing Hardrada and Tostig, on the 25th. Two days later William of Normandy, against all seaman's logic, finally set sail, landing at Pevensey on the 28th.

About three days later Harold received news of the Norman landing and the villages along the southern coast that were being laid waste by William's army. By October 5 he had marched back to London, where he quickly dispatched a message to his royal rival. On October 9 or 10 he learned of his excommunication, realizing that he and all his countrymen would be condemned to Hell if they resisted the invaders who had been blessed by the Pope.

Rejecting his brother Gyrth's offer to meet William on the field of battle, Harold decided to place the entire affair in the hands of God. He would lead the army himself and face the Normans at Hastings, an area that William had chosen for navigational reasons, on October 14. Although the Norman army numbered about 8,000, Harold had a somewhat larger force, more than sufficient to defend the ridge above where William had drawn up his men in three divisions of Bretons, Normans and Frenchmen, who were further split into groups of archers, infantry and horse. But while William demonstrated an impressive strategic ability, Harold was unable to command his motley mass, the largest Anglo-Saxon force ever to take the field.

The fatalistic Harold never issued a general order; or if he did, his men never heard him. His belief that God would render judgement during this single battle sealed the fate of all who fought with him, and the disorganized Saxons surrendered when he was killed by William and three Norman knights. (It is believed that Harold was blinded by an arrow before being hacked to pieces.)

Having lost about 3,000 men, William declared himself king, although a witena gemot had quickly elected Edgar, Harold's exiled 13-year-old brother, to take the throne. The archbishops would not support this decision, however, and they spread propaganda that God had punished Harold and England as William and his army burned and plundered a path to London. On Christmas Day 1066 the Archbishop of York crowned William at the West Minster, giving the Church's sanction to a five-year reign of terror that ended with 300,000 English, both rich and poor, being murdered or starved to death. Harsh taxes, thievery of homes and monasteries, the harrying of great tracts of land, and the disinheritance of the landowning class were accompanied by imprisonment, blindings with hot irons, castrations, and the construction of stone castles and prisons that never before had existed in England.

Early Outlaws of England

Outraged at King William's policy of parceling out seized Saxon lands to his Norman followers, some English were brave enough to organize rebellions against the crown. Sometimes these rebels were declared "outlaws," individuals placed outside the protection of the law who had no rights and could not be aided by their countrymen. Often these outcasts took to the forests of England, areas that provided refuge from the limited law enforcement of local sheriffs.

From 1067 to 1070 Eadric the Wild, a Herefordshire squire, harried the Welsh border but eventually paid liege to William, joining in his invasion of Scotland in 1072. Around 1071 Hereward the Wake, considered to be the first major English outlaw, organized a resistance that defended beseiged garrisons in East Anglia. Supported by the monks of Ely Island, and through the efforts of his wife, Alfthrida, Hereward eventually was reconciled with William. Although these local rebellions were ruthlessly suppressed, they were a great embarrassment to the Normans. With Saxon resistance nearly eliminated, William introduced the severe Forest Laws in 1079, destroying entire villages and evicting inhabitants from the New Forest, which he claimed as his royal hunting preserve.

Six years later William, maintaining a strict feudal grip on the realm, ordered his commissioners to compile a survey of all the shires of England excepting those in the far north. He desired a comprehensive record of population, ownership and tenancy, the condition and value of each tract of land, and the number of livestock on each holding. During the following year, 1086, William published this national ledger as the *Domesday Book* and demanded that all the lords and tenants-in-chief renew their oaths of fealty to him at Salisbury. A year later, after falling from his horse during a siege at Nantes in France, he died.

The Normans ruled England for another 67 years. William II, third son of William the Conqueror, became king upon his father's death, suppressing baronial rebellions in 1088 and 1095, as well as a Welsh invasion in 1098, two years before being killed during a hunt in the New Forest. He was succeeded by his younger brother, Henry, who may have engineered the "accident" that ended his life.

The reformist Henry I, nicknamed "Beauclerc," sought to better relations between the crown and its feudal tenants, but was often quite wicked. In 1101 he quelled an invasion led by his elder brother, Robert, whom William the Conqueror, shortly before his death, had appointed Duke of Normandy. In 1135 Beauclerc died of food poisoning after eating a surfeit of lamphreys near Rouen, France, leaving the kingdom to his daughter, Matilda, who had become the successor after her brother and the rightful heir, William, had drowned in 1120.

It was during this period that the concept of knightly chivalry was refined. In 1095 Pope Urban II had issued a command that all young men of good families, upon reaching age 12, should swear an oath before a bishop to defend the oppressed and care for noblewomen, widows and orphans. English knights closely patterned themselves after the French prototype—the "policeman of church and state" who was loyal first to God and then to the liege lord who held the fief on which he served. Although women earlier had been thought of as mere appendages of men, they now, thanks to the troubadours of France, began to replace the church and the liege lord as the main chivalric concern of knights. Thereafter, war was viewed as a proving ground for love as well as a way of acquiring riches and land.

At Clermont in November 1095 Urban II called for all Christians to remove the ungodly Saracens from the Holy Land, and the First Crusade departed on August 15 the following year. Destitute peasants wishing to evade the yoke of their oppressive masters joined the throng, eventually helping to recapture Jerusalem on August 12, 1099, two weeks after Urban passed away.

Enticed by the riches of the exotic Moslem world, the Normans who went on the crusade quickly abandoned religious fervor for self indulgence, contributing to an apathy that necessitated a second crusade during the spring of 1146. Desiring to retake the ground lost since the First Crusade, Pope Eugenius III designed the Second Crusade to establish militarily "the Eastern Christian Kingdom," but disorganized strategy and the various agendas of national factions within the army doomed it to failure.

When Henry I's daughter, Matilda, prepared to succeed to the English throne in 1135, she was overthrown by her cousin, Stephen, another grandchild of William the Conqueror, who had received the support of many powerful barons. A polite and gentle man who was not averse to mucking in with the peasants, Stephen did not govern with the firmness required of a king, although he was quite fearless in battle. During his reign he fought a continuous civil war with the adherents of Matilda, who finally abandoned her cause in 1148. Five years later her son, Henry Plantagenet, ruler of the Angevin Empire (consisting of the French duchies of Anjou, Touraine, Normandy and Aquitaine), raised an army to resume the war. At Wallingford in 1153 Henry and Stephen signed the Treaty of Westminster, which, upon the death of the latter, called for the English throne to pass to the Plantagenet line and not to Stephen's son, William.

The End of Norman Rule

Stephen died the following year, ending the "nineteen long winters" that had brought such misery to England. Only 21 upon his accession in 1154, Henry Plantagenet greatly regulated the power of the church, appointing Thomas à Becket Chancellor of England in 1155 and Archbishop of Canterbury in 1162. Strong and energetic, with fiery red hair and freckles, Henry, who is considered the greatest of the Plantagenet kings, was beneficent to the poor, just in legal matters, and the possessor of a staggering intellect. In 1166, exactly one century after William the Conqueror's invasion, one of Henry's legal reforms led to the establishment of the right to trial by jury—quite a change from the law practiced by the Normans. Another of his reforms, designed to curb the abuses of the clergy, led to a quarrel with Becket, who, after opposing the king a second time in December 1170, was murdered by four knights in Canterbury Cathedral. Two years after he successfully invaded Ireland in 1171, establishing an English occupation that lasted for 700 years, Henry was attacked by his rebellious sons, Richard and Geoffrey, but ruled until his death in 1189.

Although the Normans reigned in England for less than a century, every aspect of Anglo-Saxon life was altered as a result of the occupation. But amid this national catastrophe some of the changes, such as improvements in agricultural techniques and better methods of architectural engineering, were greatly beneficial.

Norman military techniques, particularly the use of the bow, also brought innovations to England, for the Anglo-Saxons had made no significant use of archery prior to the conquest. Like his Norman successors, William the Conqueror was an accomplished archer, apparently so mighty that only he could draw the string of his formidable longbow. One of the Saxon outlaws, Robert Boet, who led a band of rebels before being captured and hanged, was also an archer of some repute. Due to the Norman use of the bow, archery became an important part of English warfare long before the Hundred Years War of 1337–1453, a period previously pinpointed as the true birth of the longbow as a major weapon of great effectiveness.

Richard the Lionheart

Richard Plantagenet, third son of Henry II and Eleanor of Aquitaine, was born at Beaumont Palace, Oxford, on September 8, 1157. Tall, athletic and powerful in the arts of war, he became Duke of Aquitaine in 1174 and acceded to the throne of England upon the death of his father in September 1189. Although the English hoped he would continue the reforms established by his master politician father, Richard instead arrived in England to raise money and troops for the Third Crusade to the Holy Land.

Only three months after his coronation, Richard sailed from Dover to make arrangements for the crusade with King Philip of France. Pope Clement III had persuaded the two kings and Emperor Frederick Barbarossa of Germany to lead this new, well-organized venture to recapture Jerusalem from Saladin, the courageous Kurdish sultan who was determined to end Christian influence in the Moslem lands.

Prior to leaving England, Richard honored promises made by his late father, presenting his younger brother, John, with the counties of Cornwall, Devon, Dorset, Somerset, Derby and Nottingham, and the county of Mortain in Normandy, while maintaining control over the most important castles in these territories. By allowing John to remain in England rather than taking him on the crusade, Richard protected the future of the Angevin dynasty, but he also withheld the reigns of power to keep his brother's ambitions in check.

To govern the realm in his absence, Richard appointed Hugh de Puiset as chief justiciar and William Longchamp as chancellor, two men who soon began to quarrel. Keeping abreast of matters while abroad, Richard increased Longchamp's authority as chancellor, justiciar, and papal legate of England. One month later, on July 4, 1190, he and King Philip, leading a combined army of about 6,000, set off from Vezelay on the crusade. Seeking plunder as well as religious glory, the two monarchs agreed to split the spoils equally but quickly realized that they must divide their forces to locate adequate provisions.

During his tumultuous occupation of Sicily, in October 1190, Richard signed a treaty with the diminutive King Tancred in which he declared his two-year-old nephew, Arthur, son of his exiled brother, Geoffrey, as heir to the English throne. Four months later, Richard received word of tensions that were mounting between Longchamp and Prince John. Prior to leaving Sicily, Richard reputedly renewed his agreement with Tancred by exchanging Excalibur, the famous sword of King Arthur, for 19 ships to transport his army and weapons across the Mediterranean.

En route to Palestine, Richard captured the island of Cyprus, where his army took hostages and provisioned for the short journey to the mainland. On June 5, 1191, they set sail, reaching Tyre the next day. By June 8 Richard joined the army already laying siege to Acre, a garrison that had been targeted by the Christian forces for more than two years. The Lionheart's presence greatly inspired the weary French, Austrian and German crusaders. After the Christian army repulsed one final attack by Saladin's forces, the garrison capitulated and accepted surrender terms on July 12.

Frederick Barbarossa had died of plague in Antioch, and, as agreed, Richard planned to share the victory with Philip of France. But when Duke Leopold of Austria raised his standard over the defeated garrison, Richard, considering him to be a minor player in the siege, angrily tore it down. Denied any share in the plunder, Leopold thereafter branded Richard his enemy, while Philip, wracked by a lengthy illness, left for France on July 31.

Having demanded a substantial ransom, including a return of Christian prisoners, from Saladin, Richard became enraged when it did not arrive on time and, during the afternoon of August 20, ordered his army to massacre 3,000 captives within full view of the Moslem army. In Richard's eyes, and those of the 12th-century Christian church, the lives of unbelievers—creatures doomed to Hell—were of no human value; they were merely bargaining chips that had not prompted the appropriate response from the enemy. Ironically, Saladin was still trying to raise the money portion of the ransom when his people were butchered, cash that henceforth was distributed among his troops.

Marching his army to Arsuf, near Jaffa, Richard defeated Saladin on September 7. After opening negotiations with the defeated enemy in October, he headed to Jerusalem, where a lengthy siege eventually wore down the crusaders.

While continuing negotiations with Saladin, Richard, in mid–April 1192, received word of Prince John's continued troublemaking in England. Longchamp had held out until the spring of 1191, when he was persuaded to accept John as the heir apparent in the event that Richard died during the crusade. On September 18, 1191, the chancellor played into John's hands when his men arrested Geoffrey, Richard and John's half-brother, who had returned to England in defiance of the order that had exiled him for three years. With the clergy turned against him, and John's friends beginning an outrageous propaganda campaign, Longchamp, dressed in drag, attempted to flee the country but was jailed in Dover before managing to sail to Flanders.

   Signing a truce with Saladin that allowed both Christians and
Moslems to pass through each other's territory for a period of three
years, Richard, ill and troubled by the tense political situation in England, set sail from Acre in October 1192, bringing an end to the Third
Crusade. Discovering that all routes home appeared to be blocked, either
for political or climatic reasons, Richard was shipwrecked near Venice
before planning to pass through Austria, a domain belonging to the duke
whom he had offended at Acre. Disguising himself and his companions
as pilgrims returning from the Holy Land, Richard only stopped for
provisions when in dire need but, by the time he reached Vienna around
Christmas 1192, he could hold out no longer. Less than 50 miles from
the safety of the Moravian border, he was captured by Duke Leopold's
men and imprisoned in Durnstein Castle, set on a cliff high above the
Danube.

   For more than a year Leopold of Austria (who was excommuni-
cated by Pope Celestine III), Henry VI of Germany and Philip of France
wrangled over a ransom while Richard languished in Durnstein. In mid–
January 1193 Prince John traveled to France to pay homage to Philip for
Normandy and England, promising to marry his daughter, Alice, and
turn over the lands of Gisors and the Norman Vexin. He then consulted
Philip's father-in-law, Baldwin, Count of Flanders, who helped raise a
fleet for a proposed invasion of England. Manning the castles of Windsor and Wallingford with mercenaries from Wales and Flanders, the wily
John spread propaganda that Richard had died; but his mother, Eleanor
of Aquitaine, supported by the justiciars and barons, knew better, and
already had sent troops to the southern coast to forestall the invasion.

   On March 25, 1193, Richard agreed to pay a ransom of 100,000
marks and deliver to Henry VI 50 galleys and 200 knights for a year-
long invasion of Sicily. After he was moved to solitary confinement in
Germany, his old friend, William Longchamp, negotiated a date for his
release, provided that 70,000 marks were paid and hostages for the
unpaid balance had been delivered. Receiving letters from Richard and
Henry VI, Eleanor and the English justiciars appropriated the national
wool crop and gold and silver plate from churches throughout the realm,
as well as ordering a 25 per-cent income tax. Meanwhile, Philip of
France began attacking John's Angevin lands. When a six-month truce
was arranged in order for the English to raise the ransom money, John
was commanded to hand over three castles to his mother while retaining control over those at Tickhill and Nottingham.

During the spring and early summer of 1193, while Philip continued to threaten Normandy, Richard, from within his prison walls, attempted to negotiate an agreement between the French king and the German emperor. In June he was successful, but only after accepting a treaty with Henry VI that increased the ransom to 100,000 marks in cash and hostages worth another 50,000 marks. On July 9 Philip agreed to halt his invasion of Normandy, provided that he keep the lands already captured; and, to place a further burden on the English, he demanded that Richard pay 20,000 marks soon after his release.

On February 4, 1194, after a last attempt to renegotiate was made by Philip and Prince John, the ransom was met and Richard was set free at Mainz in Germany. After landing at Sandwich on March 13, the grateful king prayed at the shrines of Canterbury and Bury St. Edmunds before taking part in the siege of the only castle still holding out for Prince John—the garrison at Nottingham—on March 25–27. The victorious Lionheart demanded stiff ransoms from the defeated knights before retiring to Sherwood Forest for a bit of hunting. Back in Nottingham he organized legal proceedings against his treacherous brother and those who had supported the would-be king.

On April 17, 1194, Richard participated in a crown-wearing in Winchester Cathedral, where he demonstrated to the English barons that he was the true king. Less than a month later he sailed from Portsmouth for Normandy, never again to set foot on English soil. Remarkably, the provisional governments he had set up in England, Aquitaine, Anjou and Normandy had operated well during his two-and-one-half year absence on the crusade and in prison.

Richard the Lionheart spent the remainder of his life attending to Angevin matters, often quelling rebellions and the incursions of Philip of France. During the evening of March 26, 1199, while besieging the castle of Chalus-Chabrol in the Limousin, he was struck in the left shoulder by a bolt fired by Bertrand de Gurdon, a lone crossbowman using a frying pan for a shield. Intending to observe the state of the siege, Richard, wearing no armor except a helmet and carrying a rectangular shield, was caught tragically off guard. Choosing to act as if nothing had happened, he returned to his tent, where he tried to remove the bolt but only managed to snap off the shaft, leaving the six-inch iron barb inside his shoulder. Forced to call for a surgeon, Richard remained resolute as the bolt was literally chopped out in torchlight. Aware that the castle had fallen to his forces, he endured the pain of gangrene as he addressed Gurdon, forgiving the bowman for his act of self defense. On the evening of April 7, 1199, in a tent outside the walls of Chalus-Chabrol, Richard the Lionheart died, aged only 41 and one-half years. Against his orders, Gurdon, the man he had released, was flayed alive.

King John

Although Richard had sired a bastard son, Philip, who was appointed Lord of Cognac, he was unable to produce a legitimate heir with his wife, Berengaria, daughter of King Sancho VI of Navarre, whom he had married on May 12, 1191, during his stay in Sicily. By 1197, realizing that his youthful nephew, Arthur, was no fit successor, he recognized John as heir presumptive, a decision he reiterated as he lay dying at Chalus-Chabrol.

John was crowned King of England in Westminster Abbey on May 27, 1199. Less than five years later, he had lost Normandy and Anjou to Philip of France. Soon after, his quarrels with Innocent III resulted in a papal interdict against England and his excommunication in 1209. In 1213, one year after the pope declared that he was no longer the rightful King of England, John agreed to Innocent's choice of Stephen Langton as Archbishop of Canterbury.

Known for his able financial administration, John was particularly adept at levying harsh taxes, including a 1207 effort that raised the huge sum of £57,000. With the English nobles smarting at his high level of taxation, and the defeat of his army by Philip's French forces at the Battle of Bouvines in 1214, John's reign steadily led England toward disaster.

Later in 1214 the barons of the realm gathered at the abbey of Bury St. Edmunds in Suffolk to draw up demands to be presented to King John. On June 15, 1215, in a field at Runnymede near Windsor, John, averting civil war, sealed a draft of Magna Carta (the Great Charter) which included 63 clauses defining the relationship between the crown and its subjects. Wishing to end the abuse of royal power, the barons demanded reforms in taxation, foreign policy, the courts and the church. By June 19 copies of the charter had been sent to various parts of the kingdom, and barons who had renounced John once again paid homage to him.

Soon after, Pope Innocent decreed that John did not have to adhere to the demands set down in Magna Carta, and civil war broke out between the barons and the crown. In 1216, aided by the French, the rebels captured the Tower of London. Having lost a war chest loaded with money and jewels, John, "the most overrated king in English history,"[1] died at Newark Castle in Lincolnshire on October 18, 1216.

Henry III, eldest son of John and Isabella of Angouleme, was only nine when crowned in Gloucester Cathedral on October 28, 1216. In one of his wisest decisions, John had chosen two effective regents, William the Marshal, Earl of Pembroke, and Hubert de Burgh, to manage the realm until his son reached adulthood. Although the rebellious barons attempted to bring Louis, Dauphin of France, to the throne, the combined force of the coronation and the King's army brought them to heel. In 1227, eight years after the death of William the Marshal, Henry III assumed control of the realm while retaining Burgh as his chief adviser.

Robert Hod, Outlaw, and Other Rebels

During the regency period of Henry III's reign, at assizes held by royal justices in York on July 25, 1225, Robert Hod, a tenant, was listed as a fugitive owing 32s. 6d. to the Liberty of St. Peter's. At Michaelmas 1226 he was formally charged at the Exchequer in London. The next year the charge again appeared, this time naming him as "Hobbehod." In the words of J. C. Holt, "Robert Hood had fled the jurisdiction of the court. He was an outlaw. He is the only possible original of Robin Hood, so far discovered, who is known to have been an outlaw."[2]

This possible model for the Robin Hood of legend was outlawed 27 years after the death of Richard the Lionheart, the king with whom the character is so often identified. The most famous version of the legend, made popular centuries after the conflicts between Richard and John, has no basis in historical fact. As Holt argues, "[T]here is not the slightest indication that Robin played any part in English resistance to the Norman conquerors who settled in England after 1066. Of all the fictions about Robin this is the most fictitious."[3] There is a similarity between Richard and Robin, however: in the popular mind, both figures are known, not as historical realities, but as mythically romantic characters. And while we know that Richard the Lionheart truly lived, we cannot prove the same existence for Robin Hood, though the latter will continue to be indelibly linked with the former in literature, drama, and the imagination of the masses.

As the following pages demonstrate, this linkage has been established and strengthened by the historical facts about Richard I that have been woven into the fabric of the Robin Hood legend. As Lionheart biographer John Gillingham admits, "the real Richard was very like the figure of romance. He did return from crusade in disguise and was captured and thrown into a German prison"[4]—one of several actual events featured in countless versions of the outlaw tale. As Gillingham notes, Richard "was the first king since the Norman conquest to become a folk hero, a status he had achieved as early as the mid-thirteenth century."[5] Is it perhaps natural that England's most mythicized royal folk hero should become associated with Robin Hood, the nation's *most famous* folk hero? And, as far as drama is concerned, the fact that the latter is an outlawed rebel can comfortably place him within the context of the nation's most cataclysmic upheaval: the Norman Conquest, when the brutally oppressed Saxons could have used a champion as resourceful as the legendary Robin.

Although he reigned for 56 years, Henry III was an ineffectual leader, childish and irascible, and as often angered advisers as he did enemies. After marrying Eleanor of Provence in 1236, he began to award important government offices to foreigners, including three of his wife's uncles. In 1258 the English barons, fed up with Henry's blatant misrule, joined the rebellion of the Anglo-French lord Simon de Montfort, the king's brother-in-law and former ambassador, who drew up a list of suggested reforms at Oxford. Henry signed the Provisions of Oxford, thus limiting his own power, but three years later, reneged on his agreement, precipitating a civil war that led to his defeat and capture by Montfort at the Battle of Lewes.

In January 1265, with Henry as his prisoner, Montfort convened the first parliament in London, summoning four knights from each shire and two burgesses from each major town as well as the lords, bishops and abbots of the realm. Montfort was the first English administrator to include all classes (excepting serfs) in the affairs of government but, later that year, some of the barons abandoned him to support Henry's son, Edward, whose forces killed Montfort at the Battle of Evesham.

During the 1440s the Scottish historian Walter Bower wrote that a "famous murderer, Robert Hood,"[6] led a rebellion of the dispossessed in the year 1266, a date that parallels the activities of Montfort's disinherited barons who continued to oppose the crown after Henry III was reinstated. In fact, between 1266 and 1272, the year Henry III died at Westminster, a former supporter of Montfort named Roger Godberd led a rebel campaign throughout Nottinghamshire, Derbyshire and Leicestershire. In 1267 Godberd fought two engagements (one in Sherwood Forest) with Roger de Leyburn, lieutenant of Reginald de Grey, the king's constable at Nottingham Castle. Prior to his capture in 1272, Godberd may have been sheltered by Richard Foliot, a local knight who previously had helped Henry III restore order in Nottinghamshire, Derbyshire and Yorkshire, but soon after developed criminal connections that led to the confiscation of his lands. However, due to the intervention of several Montfortian knights who testified for Foliot, his estates, some of which bordered Sherwood Forest, were reinstated. These activities of Godberd and Foliot parallel events in the famous ballad "A Gest of Robin Hode," written in the early to mid-1400s (and discussed further in chapter four).

Another criminal incident related to Sherwood occurred in 1276, when two men illegally carrying bows and arrows were arrested by John de Lascelles, the steward of the forest, who, intending to turn them over to the Sheriff of Nottingham, confined them at Bledworth for the night. After darkness fell, 20 armed men broke into the house, accosted the servants, and set the prisoners free.

Two

Was Robin Hood
a Scot? (1066–1329)

From the time of the Norman Conquest until the death of Henry III, conflicts between England and Scotland were minor, short-lived affairs. During this period, clashes between the two nations were precipitated by their mutual claims on England's northern counties of Northumberland, Cumberland and Westmorland, with Scottish kings either invading or attempting to negotiate for them.

During his 36-year reign, Malcolm III, the first of the Canmore kings and the slayer of Macbeth so ahistorically glorified by William Shakespeare, attacked northern England several times. After invading Cumberland in 1071, he was defeated in Perthshire by William the Conqueror. Undaunted, Malcolm invaded the northern shires three more times before he was killed at Alnwick in 1093.

Following Malcolm's death, serious warfare between England and Scotland ceased for several decades. Embracing the overlordship of William II, Edgar (reigned 1097–1107) and Alexander (reigned 1107–24) brought peace to Scotland but also allowed the Norman feudal system to establish a foothold. Under David I (reigned 1124–53), the younger brother of Edgar and Alexander, feudalism was developed even further. Prior to being crowned King of Scots, David had accepted lands from Henry I and, by wedding Maud, a niece of William the Conqueror and daughter of Waltheof, Earl of Northumberland, he had become Earl of Huntingdon (a title later attributed to Robin Hood by some writers). King David integrated Norman ideas and customs into Scottish politics and culture, but, like Malcolm III, invaded northern England to be defeated at Northallerton in 1138. During this period Norman knights made considerable inroads, acquiring Scottish estates through intermarriages

22

with Celtic heiresses rather than seizing them by force of arms. Part Celtic themselves, these Normans were easily assimilated into Scottish culture.

In 1153 David was succeeded by his grandson, Malcolm IV, a 12-year-old who fell under the influence of Norman advisers. Twice offered aid from Henry II to quash rebellions, this Malcolm traded away the Scots claim on Northumberland in 1157. Eight years later he died, passing the kingship to his brother, William, called "the Lion" because of his standard bearing a red lion rampant on a yellow field. On the throne for nearly 50 years, he renewed the Scots' efforts to annex the north of England, particularly in 1173 while Henry was busy dealing with his rebellious sons. A year later, captured during a raid into Northumberland, William was forced to swear allegiance to Henry, thereafter holding Scotland only by permission of the English king.

Prior to embarking on the Third Crusade, Richard the Lionheart, who received 10,000 silver marks (or £7000) from William, restored Scottish independence. During Richard's absence, however, Prince John stirred up trouble on both sides of the Tweed, effectively stifling the Scottish claim on the northern shires.

While John was occupied with the Barons' War and the signing of Magna Carta, William's son, Alexander II, mounted an invasion but was defeated by English forces. When Henry III succeeded John, Alexander exchanged his claim on the north for an income from some of the estates in that region. His son, Alexander III, who ruled from 1249 to 1286, a period later referred to as Scotland's "golden age," further increased English influence by wedding Henry III's daughter, Margaret.

The Hammer of the Scots

After recapturing the English throne for Henry III, Prince Edward Plantagenet, an unusually tall man called "Longshanks," succeeded his father in 1272. Away in Palestine on the Eighth Crusade, he was not crowned until August 19, 1274, in Westminster Abbey, where, four years later, he accepted an oath of allegiance from Alexander III, who had arrived to pay homage for his lands in England. Although he accepted his position as Edward's vassal, Alexander substantially bettered the standard of living for all classes of Scots.

On the storm-lashed evening of March 18, 1286, while riding along a mountainside in Fife, Alexander, anxious to reach Yolande de Dreux, his newlywed bride, in Kinghorn, toppled over a cliff, breaking his neck on the shore below. The final Canmore king, Alexander was also the last true Scot to sit on the throne, his successors being of primarily Norman or French descent.

While Alexander ruled, Edward I, in an effort to unify the two kingdoms, had strengthened his influence in Scotland through marriages and other alliances. A remarkable administrator, Longshanks had reformed legal issues that had troubled his own kingdom for decades. A year before Alexander's tragic death, Edward's Statute of Winchester had created England's first Justices of the Peace to deal with highway robbery and local violence. A decade later, in 1295, he devised an early form of representative democracy with the Model Parliament, a partially elected body of lords, knights, burgesses and members of the clergy.

Except for border disputes, the occasional indiscretions of Scots nobles in England, and disagreements over the earldom of Huntingdon, serious tensions between the two countries had ended with the death of Henry III. But when Alexander perished tragically on the sands of Fife, the stability of Scotland died with him. Previously playing cards of diplomacy and intrigue, Longshanks now showed the ace up his sleeve. Having conquered rebellious Wales two years earlier, he was keen to add Scotland to his domain, thus truly uniting all of Britain under the Plantagenet banner.

Alexander III's only heir was his four-year-old granddaughter, Margaret, daughter of King Eric of Norway—a reality that added to the turmoil brewing over the Scottish succession. Since no female, particularly an infant one, had ever sat upon the throne, a regency composed of six nobles was quickly appointed to rule until a new king could be chosen from eligible claimants. Wasting no opportunity, Edward proposed that young Queen Margaret be betrothed to his two-year-old son, Edward of Caernarvon.

During 1290, as the Scottish guardians, the royal claimants and Edward continued to wrangle over the succession, little Margaret, while sailing from Norway to Scotland, died after a storm stranded her ship in the Orkneys. Twelve claimants, descended from William the Lion, Duncan I or Alexander II, now came forward. Two of them, descended from William the Lion's brother, David of Huntingdon, were strong contenders: John Balliol, grandson of David's eldest daughter, and Robert Bruce of Annandale, son of David's second daughter. Bruce, whose ancestor, Adam de Brus, had invaded with William the Conqueror in 1066, had been named as heir presumptive by Alexander II in 1238 but ultimately lost out when Alexander III was born three years later.

On November 17, 1292, at a court in Berwick, Edward, now calling himself "Lord Superior of Scotland," declared John Balliol the rightful heir to the throne. Before he was crowned at Scone on November 30, Balliol swore fealty to the English king, an act he repeated at Newcastle the following month. Less than three years later, however, encouraged by a committee of nobles assembled at Scone, he refused to raise troops for Edward's proposed war against Philip of France, claiming that he had paid homage under duress. When Edward retaliated by seizing his English lands, Balliol banished all English landowners from Scotland and turned over their estates, including the Annandale holdings of the Bruces, to his brother-in-law, John Comyn, Earl of Badenoch, one of the former guardians.

Robert Bruce, called "the Competitor" because of his longtime claim to the throne, passed away in 1295, leaving behind his son (b. 1253) and grandson (b. 1274), both named Robert, to continue the fight. Anxious to recapture their Annandale estates, the Bruces swore allegiance to Edward, who began his invasion of Scotland with an appalling massacre at Berwick on March 30, 1296.

Adding to the 17,000 men, women and children who were slaughtered at Berwick, 10,000 more Scots died defending their country before Comyn and a hundred of Balliol's barons were captured. In June 1296 Edward arrived in Edinburgh, where his siege engines broke the will of those manning the castle, and then moved on to Linlithgow, Stirling and Perth. Scots knights were hanged, wives and maidens raped, pregnant women disemboweled, livestock and household goods plundered.

Ironically, prior to Edward's march north, John Comyn had exacted similar Scottish atrocities upon innocent English women and children, burning churches and villages during his plundering of Northumberland. Having been thwarted in his raid into Cumberland by young Robert Bruce, who believed he was fighting not Scotland but the power of his undeserving rivals, Comyn had crossed into Northumberland seeking vengeance.

On July 2, 1296, Edward received a pathetic plea for peace from Balliol, who accused his evil committee of turning him against his English superior. The following week Balliol surrendered at Durham, where he had the red and gold insignia of Scotland torn from his tunic. Thereafter, his countrymen referred to him derisively as "Toom Tabard," the empty jacket. With Balliol packed away to prison, Edward continued his murderous march north to the Moray Firth; by the time he returned to England five months later, he had stolen the archives and regalia of Scotland, the ancient Stone of Destiny on which the nation's kings had been crowned at Scone, and the allegiance of 2,000 noblemen, clergy, burgesses and freeholders who were forced to sign what came to be known as the Ragman Rolls. Among the nobles who signed were both Robert Bruces, who soon recovered the Annandale estates. Returning to the comfort of Westminster, Longshanks truly had earned the famous epithet "Hammer of the Scots."

Sir William Wallace

Around 1274, the same year that Edward was crowned at Westminster, a brown-haired lad of Norman and Celtic, perhaps Welsh, descent was born, the second son of Sir Malcolm Wallace and Margaret de Craufurd (daughter of Sir Ranald de Craufurd of Corsbie, Sheriff of Ayrshire). The son of a chief councillor to Alexander III, Sir Malcolm possessed a love of freedom that was passed on to William when the lad was quite young.

For the first decade of his life, with Alexander III still on the throne, William enjoyed the benefits of a reign blessed by economic and political stability. After the king's tragic death, however, he may have served as squire to his father during the spring of 1287, when the guardians called up the Scottish knights to put down a suspected revolt.

Under the tutelage of his uncle, a cleric at Cambuskenneth Abbey, William learned Latin, heightened his appreciation of liberty, and developed a cunning intellect sharpened further by studying history and science, reportedly at Paisley Abbey and at a church school in Dundee (where he met his life-long companion, John Blair, who later would write a chronicle of his exploits). His studies may have resulted in his learning to read and write three languages: Gaelic, Latin and French.

In July 1291 William's father refused to take an oath of fealty to Edward Longshanks and fled with his eldest son (also named Malcolm) to hide out in the wilderness of Lennox. Some time later that year he was cut down by the blade of an English officer named Fenwick at Loudoun Hill in the Irvine Valley.

After his father's death, during a period when the Scots were ordered to hand over their castles to the English, William became involved in various skirmishes with "Southron" soldiers, including one in Dundee during December 1291. Responding to the taunts of Selby, son of the Constable of Dundee Castle, by hewing him down to the ground, Wallace escaped (reputedly by dressing in drag) to Gowrie and then to Dunipace with his mother.

Back in Ayrshire, William learned that he had been declared an outlaw. In February 1292 he hid in the relative obscurity of his uncle, Sir Richard's, home in Riccarton, where he again fell afoul of the dreaded Southrons. On February 23, while catching some trout for his uncle's dinner table, he was caught off guard (and unarmed) at nearby Irvine Water by five soldiers who demanded his hard-won harvest. Angered by his upstart refusal, one of the soldiers slashed with his sword, only to have it knocked from his hand by William's fishing pole and his head pummelled by the mighty Scot's fist. Grabbing the man's sword, William buried the blade in the hapless Southron's neck and then turned to the other four. Two of them soon joined their fallen comrade, and the remaining pair fled for their lives. Later, when the two Englishmen reported the incident to their commander, they were met with scoffs and laughter. A giant parrying swords with a fishing pole? But in an age when the average man stood just over five feet tall, there were not many like Wallace, who reportedly stood at the gargantuan height of six-feet-seven.

Now living as a roving brigand seeking shelter in the vast forest of Selkirk, William gathered together his first band of outlaws and dispossessed men, including cousins and other relatives, at his uncle's house in Riccarton. In 1296 he planned to avenge his father's murder by attacking a supply convoy led by Fenwick as it moved from Lanark to Ayr. After dropping boulders to block the progress of 180 heavily armored, mounted soldiers, Wallace and 50 lightly armed kinsmen and comrades quickly dispatched 100, causing the remainder to flee and leave behind valuable weapons, provisions, currency and 200 pack animals. Among the dead was the hated Fenwick. But Wallace had acted for reasons other than revenge. After the dust settled, he and his men transported the booty into the forest of Clydesdale, where it was distributed to all who supported his cause. Here, as in the many boundless forests of Scotland, desperate men, while sharing the rugged terrain with deer, boars and wolves, could find refuge from their enemies.

Hearing of the victory of Wallace's small motley band over a large professional fighting force, landless men, Irish exiles and outlaws from Selkirk Forest began to join his ranks. Wallace, who now was formally outlawed, became part of the rebellion against England, a conflict that gained momentum when Edward appointed three hardline officials, John de Warenne, William Ormsby, and Hugh de Cressingham, to govern Scotland. In fact, Wallace's exploits at this time became so well known that the famous poet Sir Thomas of Erceldoune (Thomas the Rhymer) composed a verse extolling his courageous virtues.

After conferring with Robert Wishart, Bishop of Glasgow, who continued to support King John Balliol, Wallace and 60 men captured the pele-tower of Gargunnock near Stirling and then headed north to set up camp in Methven Wood. Emerging from a heavily wooded hollow, the outlaws attacked a convoy from Perth, killing Sir James Butler of Kinclaven and 60 of his 90 men before burning the local castle. Pursued by Sir James' son, Sir John Butler, Wallace, armed with a formidable bow with which he had dispatched 15 of the enemy, was himself wounded under the chin by an arrow. Escaping into the recesses of Methven Wood, he reappeared a few days later to kill Butler and steal his horse. His men having scattered, Wallace swam the River Forth and walked to Tor Wood, where he was given shelter by a local woman.

At Christmas 1296 Wallace, now at Gilbank, decided to raise an army, dispersing his supporters to recruit peasants, farmers, craftsmen, burgesses, the sons of knights, small lairds and anyone else who wanted to unite against the tyranny of England. Backed by enthusiastic support, he took Craufurd Castle in Lanarkshire, where he had become attached to Marion Braidfute, the 18-year-old heiress of Lamington whose father and brother had been killed by Sir William Heselrig, the Sheriff of Clydesdale. While in Lanarkshire, Wallace continually stole into Lanark to practice the sport of killing Englishmen, carrying out a one-man genocidal campaign against the Southrons while simultaneously conducting a secret affair with Marion, who reputedly delivered the outlaw's child during the spring of 1297.

Eventually Heselrig enacted measures to check Wallace's murderous activities. Knowing that Wallace and Marion were lovers, Heselrig, who wanted his own son to marry the young woman, decided to pick a fight with the outlaw. While Wallace and some of his aides were attending Sunday mass in Lochmaben, a group of Henry Percy's men hacked off the tails of the Scotsmen's horses. Upon discovering their animals mutilated, whinnying in pain as the blood continued to flow, Wallace and his companions, joined by the bands of Sir John the Graham and Roger de Kirkpatrick, successfully hewed their way through the soldiers and then captured the castle held by the Bruces.

Further infuriated by Wallace's acts, Heselrig conspired with Robert Thorn, captain of the Lanark garrison, to bring the rebel to heel. Again taunted by English soldiers, who claimed that a priest at St. Nicholas Church had actually fathered Marion's baby girl, Wallace, hacking off the sword hand of one of them, set off a melee during which his band of 25 supporters left twice as many Southrons dead on the road. When Marion helped Wallace, John the Graham, and the other Scots escape through her back gate toward nearby Curtland Crags, Heselrig and his men killed her, burning the house to the ground.

Prior to Heselrig's savage act, Wallace had waged a sporadic campaign of murder, highway robbery, and small sieges. Now burning with vengeance against the representatives of Edward Longshanks, he was transformed from outlaw to general, vowing to kill any Englishman who crossed his path. Beyond his personal attachment to the dead Marion, Wallace could not accept the murdering of women, and he made it a point of honor to set free any females he captured during battle.

In May 1297 Heselrig returned to Lanark, certain that the furor over the murder had died down. Just before nightfall one evening, as the sheriff readied himself for bed, Wallace and 10 of his men inconspicuously entered the town in small groups. Smashing in the front door, Wallace ran upstairs and buried the blade of his two-handed sword in Heselrig's skull. With lightning efficiency his men dispatched Thorn and Heselrig's son before torching the house. A total of 240 English were killed, their women and children cast out of town without provisions.

When reports of the incident reached London, Edward, preoccupied with the war in France, regarded it as a local problem, having no clue that the murderous attack was only the first stage of a major rebellion. Soon after the Lanark murders, Wallace, Sir William Douglas (former governor of Berwick Castle) and a band of men attacked the

Scone headquarters of William Ormsby, the English justiciar, where they killed a number of his men and plundered a large booty. Ormsby escaped, however, and crossed the border into Northumberland, where Edward ordered him to raise an invasion force to be paid for, in part, by ransoms the Scottish guardians had exchanged for John Comyn and Alexander de Balliol.

As word spread throughout Scotland, more patriotic men, including nobles like Douglas who admired Wallace's bravery and brilliant strategy, rushed to join him in Selkirk Forest, transforming his outlaw band into a determined fighting force of 3,000. Robert Bruce, ignoring his pledge to Edward, favored the rebels for a time but, like Bishop Wishart and James the Steward, could do nothing but quarrel with his compatriots, each of whom had claimed he spoke for all of Scotland. Disgusted by petty in-fighting, Wallace continued to build his rebellion in the Lowlands, while the Highlander Andrew de Moray was leading an army of Gaels against English strongholds in the north.

In June 1297 Wallace was informed of the English massacre of 360 leading Scots as they had arrived at a bogus council at the Barns of Ayr. A few days later Wallace and his band trapped the severely hungover Southrons inside the barracks and burned it to the ground. Joined by a group of fighting monks led by the Prior of Drumlay, they then slaughtered 140 English troops who were quartered at the priory.

Realizing that victories for Wallace meant increased power for the Comyns and the possible reinstatement of John Balliol, Edward ordered young Robert Bruce to attack the estate of William Douglas, who was forced to abandon Wallace after his family was taken hostage. Soon after, Douglas did join a group of anti-English nobles, but when they surrendered to Sir Henry Percy's army at Irving, they agreed to exchange hostages for the retention of their lands. Douglas failed to pay up and was imprisoned in the Tower of London, where he died on January 20, 1298. By contrast, while the nobles at Irving were trying to save their own hides, a group led by Wallace killed hundreds of English and captured a fortune in booty.

After fading into Selkirk Forest, Wallace and 140 of his men headed north where they attacked the Glasgow headquarters of Bishop Anthony Bek, besieged the garrison at Perth, and sank ships at Aberdeen before joining Moray's forces in a campaign against every fortification held by the enemy. One month later Dundee and Stirling were the only castles remaining in English hands.

Focusing all their might against Stirling, the gateway to the Highlands, Wallace and Moray, now commanding a combined force of 10,000 foot and 180 horse, met up with John de Warenne's English army boasting 50,000 foot and 1,000 horse. Separated by a narrow bridge, the Scots gazed upon the superior English cavalry flying colorful pennons and mounted on majestic war horses. Intimidated by none of it, Wallace went through the motions of negotiating with two Dominican friars while deliberately insulting Hugh de Cressingham, whom he warned not to cross the wooden bridge wide enough to allow only two men abreast. The overly confident Cressingham, certain that no ragtag army of subhuman Scots could defeat Englishmen, ignored the advice and, on the morning of September 11, 1297, sent his troops across.

Having calculated the maximum number of Southrons that his force would be able to handle, Wallace waited until the most opportune moment to strike. The bloated Cressingham, further weighted down by chain mail and armor, was struck off his horse and trampled to death, as were hundreds of mounted men as they attempted to force their way through. Amid the savage carnage created by Scots forming a wall of 12-foot wooden spears (an earlier version of the *schiltrom*, Wallace's famous "hedgehog" of spears which became the basis of the British infantry formation for the next 600 years) or wielding broadswords, war hammers, pikes, axes and whatever weapons they had been able to forge themselves, Warenne fled to England, leaving his army to bear the onslaught alone. The fearsome Scots then crossed the river near Cambuskenneth and harassed the retreating soldiers as they straggled back toward the Tweed.

The Battle of Stirling Bridge was a phenomenal victory for the Scots, who accomplished a feat that no Englishman, particularly Edward Longshanks, thought possible. It was inconceivable that an army of inferior commoners, many of whom were not vassals fighting under the command of their liege lords, but volunteers, could defeat a superior force of trained knights, the flower of English chivalry and the most experienced fighters in all of Europe.

Reportedly overcome with the bloodlust of battle, Wallace had Cressingham's corpse flayed, distributing the skin among his men but saving a choice strip to use as a baldric for his five-foot sword. Moray, however, was seriously wounded and died a short time later. Having lost Stirling, the English then surrendered Castle Dundee, which had been under siege for some time.

Although impressed by his military prowess, the Scottish lords still viewed Wallace as an inferior, an outlaw whose love of freedom would prove dangerous to the feudal system from which they benefitted. But this humble young man, supported by the noble Moray, had driven the English from their nation, and his powerful supporters gathered at Perth, where they elected him "General of the Army of the Kingdom of Scotland." Moray was given the same title, but his death left Wallace as sole leader of the forces. Wallace then was knighted by one of the Scottish earls, perhaps young Bruce, and soon after used the title "Guardian of the Kingdom of Scotland."

On October 18, 1297, Wallace, intending to collect reparations from his enemies, invaded England, but his plundering of Northumberland, including an attempt to capture Carlisle Castle from the Bruces, was cut short by vicious winter weather. After heading to Durham, Wallace ended his two-month ravaging of the countryside around November 22, when he probably returned to Scotland.

Wallace, now a viceroy possessing dictatorial powers, split the nation into military districts, expecting the great barons to recognize conscription by allowing their vassals, any able-bodied males over 16, to abandon the ploughshare for the sword. To "persuade" conscripts to report without delay, Wallace had a gallows erected in every town and burgh, although only the one in Aberdeen is known to have been used. In basing his military government on classical Roman and Greek models, Wallace intended to curb the power of the nobles and other landowners. Viewing this move as an attempt to destroy feudalism, aristocrats feared he would further erode their power while increasing that of the common people. Further consternation was created when Wallace replaced all English priests with his own candidates, thus returning the Scottish church to its earlier nationalistic character.

After the New Year Edward made peace with France. Soon, Longshanks would return personally to lead his army, and the Scots could expect no aid from the French. Although many nobles disliked Wallace's increasing power, most hated the English, and not a single baron appeared at a parliament called by Edward at York in May 1298. After moving his government there two months later, Longshanks crossed the Tweed with 12,500 foot and 2,000 horse on July 3, 1298. Edward, shinily armored, sitting tall in the saddle with his hair now turned bright white, ordered a fearsome swath of destruction as his army headed toward Stirling. Forced to retreat to Edinburgh to avert starvation and disease, he soon was heartened by news that Wallace's men were not far away, holed up in the massive forest near Falkirk.

During the evening of July 21, after marching his men toward Falkirk, Longshanks was long in falling asleep, only to be awakened violently by the hoofs of his hungry horse as they came crashing down on his chest, breaking two ribs. Hiding the severe pain, he personally led his men the following morning, coming upon Wallace's schiltroms, supported by archers from Ettrick Forest and a few cavalry, in a field by the River Avon, four miles south of Falkirk.

Greatly outnumbered, with only a narrow bog to slow the advance of the English, Wallace nonetheless exhorted his men to stand their ground. The front ranks kneeling with their 12-foot spears thwarted the initial cavalry attack, but the archers and horse were soon massacred to a man. After a second charge was staved off, Edward ordered his Welsh and Lancastrian bowmen to the front, where they soon darkened the sky with a fearsome hail of arrows, slicing huge gaps in the schiltroms so the cavalry could finish the slaughter. At least 10,000 Scots, including Sir John Graham, Sir John Stewart, and nearly the entire infantry, were wiped out.

His army decimated, Wallace, in an attempt to prevent the English from regaining territory he had valiantly wrested from their grip, rode north to order the destruction of both Stirling and Perth. After he resigned his position as Guardian of Scotland, he was replaced by an unstable trio: William Lamberton, Bishop of St. Andrews; John Comyn "the Red," named Lord of Badenoch after his father had died in prison; and young Robert Bruce, Earl of Carrick. Legends abound that Bruce betrayed Wallace at Falkirk, but no evidence supports this claim; in fact, he was 50 miles away at Ayr Castle when the battle occurred, and although he and his father had aided Edward to retain their English lands, they had a falling out after Wallace's defeat. While his father, who preferred the more hospitable culture and climate of England, had always supported Edward, young Robert, born in Scotland, where he grew accustomed to the rugged lands of Carrick and Annandale, shared the Celtic sensibilities of his mother, Marjory, Countess of Carrick. Before the elder Robert, retired to his English estates and seriously ill, passed away in March 1304, the estrangement between father and son had grown irreconcilable.

Some commentators have suggested that "Red" Comyn, having fled from the field with his knights as the English cavalry charged Wallace's schiltroms, may have secretly negotiated with Edward, but this claim is also unsubstantiated. Others have speculated that the Scots would have won at Falkirk if Bruce had openly supported Wallace. The devastating defeat certainly fueled rumors about Bruce's "treachery," but any public support of Wallace on his part would have indirectly allied the Bruces with their rivals, John Balliol and the Comyns. In fact, only a few weeks after Falkirk, Bruce struck a blow against Longshanks by burning the town and castle of Ayr and leading a raid against the pele-tower at Lochmaben.

For several years Wallace reverted to the outlaw's life, knowing that, as a defeated general, he never again would receive the support of nobles who had reluctantly approved of him when he was a victorious one. Heading a loyal band of adherents, he may have returned to his old haunts in Selkirk Forest, while the Scots he had striven to free once again toiled under the feudal yoke. As suggested by documents found on him at the time of his death, he also may have traveled to France, Rome and Norway, seeking support from kings and clergy.

Edward again invaded Scotland in mid-July 1300 but, with his army starving, was forced to accept a treaty brokered by King Philip of France and effective until May 21, 1301. Prior to the invasion, the Archbishop of Canterbury had received a papal bull declaring that Scotland, being a fief of Rome, could not be occupied by the English; but the cleric did not deliver it until August 1300, when the king was at Caerlaverock, near Dumfries. Backed by his parliament and legal experts from Oxford and Cambridge, Longshanks rejected the bull and, as soon as the truce expired, sent his son, Edward, north with his own army. During 1302 the French negotiated another truce but could not enforce it when civil war erupted in their own country, and Edward was given new hope when the Pope rescinded the bull in exchange for his renewed fidelity to the Papacy.

On February 16, 1302, Robert Bruce, wishing to marry Elizabeth de Burgh, Edward's godchild and a niece of the Steward's wife, took an oath of allegiance to regain his English estates while simultaneously seeking to strengthen his ties to the Scottish throne. The following year Bruce filled William Heselrig's old position as Sheriff of Lanark, appearing loyal to Longshanks while plotting another rebellion with William Lamberton.

But Edward Longshanks knew that, as long as William Wallace remained alive, a great many Scots would continue to oppose the English.

As speculation continued to grow about Wallace's exploits, causing reality to be transformed into legend, perhaps this humble man who had risen to lead his people to freedom from tyranny was more dangerous in hiding than he was while commanding his army to victory at Stirling Bridge. Agreeing to be lenient to those Scots patriots who swore fealty to him, Edward persuaded "Red" Comyn and William Lamberton to abandon the cause of independence, and he vowed to give special consideration to whoever captured Wallace, the one patriot excluded from royal amnesty. At this point Comyn refused to take part in the betrayal of Wallace, nor would Sir John de Soulis, who soon left for the security of France.

When the ailing Longshanks was felled by a seizure during March 1305, Wallace, aided by 1000 supporters, increased his guerrilla raids against the English. As of the previous year, during which the Comyns had given up in February and the garrison at Stirling had surrendered in July, he was the only Scottish patriot still fighting the Southrons. Hired by Edward to capture the increasingly conspicuous outlaw, Sir John Stewart of Menteith, a Scottish knight whose uncle died at Falkirk, planted a spy, his nephew, often referred to as "Jack Short," in Wallace's band. Agreeing to meet Robert Bruce at the house of Robert Rae, a servant of Menteith's, on Glasgow Moor during the evening of July 1, 1305, Wallace, accompanied by his aide, Kerly, and Short, arrived to find no one there, an act he repeated every night for the next week. On the eighth night, he found, not Bruce, but Menteith and 60 men who captured him and murdered Kerly. Although Menteith assured Wallace that his life would be spared if he gave himself up, nothing was further from the truth.

After being transported to Carlisle under cover of darkness, Wallace was tossed into jail. The following morning he began the 400-mile journey to London, his legs tied beneath his horse's belly. On August 23, 1305, he was brought to "trial"—actually a propaganda farce staged to impress the French and the Papacy—at Westminster, where he was mocked as a wreath of laurel leaves was placed on his head. Charged with sedition, murder, spoliation, robbery, arson, and other sundry crimes, he was not allowed to defend himself because outlaws were excluded from protection under the law. Although he denied that he was a traitor to Edward, since he had never sworn allegiance to him, Wallace was convicted, for Edward considered his real crime to be uniting the Scottish people in defiance of the English occupation. Prior

to being delivered to the executioner to be hanged, drawn and quartered—the standard sentence for treason—he was dragged behind horses
to the Tower of London as people gathered along the route to jeer
and taunt.

At the Elms, Smoothfield (now Smithfield), Wallace, stripped
naked, was hanged but let down while still alive, only to be emascu-
lated and disemboweled, with his entrails burned before his eyes, before
the headsman brought down the merciful axe. Wallace biographer James
Mackay explains, "The hanging, mutilation and disembowelling, and
final beheading were ... regarded as death three times over."[1] After ordering Wallace's head to be dipped in pitch and placed atop a pike on London Bridge, Longshanks had similar "warnings to potential rebels" sent
to different parts of the island: his right leg to Berwick; left leg to Perth;
left arm to Stirling; and right arm to Newscastle-upon-Tyne. An unsup-
ported legend relates that monks at Cambuskenneth Abbey retrieved
the bones of the arm left at Stirling and buried them, placing the finger
bones so that they pointed toward the spot of his magnificent victory
over the English.

Hoping to cow the Scots with his merciless slaughter of Wallace,
Edward Longshanks instead created a martyr. During the Wars of
Scottish Independence, he had continually forgiven those promise-
breaking enemies who had sworn fealty, turned coat, and then sworn
again. Toward Wallace, however, the one man who fought only for the
freedom of his countrymen, caring nothing for lands, titles or thrones,
he had displayed true barbarism. Apparently, to Longshanks, showing
strength by not bowing to him at all was worse than treacherously and
cowardly bowing, then twisting the dirk of rebellion, only to *pretend* to
bow again.

Robert the Bruce, King of Scots

Six months after the execution at Smithfield, Edward Longshanks'
barbaric attempt to make an example of Wallace failed miserably. In
February 1306 Robert Bruce, while meeting with John "Red" Comyn
at Greyfriars Church in Dumfries, stabbed his rival during an argument
at the altar. Realizing that Comyn was still alive, Bruce's companions,
including Roger de Kirkpatrick, finished the bloody deed after Christopher Seton, Bruce's brother-in-law, cut down Comyn's uncle, Sir Robert,

who had attempted to retaliate. Evidently, Comyn had informed Edward of a secret pact he made with Bruce stating that each man would support the other's bid for the Scottish throne in return for possession of the victor's lands. A short time before the Dumfries incident, Edward had stripped Bruce of his guardianship, seized lands recently awarded to him and demanded payment of his father's debts that had been set in abeyance. Learning of Comyn's treachery, Bruce openly accused him before resorting to violence.

Robert Bruce had committed a sacrilegious crime and, attempting to prevent his own downfall, chose to rebel openly against England. After seizing Dumfries Castle he and his men rode to Glasgow, capturing fortifications in Clydesdale on the way. Kneeling before Robert Wishart, Bishop of Glasgow and Wallace's old adviser, Bruce prayed for absolution of his crime.

On Palm Sunday 1306, having been forgiven by the Church of Scotland, Robert the Bruce was crowned king at Scone by Isabel, Countess of Buchan (and a royal MacDuff) who, in the absence of the Stone of Destiny, placed a gold band around his head. Ironically, prior to riding to Scone as if the devil himself was at her heels, Isabel had stolen horses from her husband, a close kinsman of the murdered "Red" Comyn. Also present were the new king's four brothers—Edward, Nigel, Alexander and Thomas—now princes and leaders of the rebellion.

Seriously ill but unwilling to soften his resolve for health's sake, Edward was hunting in the New Forest when he heard of the crowning of Bruce. Carried to Westminster on a litter, he ordered the immediate mobilization of his northern forces. During the early summer he knighted 300 squires and declared his ineffectual son Prince of Wales, sending them northward with the intention of avenging Comyn's murder by subjecting Bruce and every supporter to the hideous fate of Wallace.

In the meantime, Bruce and his brothers continued to recruit dispossessed men, outlaws and other sympathizers. They dealt with the hostile MacDowall clan while attempting to subdue small revolts waged by Comyns who were persuading powerful lords to abandon Bruce's cause for their own. Opposed by many who feared the wrath of England, Bruce's forces lost Perth to Aymer de Valence, Edward's commander in Scotland and a Comyn relative, and were routed at Methven. Now more an outlaw than a king, Bruce headed for the Western Highlands and Islands, attempting to rally more Scots to his cry for independence.

In October 1306 Edward, now deathly ill, reached the Lanercost priory near Carlisle, where he awaited news from his son and other commanders in Scotland. Consumed by vengeance, he now rescinded his previous policy of offering leniency to reformed traitors. Many captured supporters of the King of Scots were executed, including his brothers, Alexander and Thomas, who were hanged, and Nigel, who was hanged, drawn and beheaded. Bruce's queen was imprisoned in England, and his sister, Mary, and Isabel of Buchan were locked in cages that hung from the castles at Roxburgh and Berwick, respectively. Bruce's daughter received the remarkably lenient sentence of being sent to a convent.

Bruce's first major military victory occurred at Loudon Hill, east of Kilmarnock, where he employed the schiltroms of Wallace to rout the forces of Valence, who returned with reinforcements to drive them into the Galloway hills. Fortunately, the thickly forested area was a natural deer sanctuary, and the hearty Gaels were able to rebuild their strength with a plentiful supply of venison.

During the spring of 1307, impressed by the performance of his faithful knights, Edward, with one foot in the grave and the other in the stirrup, mounted his black steed to ride at the head of his army as it entered Scotland. He never made it. Three miles from the border, at Burgh-on-Sands on the Solway shore, Edward Longshanks, one of the greatest Plantagenet kings and the most formidable foe the Scots would ever face, took his final hate-filled breath on July 11, 1307.

Longshanks' son, who preferred courtly pleasures to the field of battle, was concerned primarily with his own amusement and cared little for the intricacies of politics and governmental administration. He often spent his time with young men, particularly his boyhood friend Piers Gaveston, who, on June 19, 1312, was executed during a civil war in England. He did cross into Ayrshire after his father's death, but remained in Scotland only 28 days before retreating home. After his coronation in Westminster Abbey on April 24, 1308, Edward II ignored Scotland for the next two-and-one-half years, giving Bruce the opportunity to put down the remaining Comyn factions.

When Edward II finally invaded Scotland in September 1310, he found a land cleared of potential plunder and provisions by a brilliant king who had used his strength, resourcefulness and military prowess to draw swarms of supporters into his camp. With thousands of Scots tucked safely into the hills and forests, Bruce and his army avoided pitched battles while staging a number of successful guerrilla raids against unprepared English troops.

Having driven out the ineffectual Edward II, Bruce invaded England in July 1312. Forging a truce that lasted until midsummer 1313, his next threat of invasion also was staved off by a treaty that ran until September 29, 1314. By the summer of 1314, however, Edward II had pardoned the barons who rose against him during the civil war and was assembling the mightiest army in the history of the English nation. But this king was inexperienced in military strategy and, as he marched his 20,000 men north, he favored a lethargic pace and allowed little time for sleep or provisioning.

On the other hand, Robert the Bruce was an inspiring commander and a seasoned soldier who led by example, often single-handedly defeating several enemies simultaneously. He was a king who tried to become acquainted with all his men, for, rising from the status of outlaw, he never forgot how hard others had fought to help him attain the throne.

On Sunday, June 23, 1314, Bruce, sitting atop a small gray horse and sporting a coat of chain mail, faced off with Edward II on a field near the Bannock burn, a stream close by Stirling, an area the English king intended to relieve. Impressive and numerically superior but weary from their march from Falkirk, Edward's army gazed across four schiltroms at a determined foe comprised of Celts from the far corners of Scotland. Protected from behind by the hunting forest of the New Park, and on their right flank by the burn, the Scots were well set to handle a frontal attack. Like Wallace at Stirling seven years earlier, Bruce cunningly used both terrain and man-made structures when designing his battle formation.

As the vanguard of the English army led by the Earls of Hereford and Gloucester prepared to cross the ford over the burn, Hereford's nephew, Sir Henry de Bohun, rode ahead through the trees on the other side and spied a lone Scotsman on a gray horse inspecting others hiding in the woods. Spotting the golden band around the man's helmet, Bohun lowered his lance and charged ahead. Recognizing the charging knight as a member of the family who had received his confiscated lands, Bruce thundered forward, pulling his horse aside just in time to bring down his battle axe, furiously cleaving through Bohun's helmet and splintering the wooden handle before extracting the bloody blade from his opponent's chin.

A brief, ineffectual cavalry charge by the English ended just as the gloaming began to fall. The following day, the Scots, moving forward from the New Park, fooled Edward II into thinking that they were yielding, particularly when they knelt before the English horse. Sounding their trumpets, the English charged into the 12-foot line of lowered wooden spears, flooding the meadow with blood. As the Scots marched ahead with lowered spears, Edward's cavalry became unable to deploy, trapping thousands of infantry behind them. With his archers also unable to make headway, Edward then saw Bruce order his fierce Highlanders to charge, wielding two-handed claymores and long-handled Lochaber axes. As the English attempted to retreat, they were slaughtered by spearmen and archers from the Ettrick Forest. Surrounded by 500 of his knights, Edward managed to escape to Stirling.

In the greatest victory the Scots ever achieved, Robert the Bruce, leading 6,000 men, routed a force of 20,000 led by a Plantagenet king who believed he could not possibly lose to an "inferior" race. After the battle Bruce demanded ransoms for the renowned prisoners captured by his army: some he exchanged for Scots imprisoned by the English; with others he bought the freedom of his wife, daughter, sister, and Isabel of Buchan. With the enormous provisions left behind by the English army, he made presentations to nearly every family in Scotland— a gesture from a man who had paid for victory with the blood of his brothers.

Although the triumph at Bannockburn established Scottish independence and Robert the Bruce as King of Scots, the victory, which was not recognized by Edward II, did not end violent conflict with England. Bruce remained at war for the next 14 years until King Edward III, who succeeded his murdered father, signed the Treaty of Edinburgh in 1328. Bruce's brother, Edward, and James Douglas, whose father had briefly supported Wallace, led raids into the northern counties of England, burning homes and stealing cattle. Upon opening a second front against the English on the Emerald Isle, Edward Bruce was crowned High King of All Ireland on May 2, 1316, and reigned until October 1318, when he was killed during an attack on Dundalk. Although this incident ended the Bruce regime in Ireland, English power there had been broken and Western Scotland was no longer subjected to enemy attacks from across the Irish Sea.

When Robert the Bruce died on June 7, 1329, his grandson, whose birth had taken place after his mother, Marjorie, was killed in a riding accident, was crowned King Robert II; as the son of Walter the Steward, he became the first of the Stewart monarchs.

Wallace, Bruce and Robin Hood

In his impressive 1961 study of legendary medieval outlaws, historian Maurice Keen writes that William Wallace's "true story belongs rather to the annals of patriotism than of outlawry, and it is therefore with hesitation that I have included a chapter about him."[2] Other Robin Hood historians either ignore him or briefly mention him in passing, a curious fact when one considers that Wallace's real life perhaps includes more parallels to the legends of Robin Hood than that of any other outlaw on record. It is true that Robin Hood is an *English* outlaw, and it is to the history of England that inquirers have turned when searching for evidence to suggest who the real Robin might have been. But it is a Scotsman who seems to have the most in common with the legendary characterizations of Robin, a fact given further force when one considers that, upon examination of extant records, the first serious historical references to the outlaw were written by Scottish chroniclers.

In his *Chronica Gentis Scotorum*, written during the 1360s, John of Fordun presented a brief account of Wallace's exploits. Half a century later, the chronicler Walter Bower expanded Fordun's material in the *Scotichronicon*, transforming Wallace into a near-Christlike figure; and Andrew of Wyntoun, including the first vernacular account of Wallace's career in his *Metrical Chronicle* (c. 1420), offered a more humanized, less hagiographic version of the outlaw. The most well-known publication on his life, *The Wallace* (c. 1476–78), however, is not a work of history, but a lengthy narrative poem by Blind Harry the Minstrel that depicts the outlaw leader driving the English from Scotland three times before becoming a martyr on the scaffold.

J. C. Holt has amassed evidence to suggest that the legend of Robin Hood began during the mid-14th century: "The man, if he existed at all, lived even earlier.... He cannot be identified. There is a quiverful of possible Robin Hoods. Even the likeliest is little better than a shot in the gloaming."[3] Even considering this fact, Holt's dating of a possible existence for a Robin Hood may place him contemporaneously with William Wallace.

Two of the Scotsmen who chronicled Wallace's life also wrote about Robin Hood. Andrew de Wyntoun identified 1283–85 as the time of Robin's emergence, a period during which Wallace was nine to eleven years old; while Walter Bower, in updating Fordun's work, chose 1286, the time of Simon de Montfort's rebellion. The third Scottish historian to mention Robin, John Major, writing in 1521, was the first to place the outlaw during the reign of Richard the Lionheart, which, of course, eliminates a possible Wallace connection. As mentioned previously and discussed further in the following chapters, there is no real evidence for Major's claim; as Holt notes, "It was simply recycled through later versions of the tale and so became an integral part of the legend."[4]

By the time Major published his theory about Robin, the outlaw was well known throughout Scotland. For example, in 1508 Aberdeen, the Abbot and Prior of Bonacord used the aliases "Robin Hood" and "Little John" when they collected money for local charities! And by 1555 the Scottish parliament had grown so concerned with the negative effects of the legend that a prohibition against Robin Hood was enacted. Persons who impersonated the outlaw, Little John, the Abbot of Unreason, or the Queen of May within royal burghs were subjected to banishment from Scotland, while collaborators were imprisoned for five years.

Maurice Keen offers a straightforward explanation of the connection between William Wallace and Robin Hood:

> It was as a forest bandit, living free and defiant … that Wallace's own career began and ended. This part of his story is attended in historical records as well as minstrels' fiction. It is not surprising to find that the Scottish chroniclers were the first historians to take Robin Hood seriously: men of the same stamp as he were among their own national heroes.[5]

Was Wallace the real Robin Hood? Or could the story of Wallace's life have been an initial impetus for the legends?

In his 1993 study of the narrative literature of medieval Scotland, R. James Goldstein writes:

> One of the most striking aspects of the career of William Wallace is that he became a legend in his own time. While he lived, he came to the attention of several English chroniclers, and both his presence in England during his raids into Northumberland and his execution in

London enabled him to enter the popular English imagination as few individual Scots have ever done. The English government regarded him as an outlaw from the start of his career.[6]

The "evidence" that links Wallace with the character of Robin Hood developed in later legends is as follows:

1. Wallace was declared an outlaw in late 1291 or early 1292 by the English government.

2. In 1296 Wallace began to commit highway robbery against official representatives of the English crown.

3. After stealing booty from the English, Wallace distributed it among the poor in Clydesdale Forest.

4. Early in his career of outlawry, poets and minstrels, including Thomas the Rhymer, began to write and sing verses about him.

5. Landless men, exiles and other outlaws joined his band to fight against the English oppressors.

6. Wallace was sheltered by local inhabitants in a greenwood setting, the vast forests of Scotland.

7. Wallace used woodlands, particularly Selkirk Forest, to hide from his enemies and as bases from which to launch his guerrilla campaigns.

8. Wallace's lover was a woman named Marion.

9. A major enemy of Wallace, and the murderer of his Marion, was the *Sheriff* of Lanark, with whom he quarrelled and ultimately slew with a sword.

10. Wallace, with cunning and fortitude, transformed an ill-organized band of outlaws into a powerful fighting force to defeat an enemy who considered the Scots an inferior race.

11. The conflict between Wallace and Edward Longshanks was one based on race: Celts versus Anglo-Normans.

12. Wallace, once described as obtaining "his living by means of his bow and his quiver," was remarkably adept at archery and deployed archers in his battles with the English.[7] During his raid on the Perth convoy in 1296, he shot down 15 English with his formidable strongbow, which only he was capable enough to draw.

13. Wallace's conflict was with King Edward. (An early Robin Hood ballad mentions "Edward our comely king," who has been identified as Edward II.)

14. In defeating English soldiers at Irvine Water in 1292, Wallace used a fishing pole as a staff, à la Friar Tuck.

15. After the Barns of Ayr incident in 1297, Wallace was joined in dispatching his enemies by a fighting clergyman, the Prior of Drumlay, who was not averse to shedding considerable blood.

Wallace may not have been the original Robin Hood, but he comes as close to meeting the requirements as any other candidate. Realistically, over the centuries, his life probably has lent the above, and perhaps other, characteristics to the works of chroniclers, poets, minstrels and novelists who have developed and transmuted the legends of Robin Hood. For example, by the 15th century he was being referred to as "the Scottish Robin Hood," as noted in the margin of a poem written by an English monk who was a contemporary of Wallace. And a century later, the two outlaw figures were again connected in the following verse composed by an anonymous Scottish poet:

> Thair is no story that I of heir
> Of Johne nor Robene Hude
> Nor yit of Wallace wicht but weir
> That me thinks halfe so gude.

Maurice Keen writes:

The lost author of these lines had good reason for his association of Wallace with Robin Hood.... For among the stories recounted of Wallace were many which had their origin not in the magnified reverberation of historical event, but in tradition. Amongst these were many which were very similar to those told of Robin Hood and other outlaws. In essence, indeed, they are the same stories, merely associated by different authors with the name of a different hero.[8]

In his excellent 1995 biography of Wallace, James Mackay refers to his subject as a "latter day Robin Hood" on two occasions. Perhaps accepting the conventional Saxon versus Norman version of the English legend, Mackay makes an argument, not for Wallace *as* Robin Hood, but as a later real-life version of the character. In concluding his book, he writes, "Wallace in adversity became a folk hero, a cross between King Arthur and Robin Hood."[9]

Although we may never be able to prove who the real Robin Hood was, we do know that William Wallace, an historical outlaw hero, did give his life to better the lot of his countrymen. But the connection between Robin Hood and Scotland does not end with William Wallace. There are also some interesting parallels between the English legends and the life of Robert the Bruce, similarities which have led historian Jim Bradbury to suggest that the King of Scots may have been the real Robin Hood: "The case is no more convincing in any final sense than the others, but it has been ignored. Even though it may do no more than confuse the picture even further let us consider the case for no less a candidate than Robert the Bruce."[10]

Bradbury notes the period of Bruce's existence as a forest raider, the legends of his exploits that bear similarities to the Robin Hood tales, the claim of Scottish kings to the estates of Huntingdon, and Bruce's connection to a priory founded in 1130 by an earlier Robert Bruce at Guisborough, a name from which Gisbourne was derived.

The following "evidence" may be added to Bradbury's list:

1. Bruce was a true master of the guerrilla raid.

2. The exiled King of Scots relied on poached venison to keep his men alive.

3. Bruce distributed among his people the goods abandoned by the English after the Battle of Bannockburn.

4. Bruce fought many battles against "comely king" Edward II.

As in the case of Wallace, both the true exploits and legendary tales of Robert the Bruce probably influenced those who created the tales of Robin Hood. As Bradbury writes, "One could but suggest that a lost work about Robert Bruce as an outlaw hero contributed to the fund of popular stories from which the Robin Hood ballads borrowed."[11]

Was Robin Hood a Scot? Perhaps not, but it can be stated with certainty that there *have* been Scottish outlaws much like him. Certainly the facts about William Wallace and Robert the Bruce bear too many similarities to the Robin Hood legends to *not* be regarded as having connections with them. As the following chapters indicate, English historians have identified Barnsdale in Yorkshire (a location north of Sherwood Forest and Nottingham) as the most probable home of Robin Hood; in the above examination of Scotland, we have merely considered terrain just a wee bit farther north.

Three

English Rebels and Hoods (1322–1450)

During the reign of Edward II, a man named Robert Hood lived as a tenant at Wakefield manor, 10 miles from Barnsdale in Yorkshire. Using the royal porter-outlaw character of the 1400 "A Gest of Robin Hood" to guide them, some historians have suggested that this Robert Hood took part in a 1322 uprising led by Thomas, Earl of Lancaster, was outlawed, then pardoned and taken into household service by Edward II, and finally returned to a life of brigandage a year later. The fact that Edward had pardoned him in Nottingham during his royal progress of April–November 1323 paralleled the northern journey of "Edward our comely king" described in the "Gest" and proved that he was the real Robin Hood, so they thought.

However, J. C. Holt later proved that the Wakefield Robert Hood, who appeared to fit the Barnsdale Robin of the "Gest," and the Hood who was a valet to Edward II were actually two separate people, the latter being *Robyn* Hood who began his royal service *before* the king journeyed north to Nottingham. The Wakefield Robert, Holt writes, who disappeared from court records after 1317, had no provable connection to Lancaster's rebellion; while the valet Robyn, having no connection with either Barnsdale or outlawry, became unable to work and received his final payment on November 22, 1324.

One fact that suggests the possible origins of the character described in the "Gest" is the presence of the surname "Hood" in the Barnsdale area throughout the early 14th century. A contemporary of the Wakefield Robert Hood, Robert Hood of Newton, who had a son also named Robert, was listed in the Wakefield court rolls of 1308. Another family of Hoods, north of Wakefield at Sowerby, included a

John Hood who had two sons named Robert, one of whom also appears in a court record dated 1308. And, in 1309, a man named Robert Hood the Grave was "penalized ... for breaking the lord of the manor's fold at Alverthorpe ... whether he should be identified with Robert Hood of Wakefield or Robert Hood of Newton is problematical."[1]

Using surviving Wakefield court rolls, which date from 1274, and bits of earlier information, Holt has proved that Hoods resided in the area from at least as early as 1202, placing them a short distance from Barnsdale, the location most detailed in the Robin Hood legends. This connection between history and balladry, he writes, "is unlikely to be accidental. Either the Hoods of Wakefield gave Robin to the world, or they absorbed the tale of the outlaw into their family traditions or their neighbors and descendants came to associate the two."[2]

A rarer surname, "Robinhood," also existed in England by the late 13th century. In 1325 a woman named Katherine Robynhood lived in London, and a Robert Robynhood lived in West Harting, Sussex, in 1332. And, as noted in chapter one, there was the true outlaw, Robert Hod, who stirred up trouble at York a century earlier.

Also in 1332, at a parliament held in Westminster Abbey, Edward III's chief justice, Geoffrey le Scrope, described the king's concern with the growing problem of persons who, "in defiance of the law, had risen in large bands and were preying on the King's liegemen, as also on the goods of the Holy Church, on the King's justices and others; and some they took and held prisoners and made them pay heavy ransoms to save their lives."[3] Le Scrope called for action to be taken against such bands of outlaws, but little actually could be done to protect those traveling through the wilder areas of England. Whether any Hoods were among these bands remains to be seen. But two decades later, in 1354, another Robert Hood was arrested after he illegally entered the royal forest of Rockingham in Northhamptonshire.

Having staked his claim to the throne of France in 1337 (and beginning a series of military conflicts later dubbed the Hundred Years War), Edward III basked in the glory attained by his son, Edward, the Black Prince, who had defeated the French at Crecy in 1346 and soon would repeat the feat at Poitiers in 1356 to become the most feared warrior in Europe. Six years after Poitiers, William Langland wrote *Piers Plowman*, a work containing the first literary reference to the character of Robin Hood.

In 1376 tragedy struck England in the form of an infection that killed the Black Prince. The following year, his father, Edward III, went insane from senility and died. Crowned at Westminster on July 17, 1377, Richard II, 10-year-old son of the Black Prince, obeyed his advisers and levied harsh poll taxes in 1377, 1379, and 1380. Flat taxes not proportionate to individual wealth, these levies hit the poor classes particularly hard and, in 1381, more than 100,000 peasants rebelled against the crown. Led in Essex by the priest John Ball and in Kent by Walter ("Wat") Tyler, the rebels demanded the restoration of ancient rights, including a revocation of the Forest Laws and the division of Church lands among the Commons.

In June 1381 the men of Essex and Kent marched on London, burning poll tax registers, pillaging manor houses, and beheading the king's treasurer and the Archbishop of Canterbury on Tower Hill. At Mile End on June 14, Richard II, now 14, met the Essex rebels led by Jack Straw, agreeing to end serfdom and bestow an unconditional pardon on each man. At Smithfield the following day he reiterated his promises to the Kentish rebels and, when the Mayor of London, incensed at Wat Tyler's increased demands, beheaded the peasant leader on the spot, offered personally to take up their cause. Having swayed them to his side, Richard then revoked the pardons and violently suppressed those who continued to revolt. However, the poll tax was abolished and some landowners became wary of enforcing feudal duties. Like some of the characterizations of Robin Hood, Wat Tyler led common men in attacks upon the unfairness of the Forest Laws and the abuses of wealthy clerics.

From 1416–29 a man whose alias became part of the Robin Hood legends troubled representatives of both Henry V and Henry VI. While poaching in the forests of Surrey and Sussex, Richard Stafford, a chaplain at Lindfield, attributed the crimes to "Frere Tuck."

A decade later an outlaw named Piers Venables conducted a guerrilla campaign against Henry VI's government, two years after the 17-year-old king took control of the realm.

In 1450 the men of Kent rose again, this time under the leadership of Jack Cade, an Irish peasant calling himself "John Amend-All" who, like the rebels of 1381, sought the reform of clerical abuses. Supporting Richard, Duke of York, a Plantagenet heir of Edward III, the rebellion was a precursor to the Wars of the Roses, a series of civil conflicts that occurred during 1455–85. After retreating from Henry VI's forces at Blackheath, Cade defeated a royal contingent at Sevenoaks and persuaded some of the king's men to join his cause.

Deserting the mayor and aldermen of London, Henry VI holed up at Kenilworth Castle, entrusting the defense of the city to Lord Say, the Royal Treasurer and Constable of the Tower of London. On July 2, 1450, Cade beseiged the Tower and executed Say and his son-in-law, Sir James Cromer, Sheriff of Kent. Intoxicated with his easy victory, Cade allowed his men to plunder and pillage. After fighting a battle on London Bridge, the rebels were offered a general pardon by the Archbishop of Canterbury. Although most accepted the terms, Cade escaped; pursued to Sussex, he was captured and mortally wounded. Like Wat Tyler and many depictions of Robin Hood, Cade believed that the king's evil counselors had created the financial and legal oppressions suffered by the commoners.

As Stephen Knight notes, "Any precise relation to late medieval revolts and other risings is not direct, but ... the figure of Robin Hood can be used as a symbolic liberator in such events."[4] And, like the Robin Hood in most versions of the legend, the leaders of the 1381 and 1450 peasant rebellions "made their attack on particular men who were guilty of oppression, not the social system as a whole."[5]

The following chapter examines the Robin Hood of literature—of the ballads, songs and plays that sprang up during the late Middle Ages and continued through the Renaissance. As Maurice Keen so astutely writes,

> A Robin Hood who played his part on the stage of real life eludes the historian's pursuit. The quest seems fruitless, for there are woven into his myth too many strands of traditional story which are far older than the world from whose circumstances the ballad makers took their cue. But this does not mean that the ballad makers' world of the "fair forest" where the outlaw king is master is a pure figment of popular imagination.[6]

Knight agrees that historians' attempts to discover the "real" Robin Hood are trips down the wrong greenwood path; for their methods amount to "gathering a few facts together as if they form a necessary sequence, omitting all the other facts and all the absences, and so constructing an allegedly coherent narrative."[7] The many various versions of the Robin Hood legend have arisen not from "a multiplicity of focus which can readily be seen to arise from some confused dissemination of an originally 'pure' and ancient Robin Hood reality, but rather from the myth's continuous re-adaptation to a set of varying contexts."[8] It is now time to examine this "continuous re-adaptation."

Part II

Robin Hood
in Story
and Song

Four

From Minstrel's Yeoman to Playwright's Aristocrat (1400–1700)

s Stephen Knight notes, "there is no authoritative literary source" for the legends of Robin Hood.[1] After the first ballads appeared during the early to mid–1400s, the tradition perhaps developed "not so much [as] a set of transformations of an authentic single person, but rather [as] ... a forcefield of variations, of figures and fables which realize in many different and locally functional ways the concept central to the whole myth, which appears to be a resistance to authority."[2] J. C. Holt, who embraces an historical approach disallowing the possibility of "an authentic single" Robin Hood, points out that nearly all our knowledge of the medieval legend is derived from five surviving ballads and a fragment of a play: "The surviving stories ... spring, not from the point of origin of the legend, but from different stages in its growth. They emphasize different aspects of Robin's activities."[3]

All of the Robin Hood ballad makers incorporated elements from earlier outlaw romances extolling the virtues of Hereward the Wake, Eustace the Monk, Fulk fitz Warin, Adam Bell, Clim of the Clough, William of Cloudesley and others, often drawing from fictionalized elements. The first surviving literary reference to Robin, made by William Langland in *Piers Plowman* (1362), suggests that "rhymes of Robin Hood were well in circulation by this time."[4] The earliest surviving ballad manuscript, "Robin Hood and the Monk," consisting of 90 stanzas, was written in 1450. The second extant piece, a play fragment of 21 lines written on the back of a receipt, dates from about 1475, when another ballad, "Robin Hood and Guy of Gisbourne," may also have appeared. Bearing similarities to the fragment, this 58-stanza poem describes Gisbourne, disguised as a yeoman, hunting down Robin, only to be beheaded by the outlaw who then, adopting Guy's costume, rescues Little John from the sheriff. The third extant ballad, "Robin Hood and the Potter," describing Robin's defeat by a craftsman whom he challenges, appeared around 1503.

No original manuscript of "A Gest of Robin Hood" has been located. While Holt believes that it may have been composed as early as 1400, other historians accept the later date of 1450. (In either case, the original version of the "Gest" probably predates all the manuscripts described above.) Five surviving editions appear to have been derived from a single 450-stanza ballad written by an unknown author. The first of these, titled "A Gest of Robyn Hode," was possibly printed in Antwerp in 1510–15; while the second, "A Lyttell Geste of Robyn Hode," was published by the English printer Wynken de Worde, who was in business from 1492 to 1534. The other three, all printed during the mid–16th century, include corrections or additions to the earlier versions.

The "Gest" is comprised of two major stories. One, set in Barnsdale, features Robin's experiences with a knight, a group of monks, and the outlaws of St. Mary's; the other, set in Sherwood Forest and Nottingham, has Robin win an archery contest staged by the sheriff, receive a pardon from the king (whose service he enters before returning to the greenwood for 22 years), and finally dying at Kirklees when his relative, the prioress, administers poison instead of medicine. Robin is accompanied by Little John in the second tale.

"Robin Hood and Guy of Gisbourne" was first noticed in a manuscript (c. 1650) discovered in a Shropshire home by Bishop Thomas Percy of Dromore, Ireland. Subsequently referred to as the Percy Folio, this manuscript, published in *Reliques of Ancient English Poetry* (1765), also contains the ballad "Robin Hood and the Curtal Friar" and a 27-stanza fragment, "Robin Hoode his Death," which includes material similar to the concluding portions of the "Gest."

Perhaps based on the same original source as the final stanzas of the "Gest," "Robin Hoode his Death" features the ailing outlaw's visit to Kirklees (here called Church Lees), where he is bled to death by his treacherous cousin. Prior to expiring, Robin asks Little John to carry him to his grave. The content of this tale was integrated into later variations, particularly a popular 18th-century version in which Robin calls Little John with his hunting horn and then shoots an arrow from the window of Kirklees tower to mark the site of his grave. Likewise, the 1503 "Robin Hood and the Potter," which features Robin's fight with a staff-wielding craftsman, may have influenced "Robin Hood and Little John," first appearing in 1594 and later popularized in several 18th-century versions that include the famous staff duel between the outlaw and his future sidekick.

While J. C. Holt allows for the possibility of an original historical outlaw, he agrees with Stephen Knight that the various versions of the legend reflect a variety of origins:

> It is difficult to believe that these tales all stemmed from a single origin, whether in literary fiction or in the adventures of a particular person. Moreover, there is no obvious or easy method of determining which of them embodies the earliest or the most authentic account of Robin's activities. The legend is not like a settled archaeological site where the earlier deposits lie underneath the later. It is like a hoard amassed from different sources, probably at different times, perhaps for different purposes. There is no way of knowing for sure how much of the hoard remains or how haphazard that residue is.[5]

One of the most renowned elements in the legend, that of the dispossessed nobleman robbing from the rich to give to the poor, is not to be found in any of the early ballads. Another addition developed in the 18th and 19th centuries, this class-oriented theme has nothing to do with the yeoman (royal household servant) outlaw who was spoken about two and three hundred years earlier. Although Robin does help a knight recapture his lands from the abbot of St. Mary's and fight the Sheriff of Nottingham in the "Gest," he seeks to aid, not the helpless underclass, but his own associates.

By the time the Robin Hood ballads were mentioned in *Piers Plowman* in 1362, English was displacing French and Anglo-Norman as the primary literary language, allowing more people to hear the outlaw tales that subsequently were distributed in written or printed versions. And the popularity of the tales was not restricted to the lower classes, as traveling minstrels disseminated them throughout the realm, simultaneously allowing nobles, clerics and commoners to hear of Robin's exploits. Likewise, while some citizens enjoyed the tales, others spoke out against the criminality celebrated in them. Actual outlaws rarely were concerned with the effects of robbery and violence on their victims, and Englishmen who were concerned about these outrages also found much to criticize in the fictionalized versions. One man's hero is another man's villain, and the criticism of Robin Hood by all levels of society proved that the tales were not simply a product of class conflict.

The association of Robin with Maid Marian was a product of the popular May Games of the 16th century, a period during which most of the ballads began to be sung rather than spoken. Around 1500 the poet Alexander Barclay wrote of "some merry fytte of Maid Marian or else of Robin Hood," but he did not actually tie the two characters together. The May Games accomplished this by naming Robin and Marian King and Queen of May. Play games at other times of the year featured Robin, Little John and bands of followers collecting coins from spectators. The first surviving play, based on portions of "Robin Hood and Guy of Gisbourne," was performed in 1475.

Proving that royalty also was interested in the outlaw, Henry VIII became involved in the Robin Hood games during the early 16th century. In 1510 he and 11 nobles, dressed in gaming attire, broke into Queen Catherine's bed chamber; and near Shooters Hill in 1515 a lavish feast for Henry and Catherine was enacted by 200 revelers dressed as Robin and his yeomen. During the lengthy reign (1558–1603) of Henry's daughter, Elizabeth I, the conception of the outlaw character was altered even further to fit him into the current political climate.

In 1589 William Warner's pastoral poem "Albions England" transformed Sherwood's peasant bandits into "merry men," enthusiastic individuals who were happy to fight for their leader and nation. Here Robin's greenwood supporters rallied round him, not out of last ditch desperation, but because it was the jolly good thing to do—a characterization that would become an integral element of later stories, novels and dramas. Specific merry men such as Little John and Friar Tuck were soon joined by others, as in the 17th-century broadside "Robin Hood and Allen a' Dale."

Several dramatizations of the legends became popular after the plague ravaged London in 1592. In an effort to safely avoid references to recent events and current politics, playwrights transformed Robin into a supporting character who offers little resistance to established authority. Produced during 1592-93, *George a' Greene* incorporated events from "The Jolly Pinder of Wakefield," while *The Famous Chronicle of Edward I* (1593) incorporated material from the "Gest" with a Robin Hood play game.

Commissioned to write a Robin Hood play in 1598, Anthony

Munday fashioned a version of the legend that subsequently was accepted by dozens of dramatists and novelists, a mutation that remains prevalent four centuries later. Receiving £5 from producer P. Henslowe, Munday's work eventually was staged as two separate plays, *The Downfall of Robert Hood, Earle of Huntington* and *The Death of Robert Hood, Earle of Huntington*. Mindful of the interests of his noble benefactors, Munday, setting his drama during the absentee reign of Richard the Lionheart, portrayed Robin as a dispossessed aristocrat who becomes, not an anti-establishment rebel who rallies commoners against royal corruption, but the outlaw lord of Sherwood Forest. Curiously, Prince John was depicted as a defender of Robin who also became a Sherwood outlaw when King Richard returned to curb his royal ambition. With *The Downfall* Munday mythically connected Robin with Richard and the earldom of Huntingdon, and strengthened the conservative depiction of the outlaw as a friend of the legitimate crown, further eroding the enemy of authority depicted in the early ballads. He also changed the maiden's name to Matilda, adding the surname fitz Walter and expanding the love interest. Although he gave Robin little to do in *The Death*, Munday already had pioneered the characterization that would influence generations of historians hunting for the real Robin and dramatists depicting the romantic one.

A year after Munday's dramas appeared, Robin as Earl of Huntingdon returned in *Looke About You*, a parody by an anonymous playwright. Set during the reign of Henry II, this seminal Robin Hood comedy featured a non-outlaw sans merry men who is harassed while dressed in drag. William Shakespeare also involved Robin in light-hearted contexts in two of his plays, *As You Like It* and *Henry VI* (both published in 1623).

In 1622 an edition of Michael Drayton's *Poly-Olbion* used Robin's outlaw life to teach a moral lesson. Influenced by Drayton's work, Ben Jonson's unfinished play *The Sad Shepherd: A Tale of Robin Hood*, written during the 1630s, presented the outlaw as a lord who acts the good host at various forest functions and carries on a romantic liaison with Maid Marian. A major ballad, "A True Tale of Robbin Hood: A brief touch of the life and death of that Renowned Outlaw, Robert Earle of Huntington, vulgarly called Robbin Hood who lived and died in 1198," by Martin Parker was published in 1632. By this time the connection of Robin with Huntingdon was becoming widely accepted, as was the metamorphosis of the outlaw "away from a collective and anti-authoritarian rebel into a figure much more consistent with the centralized, Protestant and money-oriented state."[6] Combining Munday's version of the legend, including a characterization of William Longchamp, with bits from the "Gest," Parker involved Robin in minor, politically palatable events, reflecting the subversion of the original medieval character that occurred during the late 16th and early 17th centuries. Stephen Knight adds:

> The power of royalty was too great for the Elizabethan playwrights to go far in making Robin the libertarian enemy of princely oppression ... it would not be fully realized until the weight of history and the growth of bourgeois democracy had made royalty an easier target than in the period of autocracy. In those circumstances the hierarchical idealisms of Elizabethan and Jacobean neo-pastoral produced the hero's own inactivity, and that was the pattern that continued throughout the light theatrical modes of the eighteenth century.[7]

A century after the death of Elizabeth I, the original conception of the forest outlaw, including elements that may have been based on a real Robin Hood, William Wallace, Robert the Bruce or other medieval rebels, had been trodden under by 300 years of revisions. J. C. Holt writes:

> By 1700 the accession of secondary material to the legend was largely at an end. Repetition had overtaken invention. The printed versions of the ballads established a kind of canon.... The tale was still vigorously alive. But this was at the cost of becoming totally fictional. Whatever the historical reality, of political detail or social immediacy, that lay behind the original tale, it was lost amidst the jumble of new names, relationships and circumstances required by artistic or commercial convenience.[8]

But while the tradition was becoming solidified as conventional fiction in England, far north of the border, another real-life Scot was carrying out campaigns of lawlessness and, like Wallace and Bruce before him, distributing the spoils among the commoners under his care. Declared an outlaw for living up to his own code of honor, he eventually would become known as the "Robin Hood of the Highlands."

Five

Robin Returns to Scotland (1671–1734)

Descended from the chieftains of two prominent clans, Robert Roy MacGregor was born at the head of Loch Katrine in the southwest Highlands in February 1671. On March 7 of that year he was baptized into the Protestant faith by his proud parents, Donald Glas MacGregor, a chief of the Dougal Ciar sept of Clan Gregor, and Margaret Campbell MacGregor, an experienced mother of two sons, Duncan and Iain, and a daughter, Margaret, all of whom were much older than the newborn lad.

In remote, nearly inaccessible Glen Gyle, located in the mountains between Loch Katrine and Loch Lomond, Rob grew up in a peaceful time devoid of clan warfare and civil strife. Educated in literature, history and politics by the Gregorach, or men of the clan, at ceilidhs held at his home or in the turf houses of other clansmen, his years of learning were accompanied continuously by singing and the skirling of the Highland bagpipes.

Scampering around on hard earthen floors covered with the dung of animals that shared their dwellings, Highland children—the one-third who survived infancy—went barefoot even in winter. While young boys learned to fish, round up Highland cattle, ponies and sheep, and grow barley, flax and oats, they also attended informal public schools set up in local barns and outbuildings. Combined with his interest in reading and writing, this type of study allowed Rob to develop a mastery of Lowland Scots and English, as well as his own Gaelic language. He also reputedly became familiar with French and Latin.

As a lad Rob also began to develop a prodigious talent for swordplay. During the yearly "call to arms" drill that was required in times of peace, he engaged in daily broadsword practice, using an ash stick until he reached 16, when his father presented him with his own broadsword, dirk, targe, gun and two pistols. Now able to wield the real Highlander's steel, Rob constantly sharpened his skills until no one else could match his prowess. He also became a proficient archer while joining Duncan and Iain in the hunting of red deer.

Like most clansmen, Rob was the very picture of physical fitness, having developed a sturdy physique while trekking up to 30 miles per day driving cattle over wild moorland and braes. Of only average height—perhaps 5'4"—he was exceptionally broad-shouldered, with muscular legs and long arms that served him well while wielding the broadsword and targe. Living for days at a time out in the elements, sleeping on the rocky ground in his plaid, he developed the acute sensual understanding of nature indigenous to the Scottish Highlander: the ability to gather information from earth, sky, rain and the behavior of animals. Before he was 20 he could spot tracks others were incapable of seeing, a talent that would serve him well during his career as a professional cattle reaver.

All classes of men were involved in the "lifting" of cattle deemed common property by the Highlanders. A traditional activity of the region, reaving was not considered a crime. Acts of highway robbery and other forms of personal thievery feared in the Lowlands and throughout England were almost completely unknown in the Highlands.

Authorized by the government, Highland Watches, forerunners to what later became known as protection rackets, collected "blackmail" (or black rents) from farmers to guard their cattle herds from raiders. If farmers chose to forego this insurance, the Watch failed to protect their stocks, and depredations quickly followed. In 1658 the MacGregors had been authorized to operate their own Watch in the Lennox, an area in western Scotland once comprising Dunbartonshire and portions of Stirlingshire, Perthshire and Renfrewshire.

Rob Roy's early training as a reaver and retriever who tramped his way across Scotland in every sort of weather conditioned him well for his first major act of rebellion, an incident forced upon him by the political loyalty of his clan. Having taken an oath of allegiance to King James II of Scotland and VII of England, the MacGregors remained loyal to the Stewart monarch after he abdicated in the wake of the Whig's Glorious Revolution in 1688. The following year Rob, required by Highland custom (as a youngest son) to accompany his father on military campaigns, joined Donald Glas and other clansmen at Dalmucomar to declare their support for the Jacobite cause. Knowing that James' successor, Dutch King William, thought of the clans as nothing more than groups of ignorant savages, the Highlanders wanted to preserve their ancient way of life, a culture accepted by the Stewarts but doomed to extinction by the Whigs.

On July 27, 1689, Rob and his father fought at the Battle of Killiecrankie, a Jacobite victory spoiled by the death of their valiant general John Graham, Viscount Dundee. Following the subsequent Jacobite defeat at Dunkeld in August, Rob's brother Duncan was captured, as was Donald when he led a raid on the stock of William Cochrane, the Whig Laird of Kilmaronock, who had withheld his blackmail. After being held at Stirling Castle, Donald was transferred to the Edinburgh Tolbooth in January 1690, but Duncan was released two months later; since he had not sworn allegiance to the Stewarts, he was able legitimately to take the oath to King William. Meanwhile, Rob tended to the family farm until his brother Iain returned, following the close of the rebellion at the Haughs of Cromdale.

Troubled by her husband's imprisonment, Margaret MacGregor died in September 1691. Shortly thereafter, Donald swore allegiance to William, and government troops seized his rents to pay for his incarceration—events that instilled in Rob a lifelong hatred of Whigs; in fact, Highlanders in general considered the term "Whig" to designate a stilted, cold-hearted, pompously selfish man.

At the close of that month, Rob, joined by men from Glengyle, Craigrostan, Arklet, Strath Gartney and upper Balquhidder, carried out a major cattle raid at Buchlyvie which later came to be known as "The Harrying of Kippen." Determined to raise enough ransom to free his ailing father, Rob was outraged by Sir Alexander Livingston's (the Earl of Linlithgow) refusal to pay his mail to the Glengyle Watch; in return, the young reaver developed a plan to lift the nobleman's 200 cattle as they were driven to his east-country estate. The successful raid made Rob a well-known figure in western Scotland and increased the popularity of Clan Gregor.

On October 1, 1691, Donald Glas was released from prison. His oath of allegiance to King William was only one of many being sworn by Highland chieftains who were required to do so before New Year's Day 1692. Echoing the outrage of many throughout the land, the MacGregors were appalled when Alasdair, chief of the Glencoe MacDonalds, being unable to make his submission at Inverary due to severe weather, was beset by a troop hired by the government and led by Rob's uncle, Captain Robert Campbell of Glenlyon, who massacred 38 members of the clan, including the chief, two women and a six-year-old child.

On New Year's Day 1693 Rob married Helen Mary MacGregor, a black-haired, dark-eyed distant cousin from the farm of Corryheichen, 15 miles south of Balquhidder. Shortly afterward, Rob's joy turned to fury when he and his bride were forced to drop their surname. Repeating an act that had occurred earlier in the century, the government proscribed, or forbade the further use of, the name MacGregor. Perhaps the growing stature of Clan Gregor and the power of the Glengyle Watch prompted this act, but whatever the reason, no MacGregor could outwardly use his surname without being arrested.

Considering family ties to be of paramount importance, Rob chose his mother's maiden name, a move that gained him the guardianship of Sir John Campbell, Earl of Breadalbane, chief of the mid-Scotland sept of Clan Campbell and the rival of Lord John Murray, Secretary of State for Scotland, landlord of Balquhidder and chief of the clan most hated by the MacGregors. Captain Archibald MacGregor of Kilmanan, who became chief of Clan Gregor in February 1693, took the surname Graham, as did Mary's family, while Rob's brother Iain chose Murray, perhaps due to a territorial affiliation. Following the proscription, the Glengyle Watch assessed each farm under its jurisdiction in an attempt to persuade more cattle owners to buy insurance.

On January 4, 1694, Archibald moved Rob and Mary to Inversnaid in Craigrostan, an area between Ben Lomond and the northeastern shore of Loch Lomond that supported 150 families. Soon after, vicious weather and poor harvests led to a murderous famine that wracked most of Scotland for the rest of the decade, killing Rob's brother Iain in 1700. Rob and Mary's first two sons, James and Coll, were born during this period (in 1695 and 1698, respectively), and soon were followed by Duncan (in 1704) and Ranald (in 1706).

In December 1701 Archibald, now dissipated from years of alcohol abuse, sold 6,720 acres, including Craigrostan, the township of Knockyle, the western flank of Ben Lomond and the west end of Loch Arklet, to Rob. At this time Rob began to demonstrate the compassionate nature that later would reach legendary proportions. To Rob and other Highlanders, human beings and their land were inseparable, and his purchase of Craigrostan meant that he now accepted responsibility for the welfare of its tenants, a regard heightened by the misery wrought by the recent famine.

When Donald Glas passed away in 1702, Rob, as his only surviving son, became Tutor of Glengyle (the effective leader of Clan Dougal Ciar) until the late Iain's son, Gregor, reached adulthood and could accept the responsibilities. Without batting an eye at this increased burden, Rob placed Iain's widow, Christian, and her four children under his care. In March 1703 Rob's generosity was demonstrated when he purchased for Gregor 6,400 acres of Glen Gyle from James Graham, Marquis of Montrose, who had been investing in his cattle enterprise.

By the end of the decade Rob was greatly respected throughout the Highlands and Lowlands, by gentlemen and commoners alike. His business had thrived, allowing him to acquire more properties, including the lease on Monachyle Tuarach, a farm south of Loch Doine in Balquhidder, for Gregor's brother Donald in 1707.

Although he still involved himself in Jacobite matters, Rob did not officially join those intending to rise against Queen Anne (who had succeeded William in 1702) during the spring of 1708. When the French invasion force, including James Edward Stuart, son of King James II and VII, was halted by a ferocious storm, the rebellion was aborted and the Scots returned to their homes.

The Making of an Outlaw

Rob's prosperity continued until April 1711 when a tragic incident sparked a series of events that reduced the Captain of the Glengyle Watch and Laird of Craigrostan into a Robin Hood of the heather. Having borrowed £1000 sterling from the Marquis (now Duke) of Montrose, Rob had entrusted bills of exchange to his man Duncan MacDonald and sent him with drovers to purchase herds of cattle to fatten up for the next year's trysts. In May an agitated drover returned to Craigrostan, reporting that MacDonald had decamped with the money, presumably after buying the cows and selling them for a tidy profit.

Montrose, who split profits with Rob but demanded that the debtor absorb all losses, was furious. Having mortgaged a portion of Craigrostan to the duke, Rob set out to find MacDonald and persuade his own debtors to settle up. But Montrose, having no understanding of Highland honor and mistakenly believing that Rob intended to cheat him, ordered his capture. Rob met with Montrose's factor, James Grahame of Killearn, to begin settling the debt, but the duke demanded immediate payment in full, knowing that the Highlander's inability to do so would give him the power to sieze the mortgaged section of Craigrostan.

Ordered to appear in court at Glasgow, Rob instead set out once more to collect money for payment to Killearn. Commanding his factor to bill Rob for interest above any sum offered, Montrose continued to distort the case, and in early October 1712 an arrest warrant was issued. However, through Killearn, Montrose offered to forgive the debt if Rob would present evidence that John Campbell, Duke of Argyll, had been or currently was involved with the Jacobites. Rob refused to bear false witness against another man, thereafter appealing for aid from Argyll and John Murray, Duke of Atholl, both of whom failed to reply. On February 28, 1713, Robert Roy MacGregor Campbell was officially proclaimed an outlaw, losing all rights and claims to his goods and lands. About a week later, Montrose, who also held the office of Sheriff for Dunbartonshire, ordered a troop under Killearn's command to evict Rob and his family from Craigrostan and to seize all movable property and livestock.

Sailing up Loch Lomond to Inversnaid, Killearn and his men discovered only Mary and some of the children at home, for Rob had holed up 20 miles north at Corrycharmaig, a property he had leased from the Earl of Breadalbane. Killearn ordered some of the men to eject Mary and the boys from the house and confiscate the furnishings and clothing, and others to remove all grain and farming equipment from the outbuildings. Contrary to legend, the house was not burned, but destroyed by the troopers so that only the outer walls were left intact. Outraged that Montrose and Killearn had stooped so low as to terrorize a woman, Mary stood up to the factor and was pummelled in return (popular folklore suggests that she was raped, although most historians consider this story apocryphal).

At the time of the attack that cold March evening, no one in the area was able to help Mary and the lads. Gregor was five miles away at Glen Gyle, while Mary's father and uncles were at Corryarklet, three miles distant. On his way home with some hard-earned money for Killearn, Rob heard news of the outrage from members of Clan Buchanan. His anger growing with every hoof-fall of his horse, Rob reached Craigrostan to discover that his family was safe at Portnellan, but the sight of his ruined home hit him like the rush of a Highland storm. It was at this very point that Rob, now aged 43, truly became the Robin Hood of the Highlands—a fact vividly described by biographer W. H. Murray:

He was gripped by a wild rage of spirit. They, the men of stone, had done this harm to him and his, and they had done it to his name and clan and race for centuries: men of law, state, property, and of stone hearts. He would fight them till he died. They had not destroyed him but changed him. Never again would he live his life as a straightforward Highland cattleman or trusting patriot. These men like Montrose, so secure in great properties or positions that they felt free to wring human dignity out of men, and debase them for a quick gain, were an enemy worthy of hatred. He could outmaneuvre them. He could strike at them without compunction. Never need he scruple to turn against them their own weapons of deceit, faithlessness, and dissimulation—new arts to him but learned from masters. Montrose had sown the wind but would reap the whirlwind.[1]

A month after Killearn's attack on Inversnaid, Rob appeared at Finlarig Castle to meet with the Earl of Breadalbane, who, anxious to strike a symbolic blow against Montrose, presented him with the lease to Auchinchisallen in Glen Dochart, deep within Campbell territory where no Graham would send troops. After making one last unsuccessful effort to persuade Montrose to accept payments on the debt, Rob organized a band of men, including his former gillie, Alasdair Roy MacGregor, to raid Montrose's lands, reave his cattle and collect the tenants' rents before Killearn had an opportunity to do so. Presenting the tenants with receipts for rents paid to the duke, Rob never harmed their personal property and often gave them the spoils of his raids. When hearing of a poor farmer or wife scheduled to be turned out by Killearn, he would arrive before the scheduled eviction to place a bag of coins in the grateful tenant's hand.

And while Rob had become a real Robin Hood, Sheriff-depute Killearn's severe treatment of tenants made him a veritable Sheriff of Nottingham. Murray writes:

> From this time began the many acts of compassion for the poor that gave popular comparison to Robin Hood. They were attested by contemporaries and no legend of romance. If the poorer people had been left too short of winter grain taken for rent, Rob raided the Buchanan girnels and distributed grain where most needed. His charity no doubt began at home, but it spread out. It is easier to be generous with other people's property than one's own, but Rob had no property of his own, apart from the clothes on his back, and his sword, dirk, gun and pistols. In the days when he did have money, he had been generous with that too. He can be given credit, then, for staying true to himself.[2]

Rob Roy was Robin Hood indeed: outlaw; campaigner against corrupt, self-interested, over-taxing nobles; a man who robbed from the rich and gave to the poor.

When the Jacobites resurrected their plans for rebellion upon the succession of King George I of Hanover in 1714, Rob combined his campaign against Montrose with further support for the Stewarts, hoping that a successful rising would lead to the reinstatement of his lands. He was present at the Jacobite war council on the Braes of Mar on August 15, 1715, and helped raise provisions during the early days of the rebellion, which began at Braemar on September 6. He was wounded while fighting at Inverary in October, and served as a geographical adviser, messenger and reconnaissance man for John Erskine, the Earl of Mar, the dedicated but ineffectual general who led the rebels.

During the rising, Scotland was ruled by two men known intimately to Rob: the Dukes of Montrose and Argyll, who were Secretary of State and Commander-in-Chief of the Hanoverian army, respectively. The Jacobites experienced some early successes, including Mar's capture of Perth on September 14, and a recruitment that increased their ranks to 10,000 by early November.

Rob's major contribution to the campaign occurred in mid–November 1715, when he led 250 Gregorach southwest from Strath Allan to reconnoiter the Fords of Frew on the River Forth, at which the main body of Mar's army was to cross prior to attacking Argyll's forces. Unfortunately, Argyll caught wind of the plan and decided to cut off the dallying Mar before he could reach the Fords; marching his 3,500 troops north to the Sheriff Muir above Strath Allan, he met Mar in an indecisive battle. By the time Rob heard the news and hastened to the scene, the battle of Sheriffmuir was over. The following day each side claimed victory, but Mar's army never advanced farther south. After two more months of inactivity, including James Stuart's arrival at Peterhead to discover that the rebellion was over, the remaining Jacobite fighters returned to their homes. The government executed some noblemen who played conspicuous roles in the rebellion, but a general amnesty was granted to those who agreed to hand over weapons and provisions.

After the debacle at Sheriffmuir, a legend criticizing Rob's inaction at the battle quickly spread throughout Scotland and persisted for many years, particularly after Sir Walter Scott published the rumor as fact in two of his books. Although he had arrived too late to salvage Mar's inept handling of the affair and realizing that a further attack without organized support would result only in the senseless slaughter of the Gregorach (the kinsmen he had sworn to protect with his own life), Rob was viewed as a coward and a plunderer of the dead. Worse yet, Rob's status as an outlaw excluded him from the government's amnesty; and with the Jacobite defeat, his dread enemy, Montrose, became supreme ruler in Scotland.

During the spring of 1716 Rob sent Mary, who was pregnant with their son, Robin Oig, away from Auchinchisallen to Glen Gyle in the care of Alasdair Roy. Soon after, a Hanoverian troop plundered and burned the house, but Rob and some of the Gregorach picked off a few soldiers before setting off for Glen Chaorach.

Again approached by Montrose to produce evidence against the Duke of Argyll, Rob remained true to form, refusing ill-bought amnesty before heading to Inverary to seek protection from Argyll himself. Making a public demonstration of submission by giving the Duke some useless, rusty weapons they had gathered before arriving at the castle, Rob and his men then returned to Inversnaid and recruited more clansmen for a series of raids on Montrose's lands. In late September 1716 Rob's house again was torched, but the Gregorach, having received word of the reprisal, escaped unscathed.

With Mary, Duncan, Ranald, and the infant Robin Oig safely lodged at Loch Katrine, Rob took the heat off his homeland by returning to Argyll and, aided by six gillies, built a new house in upper Glen Shira, a remote area accessible only by a direct route through Inverary. Although he no longer could live with his wife and sons, he did make occasional visits while passing through to lift Montrose's cattle and sheep.

On November 19, 1716, Rob finally caught up with the heartless Killearn, ready to repay him for the destruction of Inversnaid and the eviction and brutalizing of Mary. At an inn at Chapellaroch near the Fords of Frew, Killearn was playing host to tenants who had paid their rents earlier in the day; upon hearing that Rob was nearby, he quickly tossed his money bag into a loft and returned to his dram. Seconds later Rob burst in and the Gregorach wasted no time finding the satchel, from which £3000 was lifted to pay for the attack on his home. Killearn then was marched 20 miles north to Portnellan and ferried out to the small island of Eilean Dhu in Loch Katrine. At Rob's insistence the factor penned a letter to Montrose requesting that his captor be forgiven any further debt and that additional reparations be paid for Craigrostan.

Although Montrose was mildly concerned about the safety of his reliable factor, he was not willing to pay ransom and left Killearn to his own devices. Unwilling to sink to the cruel level of his Lowlander enemies, Rob then took the flabby Killearn, who was no fighter, to Kirkintilloch and returned his account books before releasing him.

To avoid capture Rob rarely stayed in one place for long, but his luck ran out in April 1717 when he chose to spend a night in a house at Balquhidder. Receiving word that Rob was in the area, a troop led by Montrose surprised him while he slept wrapped in his plaid; bound with a leather belt, he was placed on a horse and surrounded by dragoons headed for Stirling. While crossing the Fords of Frew, Rob's guards were forced to release the belt and tether him to James Stewart, one of Montrose's tenants who, unbeknownst to them, had once benefitted from the prisoner's Robin Hood-like activities. Halfway across the river, Rob plunged into the icy water, discarded his plaid, and dived under as far as he could; with his tartan drawing the troopers' fire, he swam to the north shore and escaped.

With every unconquerable move he made, Rob became more like Robin Hood. Murray writes:

> From this time onward, Rob Roy became in the public mind a legendary character, whom neither kings, generals, dukes, sheriffs, nor their armies, were able to capture for the gallows, who repaid enemies intent on his death with forbearance, at least in regard to their own lives, who gave to the poor the food and justice their masters withheld, and managed all this with an easy insouciance, which people envied him. The insouciance was far away from the truth—a heavy toll was being taken of Rob's superb constitution and spirit—but the rest was too near the truth for Montrose's liking. He confessed himself beaten and gave up the pursuit.[3]

However, Montrose's defeat encouraged others to try their hand at laying the Highlander by the heels. But like those characters in the legends who are incapable of capturing Robin Hood, "The lesser men posed little threat to Rob Roy in his own country. They were either fools or ignorant, having no conception of Rob's complete mastery of his environment."[4] To maintain this edge on his would-be captors, Rob had to stay on the run, never able to see Mary and the boys for more than a few hours at a time.

In early June 1717 the Duke of Atholl, wishing to regain favor at King George's court, set out to seize Rob. Promised protection by the duke, Rob, who wanted to establish a new cattle operation at Inver-lochlarig Beg, one of Atholl's farms, agreed to meet at Dunkeld; but when Rob again refused to defame the Duke of Argyll, he was thrown into a cell at Castle Logierait in Perthshire. But Rob being *Rob*, he managed to get his jailers drunk and, aided by a Gregorach gillie, escaped on horseback before a troop could arrive to take him to Edinburgh.

By the autumn of 1717 Rob was basing most of his operations in Balquhidder. While he was visiting Mary at Monachyle Tuarach, a troop hired by Atholl surrounded the house and ordered him onto a steed in the middle of a double line of cavalry riding south to Stirling. At Loch Lubnaig the troopers were forced to stretch their formation into single file while riding along a narrow path skirting the edge of a sheer cliff. When the horse behind Rob refused to continue, he watched carefully as those in front of him trotted on; dismounting, he pulled himself onto the bank above and quickly disappeared into the woods.

Thereafter, no official army personnel were used to pursue Rob Roy; this daunting task was relegated to private troops hired by noblemen and other independent companies. Montrose had already given up, but Atholl made one last effort, commanding 20 horsemen to Balquhidder, where they were ambushed and sent packing by Rob and a small band of Gregorach at the pass of Glen Ogle.

The construction of a barracks ordered by Montrose began at Inversnaid during the spring of 1718. On August 8, a group of clansman walked up to the structure and calmly knocked on the door before carrying off the entire party of builders. Unable to receive a positive identification of the kidnappers, Montrose and his subordinates shifted both blame and personnel, but by the winter of 1719, the barracks finally was completed.

Annoyed by the presence of a fort on the site of his former home, Rob ironically benefitted from the sense of security the government gained from the project. The area was now protected from the legendary outlaw—so the crown believed—and Rob settled down with Mary at Monachyle Tuarach before building a new house at Inverlochlarig Beg.

Although Rob now was able to return to farming and cattle reaving, he again supported the Jacobites in 1719, when a rising was planned in coordination with Spaniards anxious to regain Italian lands lost to the English in 1713. Accompanied by 40 men, Rob joined them at the abortive Battle of Glen Shiel, and then destroyed a store of government arms before returning to Balquhidder. The entire "rebellion" was little more than an inept broadsword swipe in the night.

In 1723 Rob truly became a living legend upon the publication of Daniel Defoe's novel *Highland Rogue*, a fictionalized account of his exploits, the first entry in a trilogy about famous villains that later included *Jack Shepherd* and *Jonathan Wild*. Interestingly, the book was a favorite of King George and became the subject of much discussion at the English court. As a result of its popularity, Rob was even more feared throughout the realm, and Argyll, who now was favored at court, persuaded the proud Highlander to meet with him and Montrose, reportedly in London. This successful gathering, together with the death of Atholl the following year, gave the 53-year-old Rob a new lease on life.

In 1725 many of the Jacobite chiefs made submissions to General George Wade, commander of the army in Scotland, in return for the king's amnesty. A letter supposedly written by Rob on September 15 of that year, in which he claims he was forced to support the Jacobites while secretly sending military information to Argyll, has been proved to be a document sponsored by Argyll and perhaps written by the duke's lawyers in Edinburgh. W. H. Murray suggests that Rob "signed without care, reckoning that since all submissions now made were false to the core, he need have no scruples about a formal letter meant for Wade's eyes only."[5] The next year Rob, receiving a pardon, was no longer an outlaw.

In 1729 Rob made the last of his conversions by abandoning the Protestant faith for Catholicism and giving up reaving to seek forgiveness for his years of lawlessness. His nephew Gregor, commanding a Watch authorized by the government, now collected the blackmail. Working on the farm at Inverlochlarig Beg until December 28, 1734, Rob, wearing his plaid, dirk and pistols while the Gregorach piper skirled the lament "I Shall Return No More," passed away sitting upright in a chair. Even dying at the ripe old age of 64, the honorable outlaw could not bear to let his enemy—in this case, John MacLaren of Invernenty, who had arrived to discuss improving relations between them—catch him in a vulnerable position. He lies to this day in the old churchyard of the Kirk of Balquhidder.

Most legends about outlaws, including those of Robin Hood, feature intense physical violence. The life of Rob Roy MacGregor, like that of the many characterizations of Robin Hood, was filled with violence, yet Rob never fought to the death in any of his 22 recorded duels. A major tenet of the Highlander's code of honor was to duel only until "first cut," or to concede victory to the man who was resourceful and skillful enough to draw the other's blood.

One of Rob's most well-known duels occurred at Arnprior, the home of John Buchanan, located between Buchlyvie and Kippen. Here, after downing a few drams, Rob insulted Henry Cunningham of Boquhan, a Lowland fop whose overt effeminacy and pretentious manner caused the Highlander's blood pressure to rise. Outside on Shieling Hill, Rob, not knowing that this *exquisite* was also a fearsome swordsman, failed to prepare himself and was driven off the field, thus sustaining the one and only documented loss of his duelling career.

Contrary to the novels, dramas, and motion pictures that depict him as a lethal duellist, Rob Roy was so driven by Highland honor—unwilling to adopt the iniquitous methods of his enemies, including slander and out-and-out murder—that he often risked his life and the security of his family to remain true to the code. He even freed Killearn, the man who had destroyed his home and abused his beloved wife, because he would not succumb to vengeance. His dedication to this philosophy also kept him aware of his roots and led to his fame as a Robin Hood who was the benefactor of commoners across the land. Murray writes:

> The men of great Lowland estate could bring themselves on occasion to fight and die for religious convictions or political beliefs, but lived divorced from the people, unable to bridge the social gulf as Rob Roy could from his life in the clan lands. They were careless of the plight of the lower orders. They turned a cold eye on men, women, and children, whom they considered public trash, without human rights, and not like cattle to be held in some esteem. Rob Roy was a more civilized man than the lords of his day in one important respect. His concern for the common man was unfeigned. He had lived as they did. He could not have brought himself to inflict on people the inhumanities approved by men of power.[6]

After all he suffered at the hands of those who mistook his Highland lifestyle, conception of honor, and cattle reaving (which was an institutionalized practice) for cowardice, perjury, fraud and extortion, Rob Roy in the end was able to win his battle and regain a home and land without paying his enemy with the betrayal of another man. Even in his greatest time of trial, when he could not see his own family or merely spend a night under a leaky roof of thatch, he made other families' lives more comfortable with a bag of coins or a side of beef. After the 1715 Jacobite Rebellion, when General Wade's road-building program rolled into the Highlands to carry on a cultural decimation that would reach a high point 30 years later, Rob was striving to preserve what he viewed as a more honorable way of life.

Did Robin Hood exist? The spirit of the legend certainly did—in Robert Roy MacGregor.

Six

Storybook Outlaws
(1771–1900)

Five years before Rob Roy drew his last breath, an infant christened Walter Scott was born in the Borders of Scotland. Other than becoming a writer to the Signet Library in Edinburgh, a cathedral-like building originally established to house Scots law books and statutes, Scott's greatest achievement was siring a namesake who has been called "the most popular novelist of all time."

Born in Edinburgh in 1771, Walter Scott the younger was stricken with polio at the tender age of 18 months. Prevented from engaging in activities enjoyed by most children, the lad spent his formative years with his grandfather at Sandyknowe farm near Kelso, where he rested his lame right leg while developing a fascination for the traditional Border ballads and songs he heard performed by his relatives and the local folk.

While young Scott was absorbing the lively culture that would guide the rest of his life, another future novelist of historical bent was born in Edinburgh during the momentous year of 1776. And, like Scott, little Jane Porter, sired into a prosperous family, was regailed with traditional songs and tales while still a wee bairn in the nursery. Lullabies extolling the martyrdom of William Wallace were dramatically supported by an old serving man who recounted the battles of Stirling and Bannockburn while laying out family repasts in the dining hall.

When Miss Porter was one, six-year-old Walter Scott returned to Edinburgh and, in 1779, entered the High School, where he studied Latin Literature and began writing his own poetry. From 1783–86 he attended Edinburgh University, and after serving a three year apprenticeship with his father, returned there to study law. In 1792 he was accepted by the Scottish Bar, the Faculty of Advocates, and began a distinguished career that included life-long stints as Sheriff-Depute of Selkirkshire and Principal Clerk to the Court of Session, Scotland's highest civil court.

During Scott's student days a comic opera, *Robin Hood, or Sherwood Forest* (1782), was staged at the Theatre Royal in London's Covent Garden. With a libretto by Laurence McNally and music by William Shield, this production furthered the romantic, conservative depiction of the outlaw firmly established a century earlier. A few years later Anthony Munday's 1598 characterization (the dispossessed aristocrat who aids Richard the Lionheart) was resurrected by Joseph Ritson, who collected and published the major texts on the outlaw myth in 1795, prefacing the collection with his essay "The Life of Robin Hood."

Ritson took Munday's late 12th-century character, called him Robert Fitz Ooth, Earl of Huntingdon, born at Locksley in 1160, and reshaped him according to his own radical political views. Although many revolutionary thinkers of the time believed that Anglo-Saxon England was much more egalitarian than the "Norman yoke" that supplanted it, Ritson did not express the outlaw's activities in purely Saxon versus Norman terms, and even claimed that Robin was descended from a Norman lord.

Fascination with Tradition

Like his predecessor Robert Burns, whom he met at a dinner in Edinburgh during the winter of 1786-87, Walter Scott performed his governmental duties while indulging a true love for poetry, literature and music. Burns' dedication to his muse subsequently resulted in Scotland's two national songs, "Auld Lang Syne" (1791) and the anthem "Scots Wha Hae" (1793), whose first two stanzas forever immortalize the outlaw leaders of the Wars of Independence and their eternal enemy:

> Scots, wha hae wi' Wallace bled,
> Scots, wham Bruce has aften led,
> Welcome to your gory bed
>   Or to victorie!
> Now's the day, and now's the hour:
> See the front o' battle lour,
> See approach proud Edward's power—
>   Chains and slaverie!

Sharing Burns' penchant for re-working traditional songs, Scott published his famous *Minstrelsy of the Scottish Border*, a marriage of old material and his own literary embellishments, in 1802-03, and he followed this with a prolific array of long poems imitating traditional ballads and medieval romances.

During this same period one of Britain's premier poets, William Wordsworth (1770–1850), composed "Rob Roy's Grave," a work literarily linking the Scottish and English outlaws:

> A famous man is Robin Hood,
> The English ballad singer's joy!

A decade later Scott became immensely successful as "the father of the historical novel," principally writing about Scottish subjects, although his first works were published anonymously. After his first novel, *Waverly*, proved a huge hit in 1814, he published his future works under the pseudonym "the Author of *Waverly*" and later was dubbed "the Great Unknown."

The Scottish Chiefs

Interestingly, five years before *Waverly* proved a sensation, Jane Porter had published *The Scottish Chiefs*, her mammoth historical novel based on Wallace's exploits during the Wars of Independence. As an adolescent she had heard detailed accounts of Sir William's heroic acts from Luckie Forbes, a pious neighbor, and these narratives had inspired her to research any written records or tales chronicling the years 1296–1305. She read John Barbour's *The Bruce*, Blind Harry's epic poem, Thomas the Rhymer's verses, and letters penned by Edward Longshanks himself.

While living in an English cottage at Thames-Ditton, Porter crafted a highly romanticized, staggeringly thick but eminently readable fictionalization of Wallace containing enough fact to make it acceptable to those seeking more than just a rattling good yarn. In 19th-century fashion, Wallace, of course, is a paragon of virtue, a man who is sparked to revolt when agents of the tyrannical Longshanks murder his Marion. All the blood and thunder of the genre are there, including embellished dramatizations of the battles of Stirling and Falkirk, the self-interested

wrangling of the Scottish nobles, Bruce's conflict with his father, and
Wallace's tragic end (he is merely hanged).

Whetting the appetites of European readers for Scott's style of historical writing, *The Scottish Chiefs* was the early 19th-century equivalent of a blockbuster, lauded throughout Great Britain, translated into
many languages, and a favorite tome of royals across the Continent
(with the exception of Napoleon, who reportedly banned it). Although
successive generations have considered the novel (particularly a 1921
edition beautifully illustrated by N. C. Wyeth) as children's literature,
Porter's mixture of fact and romanticism, particularly her inclusion of
fabricated female love interests for Wallace, anticipated similar depictions of Robin Hood and other outlaw heroes throughout the remainder
of the century and into the next.

Rob Roy

During the spring of 1817 Walter Scott began planning a novel
loosely based on the exploits of a certain reaver and retriever who, dur-
ing his childhood, had been described to him by Alexander Stewart of
Invernahyle, an old man who claimed to have fought Rob Roy Mac-
Gregor with broadsword and targe decades earlier. After visiting Loch
Lomond and a cave at Inversnaid supposedly frequented by Rob, Scott,
using the 1715 Jacobite Rebellion as a backdrop, integrated general facts
and a few specific events from the Highlander's life into a tale about
Frank Osbaldistone, the son of a London merchant who is banished to
Northumberland when he refuses to follow in his father's mercantile
footsteps. At Osbaldistone Hall, Frank earns the enmity of his cousin,
Rashleigh, a Jacobite plotter who attempts to ruin the London business
and destroy Frank's relationship with Diana Vernon. Diana, along with
Bailie Nicol Jarvie, a Glasgow merchant, persuades the outlawed Mac-
Gregor to end the intrigues. In the end Rob kills Rashleigh, who has
informed on the Jacobites, and retrieves the funds stolen from William
Osbaldistone. Free to marry Diana, Frank is reconciled with his father,
who makes him Lord of Osbaldistone Manor.

Published by Archibald Constable in a three-volume first edition
of 10,000 copies on December 31, 1817, *Rob Roy* was an enormous success for "the Author of *Waverly*," who contributed further to burying
the true facts about the outlaw under the weight of popular legend. For

here Rob is only one of many primary characters in a tale dealing with the transformation of material interests in Scotland during the 18th century, a championing of a new commercial society at the expense of a traditional one.

Although the novel is titled *Rob Roy*, it focuses on Frank Osbaldistone, who, in old age, recalls his exploits for his business partner. In fact, the outlaw is not referred to as Rob Roy until midway through the 39-chapter saga, being known only as "Mr. Campbell" in its earlier stages. Additionally, Scott's depiction centers primarily on his cattle thieving and Jacobite intriguing, although Rob does prove heroic by assisting Frank and Diana. Perhaps the most unfortunate element in Scott's fictionalization is his portrayal of Rob's wife (here called Helen) as a stern, obnoxious and violent woman.

Two passages are of particular interest. In chapter 26 Bailie Jarvie compares Rob to both Robin Hood and William Wallace; and in the novel's penultimate paragraph, Frank Osbaldistone, with a fair degree of historical accuracy, narrates:

> I often visited Scotland, but never again saw the bold Highlander who had such an influence on the early events of my life. I learned, however, from time to time, that he continued to maintain his ground among the mountains of Loch Lomond, in despite of his powerful enemies, and that he even obtained, to a certain degree, the connivance of government to his self-elected office of Protector of the Lennox, in virtue of which he levied black-mail with as much regularity as the proprietors did their ordinary rents. It seemed impossible that his life should have concluded without a violent end. Nevertheless, he died in old age and by a peaceful death, some time about the year 1733, and is still remembered in his country as the Robin Hood of Scotland, the dread of the wealthy, but the friend of the poor, and possessed of many qualities, both of head and heart, which would have graced a less equivocal profession than that to which his fate condemned him.

On January 17, 1818, less than three weeks after *Rob Roy* was published, a stage version opened at Edinburgh's Pantheon Theatre, where it remained for six performances. Later that year other dramatizations, including George Soane's *Rob Roy, the Gregaroch*, and a London production by actor, writer and Scott enthusiast Daniel Terry, appeared.

Running for 32 performances at London's Covent Garden, Isaac Pocock's *Rob Roy MacGregor; or, Auld Lang Syne*, featuring music by Devon composer John Davy, then moved to Edinburgh, where it opened at the Theatre Royal on February 15, 1819. As Bailie Jarvie, the impressive Charles Mackay went on to play the part more than 1,100 times, including a royal command performance for King George IV during the monarch's two-week visit to Edinburgh in August 1821. Having participated in arranging the reception, Scott met the king upon his arrival at Leith Roads and later shared some Highland whisky with him. George enjoyed the play immensely and made certain to send a note of gratitude to Scott before departing for London the following day. One year later Pocock's popular adaptation was revised by W. H. Murray and performed as *Rob Roy*.

Several other stage adaptations appeared over the ensuing century. Another version of *Rob Roy MacGregor; or Auld Lang Syne* was performed as an opera in 1820, and was followed by *Gregaroch, the Highland Watchword* (1831); *Rob Roy* (c. 1832), a Parisian opera with music by Friedrich von Flotow and libretto by Dupont and Desforges; *Rob Roy* (1859), with Henry Irving as Rashleigh at Edinburgh's Theatre Royal; *Rob Roy* (1867), a Drury Lane opera featuring Sims Reeves; *Robbing Roy; or Scotched and Kilt* (1879), a parody by F. C. Burnand with music by H. C. Stephens; and *Rob Roy* (1905) by J. R. Park.

As an introduction to the novel, Scott included a history of Rob Roy that contains as much legend as fact. This work also was published under the title "Historical Account of the Clan MacGregor" in *The Quarterly Review* and in the book *Manners, Customs, and History of the Highlanders of Scotland & Historical Account of the Clan MacGregor*. Although Scott's knowledge of the Highlands was colored by a Lowlander's romantic notions, his interest in Rob Roy was considerable, as evidenced by the private collection of armaments he displayed at Abbotsford, his neo-Baronial mansion on the southern bank of the Tweed near Melrose in Roxburghshire: amid weapons such as the hunting knife of Prince Charles Edward Stuart ("Bonnie Prince Charlie"), the pistols of John Graham of Claverhouse ("Bonnie Dundee"), and the sword of James Graham, 1st Marquis of Montrose, were Rob's own broadsword, dirk, gun and sporran. Elsewhere in the mansion hung a portrait of the outlaw.

Ivanhoe

> "Call me no longer Locksley, my Liege, but know me under the name which, I fear, fame hath blown too widely not to have reached even your royal ears—I am Robin Hood of Sherwood Forest."

After *Rob Roy*, the prolific Scott, anxious to earn more money to pour into Abbotsford, wrote three more Scottish novels—*The Heart of Midlothian* (1818), *The Bride of Lammermoor* (1819) and *A Legend of Montrose* (1819)—before turning to an entirely different subject to challenge his literary and historical prowess: the conflict between Richard the Lionheart and Prince John in late 12th-century England. Scott possessed a formidable knowledge of his own nation during the 17th and 18th centuries, but did he know enough about *English* events that occurred more than five centuries earlier? Regardless of the monumental task he assigned himself, he believed his readers might be growing tired of Scottish matters; he wanted to offer them a new setting while simultaneously tackling the problems created by the feudal order firmly established by the Normans.

The result of his literary experiment, *Ivanhoe*, was completed on August 19, 1819, and published by Constable in a two-volume first edition of 10,000 copies. Priced at 30 shillings, it sold out in less than two weeks. This time around, Scott wanted to use the *nom de plume* Laurence Templeton, but Archibald Constable persuaded him to stick with the tried and true "Author of *Waverly*."

However, Scott added a "Dedicatory Epistle" (to the "Rev. Dr. Dryasdust, F.A.S."!) to the beginning of the novel, signing it "Laurence Templeton." In this preface, he links the English legend with the Scottish outlaws when he writes, "The name of Robin Hood, if duly conjured with, should raise a spirit as soon as that of Rob Roy; and the patriots of England deserve no less renown in our modern circles, than the Bruces and Wallaces of Caledonia."

Ivanhoe opens in an ancient Yorkshire forest inhabited by "bands of gallant outlaws." Scott's inclusion of Robin Hood (called "Locksley" until chapter 40, when the outlaw reveals his true identity to Richard the Lionheart) in a major work of prose fiction was an innovation at the time—a literary device that became rather commonplace thereafter. Like other tales of Robin Hood published after the appearance of Ritson's influential "history," the novel situates the outlaw at the center of a Saxon versus Norman conflict, although in reality this national calamity had ended decades earlier. However, in chapter one, Scott immediately sets the stage for his continuation of this racial rivalry:

Four generations had not sufficed to blend the hostile blood of the Normans and Anglo-Saxons, or to unite, by common language and

mutual interests, two hostile races, one of which still felt the elation
of triumph, while the other groaned under all the consequences of
defeat.

The "groaning" of the defeated is represented by Cedric the Saxon,
a descendant of Hereward the Wake who cannot accept the reality of
more than a century of Norman domination. Early in the tale, at Cedric's
domain of Rotherwood, the ensuing conflict is established by the major
characters: disguised as a pilgrim having returned from the Holy Land,
Sir Wilfred of Ivanhoe, the disinherited son of Cedric, hears himself
identified as the enemy of Brian de Bois-Gilbert, a Norman knight who
jousted with him in Palestine; and when Ivanhoe offers his seat to Isaac
of York, a Jew despised by the others, he establishes a relationship that
evolves throughout the novel. Also present at Rotherwood is Rowena,
Cedric's ward, who loves Ivanhoe but is intended to be the bride of
Athelstane, the Saxon's heir. The affairs of these characters, developed
in extensive detail by Scott, are backgrounded by the Richard the Lionheart–Prince John struggle.

A mysterious black knight who allies himself with Ivanhoe (known
as "the Disinherited Knight") at Prince John's tournament in Ashby and
later joins Locksley in besieging the Normans (including de Bois-
Gilbert, Reginald Front-de Boeuf [John's intended recipient of the Ivanhoe estate] and Maurice de Bracy [a mercenary leader who conspires
to kidnap Rebecca, Isaac's beautiful daughter]) is later revealed as King
Richard, who, until the final chapters, is still believed held by Leopold
of Austria. When Rebecca is condemned to death for practicing witch-
craft (actually medicine), Ivanhoe, as the Jewess' champion, and Richard
hasten to her assistance. In the ensuing joust, de Bois-Gilbert, who has
developed a forbidden love for the Jewess, dies "a victim to the violence of his own contending passions." Having regained his throne,
Richard attends the wedding of Wilfred and Rowena, "a pledge of the
future peace and harmony betwixt two races, which, since that period,
have been so completely mingled, that the distinction has become wholly
invisible."

The distinction between Saxon and Norman actually had become
quite invisible to the freemen of England before the Angevin Richard
the Lionheart sat upon the throne. However, Scott qualifies his depiction of the racial conflict by placing much of the Saxon patriotism within
Cedric, who remains dedicated to a long-lost cause.

Scott's King Richard is a much more complex character than later depictions of the monarch in similar Saxon versus Norman tales. Here he actually returns to England, fights valiantly, and then commands Robin Hood and the merry men, rather than merely being ransomed and protected by the outlaws.

Interestingly, Robin Hood (depicted as a yeoman) is a more visible character than Ivanhoe, who either lies wounded or disappears for much of the lengthy tale. With his jousts at the beginning and end, Sir Wilfred provides a dramatic frame for Locksley and Richard's heroics in between. But with Ivanhoe cast as the title character, Robin is only a supporting player, "a marginal version of the outlaw hero" who "acts as military support and security officer to the forces of good."[1] Scott borrowed only a few elements from the traditional ballads, but created several events, including the archery contest at which the outlaw demonstrates his prowess, that subsequently became part of most Robin Hood fiction and drama.

The most interesting social aspect of *Ivanhoe* is Scott's depiction of the Jewish characters, perhaps the most positive up to that time. At first, Isaac is cast as the stereotypical moneylender, but as Scott develops the narrative, he shows us that it is the Christian society around Isaac that prevents him from being anything else. As Scott biographer Edgar Johnson writes, "The existence of the Jew as outcast and scapegoat indicts the society that rejects him."[2] Isaac and the other Jews are not the only disinherited and despised characters who populate *Ivanhoe*, for most of the other major characters also fall within this group, most notably Locksley and the Saxon outlaws, Ivanhoe himself, and (for a time) King Richard the Lionheart.

Today, Scott's prose, steeped in historical detail, may be rough jousting for readers accustomed to more economical writing styles. But, as Johnson writes, in *Ivanhoe*: "The critical insight into the virtues and the shortcomings of the feudal system and the code of chivalry is acute and in the main just. Both as a work of literary imagination and as a feat of historical reconstruction, the novel is an impressive achievement."[3] In many ways, Scott's version of the Robin Hood legend, for better or worse, has been more influential than any other.

Awarded a baronetcy in 1820, an event coinciding with the success of *Ivanhoe* but earned through his discovery of the Scottish regalia lost since the British Civil Wars of 1638–50, Scott prospered until an economic crisis wracked Britain during January 1826. Having invested in the publishing and printing companies that produced his books, he lost heavily; but rather than declaring bankruptcy, Scott chose to pay off the debt by increasing his already formidable literary output. Recovering financially but destroying his health, he suffered four strokes and passed away on September 21, 1832.

Not surprisingly, several other writers attempted to catch Scott's prominent coattails as the great novelist sped on with his career. Although Thomas Love Peacock had begun *Maid Marian* before *Ivanhoe* appeared on the stands, he heavily revised his manuscript before it was published in 1822. Although this juvenile-oriented novel borders on parody, it successfully merges many of the earlier ballads collected by Ritson; and its structure—including the outlaw's love for Marian and the return of Richard—predated that incorporated into most future fictionalizations of Robin's exploits.

Six years after Scott was laid to rest at Jedburgh Abbey, Thomas Miller's stilted juvenile tale *Royston Gower* (1838) aped *Ivanhoe* by casting Robin Hood and his men as the military support of a soldier, this time fighting against the abuses occurring during John's actual reign as king. Serialized from 1838–40, Pierce Egan's action oriented *Robin Hood and Little John: or, The Merry Men of Sherwood Forest* was hugely popular, repeating the Earl of Huntingdon characterization, vivid scenes of medieval warfare, and Scott's Saxon versus Norman thematics. Writing in 1843, G. P. R. James joined Scott and Miller in presenting the outlaw in minor mode, here as captain of Simon de Montfort's archers at the battle of Evesham.

Two-dimensional depictions of Robin continued as each success bred a hasty imitation. Borrowing Miller's title and Egan's content, Joachim Stocqueler, in 1849, published his now obscure *Maid Marian or, the Forest Queen*. Three years earlier he had contributed *Robin Hood and Richard Coeur de Lion*, an absurd pantomime devoid of nationalist elements in which, in a reversal of Elizabethan style, the outlaw and his men were all portrayed by women. Other stage melodramas and satires, some of which incorporated the Saxon versus Norman theme, including John Oxenford and G. A. MacFarren's jingoistic *Robin Hood: An Opera* (1860), followed.

By the latter decades of the 19th century, two types of popular Robin Hood fiction began to appear, as some authors continued to write for adults and others specifically targeted an adolescent audience. Some entries in the latter category include Richard Lewis' *Life and Adventures of Robin Hood* (1865), George Emmett's *Robin Hood and the Outlaws of Sherwood Forest* (1869) and "Forest Ranger's" *Outlaws of Sherwood Forest* (c. 1870), but perhaps the most popular and influential children's version is Howard Pyle's *The Merry Adventures of Robin Hood of Great Renown in Nottinghamshire*, first published by Constable in 1883 and perpetually available in several editions.

A gifted and successful illustrator, Pyle occasionally wrote fiction, including a major book on King Arthur and his knights, to accompany his drawings. At the age of 30 he produced the text and 23 now-legendary, full-page illustrations that have provided inspiration for dozens of subsequent storybooks, novels, dramatizations and motion pictures. The enormous success of Pyle's work was due to his straightforward integration of familiar action-oriented Robin Hood stories, but also to his timing, as the publication of *The Merry Adventures* coincided with the acceptance of English literature as a required subject by the British education industry. School teachers and administrators turned to the Robin Hood tales as a means of providing students with an easy-to-understand, positive overview of their English heritage.

Pyle's text includes all the events now considered essential to the legend: Robin and Little John's fight over the stream; Robin's winning of the golden arrow at the Sheriff of Nottingham's archery tournament; the lavish feast in Sherwood Forest; Friar Tuck carrying Robin across the stream; Robin's slaying of Guy of Gisbourne; Robin's waylaying of the disguised King Richard; and the Lionheart's pardoning of Robin and his merry men, who also include Will Scarlet, Allan-a-Dale, and Midge the Miller. Also featured are Sir Richard of the Lea and Robin's shooting of the final arrow before his death at the Priory of Kirklees.

Twenty years later, *Bold Robin Hood and His Outlaw Band*, a similarly impressive text-and-pictures effort containing much of the same content, was created by Louis J. Rhead, an English writer-artist popular with young readers during the early 1900s. Rhead's hero is the noble Robin Fitz Ooth, son of the Earl of Huntingdon, but really "a yeoman at heart" who feels an affinity for the local peasants.

Rhead's unadorned style is the most admirable of the Victorian versions, and his spare use of lethal violence suggests his influence on later cinematic adaptations. He apes Pyle's structure, but pares down the content, suggesting the continuous literary streamlining of the legend that would reach its zenith in the hands of popular screenwriters.

Part III

Robin Hood
on the Screen

Seven

Shadows of Sherwood: Early Silent Films (1908–1913)

In 1908 *Sherwood*, a nostalgic, entirely fictional play by Alfred Noyes, was followed by the outlaw's screen debut in two one-reel productions: Kalem's *Robin Hood* and Clarendon's *Robin Hood and His Merrie Men*. The latter film, directed in England by Percy Straw from a screenplay by Langford Reed, featured Robin wooing Maid Marian and forming a band to save a condemned man from the gallows.

A seminal "Scottish Robin Hood" film, *Rob Roy*, an adaptation of Scott's novel directed by Arthur Vivian, was released by United Films in 1911. The first three-reel feature ever produced in Great Britain, it was filmed entirely in Scotland and starred John Clyde as Rob, Theo Henries as Helen MacGregor, Durward Lely as Francis Osbaldistone, and W. G. Robb as Bailie Jarvie.

Robin Hood made several appearances during 1912, most prominently in Henry Gilbert's popular novelization, and in John Drinkwater's play *Robin Hood and the Pedlar*, but also in the first three-reelers based on the legends. British and Colonial's melodramatic, *Ivanhoe*-inspired *Robin Hood—Outlawed*, directed by Charles Raymond and starring A. Brian Plant as Robin and Ivy Martinek as Marian, incorporated the outlawed nobleman depiction and featured the Merry Men rescuing the maiden from Sir Hubert de Boissy (Jack Houghton), an iniquitous knight.

The first Hood feature produced in the United States, Eclair's *Robin Hood* was filmed in California during 1912 and released the following year. Based on Reginald de Koven's 1890 musical, it established the popular cinematic theme of the outlaw fighting Sir Guy of Gisbourne for the hand of Maid Marian. Another 1912 production released in the United States in 1913, Kinemacolor's *Robin Hood*, was based on Howard Pyle's popular novelization. Shot on location in Sherwood Forest, it was the first Hood film to focus heavily on Will Scarlet, who, while courting the Lady Christabel, ran afoul of her sheriff father, Baron Fitz Alvine, and was outlawed. Jousting with Friar Tuck and falling in with Robin and his men, Will returned to Fitz Alvine's castle in force and, after being captured and sent to the gallows, was rescued in the nick of time by Robin (who is merely a supporting character in the film). Utilizing a primitive early color process, this film, originally released in Great Britain as *In the Days of Robin Hood*, was well received by the American press. In his August 22, 1913, *Variety* review, "Corb" wrote, "As runs the spirit of the famous old-time tale, so, in the main, run the incidents selected for the composite of it in colored filmdom."[1]

Three more Hood films were released during 1913. Thanhouser's *Robin Hood*, a four-reeler shot in California, featured the archery contest and King Richard's incognito visit to Sherwood. This effort was joined by legitimate feature adaptations of *Ivanhoe* produced on both sides of the Atlantic.

Written and directed by Herbert Brenon, who also played Isaac, Independent Moving Pictures' *Ivanhoe* featured popular star King Baggot as Sir Wilfred, Leah Baird as Rebecca, Evelyn Hope as Lady Rowena, and W. Thomas as Robin Hood. Zenith Films' British version, curiously released in the U.S. as *Rebecca the Jewess*, was directed by Leedham Bantock and starred Lauderdale Maitland as Ivanhoe, Edith Bracewell as Rebecca, Nancy Bevington as Lady Rowena, and Hubert Carter as Isaac.

In a mere five years, films based on the outlaw's exploits—derived not from the ballads but from popular literature and stage adaptations— already had established the content and thematics that would become essential components in the action-oriented Robin Hood genre. The Saxon versus Norman conflict solidified by Scott became a familiar environment in which archery contests, castle sieges, horse chases, duels, and, most notably, the romance between Robin and Marian and the related clash between the outlaw and a Norman villain, often Guy of Gisbourne, were played out again and again.

Eight

No Heavy-Footed Englishman: *Robin Hood* (1922)

On August 28, 1921, Douglas Fairbanks released his sixth film for United Artists, *The Three Musketeers*. Two years earlier he had formed the new distribution company with Charles Chaplin, D. W. Griffith and Mary Pickford, whom he married in 1920. Now Mr. and Mrs. Fairbanks' popularity was on the increase, a fact proven by a film magazine's report that each of them was earning a tidy $19,230.77 per week!

The success of *The Three Musketeers* and his performance as D'Artagnan inspired Fairbanks to produce and star in another epic adventure film. First he and Mary selected *When Knighthood Was in Flower*; after William Randolph Hearst bought the rights for his beloved Marion Davies, the Fairbanks next considered *Romeo and Juliet*, but an adaptation of Shakespeare's famous play would have had to be a tragedy in which both of them die—certainly not an acceptable turn for America's Sweetheart and her agile, heroic husband. And although Mary was only 28, Doug was 38—perhaps a bit too old to play a star-crossed teenager.

Unable to agree on a property, they shelved the idea of starring together. Instead, Fairbanks paid $90,000 for the rights to Owen Wister's best-selling Western, *The Virginian*; but then, realizing that his trademark acrobatics and derring-do would not mix with the laid-back cowboy character, he re-sold it for a profit. For Fairbanks had typecast himself as the larger-than-life, energetic, over-the-top hero; and whether he was playing D'Artagnan, Zorro, the Thief of Bagdad, the Black

Pirate, or the Man in the Iron Mask, he always was the ever-grinning
Doug, thrusting his right hand into the air, leaping into action, and
bouncing all over the set. In each film only his costume was different.
And his Robin Hood is no exception.

When *The Virginian* was sold off, Fairbanks' associate Edward
Knoblock suggested *Ivanhoe*, but the actor wasn't interested. Devising
a variation on Scott's sprawling tale, Fairbanks' brother Robert and
director Allan Dwan mentioned the Robin Hood legends, but again
Doug shot it down: "I don't want to look like a heavy-footed Englishman tramping around in the woods."[1] Of course, he wanted to look like
Douglas Fairbanks. Nevertheless, Lotta Woods handed him some extensive "research" material containing all the romantic ingredients of the
popular novels: the Merry Men, the villainous Sheriff of Nottingham,
the iniquitous Prince John, beautiful Maid Marian, and the robbing the
rich to give to the poor angle.

After more brainstorming sessions, Fairbanks still could not make
a decision on which story to film. Fond of Alexandre Dumas' tales, he
thought of following *The Three Musketeers* with *Chico the Jester*, but
this idea also was abandoned. Then, on New Year's Day 1922, he gathered together his staff, including Robert Florey, and, standing before
them in grand cinematic fashion, rapped the meeting table with his fist
as he announced that *Robin Hood* would be the most monumental film
he would ever make. Having discovered that the old Goldwyn Studio
at Santa Monica and Formosa was for sale, he intended to buy it to con-
struct mammoth medieval sets and stage a grand jousting tournament,
à la *Ivanhoe*. When his brother John asked about the cost, Fairbanks
replied, "That's not the point. These things have to be done properly,
or not at all."[2]

The Goldwyn Studio was purchased by the Fairbanks brothers for
$150,000, but when their backers turned down the expensive plans for
Robin Hood, Doug decided to pay for it himself. Setting his pre-pro-
duction staff to work on detailed research into the reign of Richard the
Lionheart, a story outline, shooting schedule and budget (which was
estimated at $1.5 million), Fairbanks, before heading to Europe with
Mary, hired Wilfred Buckland to design the imposing sets, Mitchell
Leisen to create the hundreds of costumes, and Arthur Edeson as direc-
tor of photography.

Aided by 500 construction workers, Dwan, who had agreed to
direct, and Robert Fairbanks oversaw the building of the castle on the

Robin Hood (1922). Douglas Fairbanks is far more subdued in this publicity still than in the film.

Goldwyn lot. Made of large rocks, chicken wire and plaster, the enormous structure included cavernous rooms lighted by the sun and huge reflectors, a drawbridge powered by a gasoline engine, and a full-scale moat. Leisen's crew began making the costumes, including armor of heavy canvas and chain mail of hemp, all covered with thick silver paint.

Having returned from New York after his European jaunt, Fairbanks was met at the train station by Robert, who informed him that the $250,000 castle was finished and ready for filming. Doug then asked if the medieval structure was "big enough to look realistic," but he was not prepared for the gargantuan 90-foot edifice—the biggest set ever built in Hollywood—that awaited him in Santa Monica. Shaking his head in disbelief, Fairbanks expressed the fear that his character would be swallowed up by such a monstrosity. Believing there was no way he could compete with it, he canceled the production.

Having spent a quarter million of his personal fortune, Fairbanks hoped that another company would take the 10-acre castle off his hands. But when Chaplin surveyed the place, he turned to his friend and said, "Magnificent. What a wonderful opening for one of my comedies: the drawbridge comes down, and I put out the cat and take in the milk."[3]

A few days after shelving *Robin Hood*, Fairbanks walked over to the set with Allan Dwan, who had been thinking of ways to persuade him to resume production. Inside the castle, Dwan led him through the immense hall and up a spiral staircase to the balcony. Describing a scene in which Robin would stand in exactly the same spot, Dwan pointed to one side, indicating the entrance of the Sheriff's men and how they would trap the outlaw on the stairs. Standing on the railing of the balcony, Dwan asked, "Now what do you think you do?"

Totally disinterested, Fairbanks had heard enough. "How do I know? Fall on my ass, I suppose," he grumbled.

"You see those curtains?" Dwan countered, waving his hand toward a 50-foot drapery that hung beside the staircase. "Watch." Leaping off the balcony, he landed in the curtain and then slid all the way down to the stone floor.

When Fairbanks, now sporting his trademark grin, asked Dwan just how he had performed the astonishing feat, the director pulled back the curtain to reveal a long metal slide that he and Robert had designed. Not about to be upstaged by his associate, Doug, nattily attired in suit and Homburg, leaped onto the device himself and slid to the floor—then called in everyone to watch him slide down again. From that moment on, Fairbanks, his ego swelled to a size larger than the castle, was enthusiastically committed to making *Robin Hood* his magnum opus.

Heavily influenced by *Ivanhoe*, Fairbanks (using the *nom de plume* Elton Thomas) wrote the screenplay under the editorial supervision of Lotta Woods. Edward Knoblock, who earlier had suggested filming Scott's novel, acted as literary consultant. Opening with a shot of castle ruins, a title card reads, "History—in its ideal state—is a compound of legend and chronicle and from out of both we offer you an impression of the Middle Ages." Here, Fairbanks gives himself license to mix a modicum of history with material gleaned from *Ivanhoe* and the popular 19th-century storybook versions of the legend, all squarely set within the reign of Richard the Lionheart (played with scenery chewing glee by the ever bombastic Wallace Beery).

The film opens with the "impulsive, generous and brave" Lionheart at a tournament, viewing a joust between the Earl of Huntington (Fairbanks, wearing his usual 1920s mustache!) and Sir Guy of Gisbourne (Paul Dickey), one day before he is scheduled to lead a crusade into the Holy Land. Also in attendance is Prince John (Sam de Grasse) who is immediately shown to be a treacherous villain with plans of usurpation. Triumphant in combat, Huntington is proclaimed second in command on the crusade. But when Lady Marian Fitzwalter (Enid Bennett) presents him with a ceremonial crown, Huntington reveals a phobia (and enacts the first of the film's endless episodes of ludicrous anachronisms) when he admits, "Exempt me, sire. I am afraid of women." (Fairbanks' writing style merely was an extension of his leaping, grinning, and arm-thrusting overacting technique.)

But Richard will have none of Huntington's gynephobia and, during the succeeding feast, has him tied up and pawed over by a bevy of young women. In classic Fairbanks style, the Earl manages to escape their grasp in time to rescue Marian from the evil clutches of Gisbourne and Prince John. Here, material borrowed from the 19th-century tales is merged with typical 1920s romantic twaddle as the smitten Huntington speaks of his "knightly priviledge" and concedes, "I never knew a maid could be like you." Rather than depicting Huntington as an outlaw who develops an interest in women when he falls in love with Maid Marian, Fairbanks offers a ridiculous woman-fearing acrobat who experiences an instant revelation after he protects her virtue.

As the crusade begins the next morning, Richard is unable to find his right-hand knight, who is up on a battlement, continuing his romantic

Robin Hood (1922). **Robert, Earl of Huntington (Douglas Fairbanks), receives a ceremonial crown from Lady Marian Fitzwalter (Enid Bennett) before leaving on the Third Crusade.**

pursuit! In a totally ahistorical moment of Victorian melodrama, John orders Gisbourne to make certain that the King and his Earl do "not return from the Holy Land." Offering Sir Guy Marian's hand in exchange for Huntington's head, the Prince absurdly continues to plot his way to the throne. During his subsequent reign of terror and taxation, he razes and burns Huntington's castle.

When he receives a note written by Marian, Huntington plans to return to England, telling the King that he cannot stand to be away from his love. Believed to be jesting, he heads for home, first sending a note by carrier pigeon that is intercepted by Gisbourne's falcon. Gisbourne then shoots Huntington with a crossbow bolt and shows the note to Richard, who imprisons him for desertion. To complete his pledge to Prince John, Gisbourne then begs for the death penalty.

John soon learns of Marian's part in the affair, but after the maid goes into hiding, he assumes she is dead. Meanwhile, one of Huntington's confederates frees him, and they vow to return to England. At this point—90 minutes into the film—the outlaws of Sherwood finally appear, declaring that they need an effective leader to weld them together. And, in Palestine, King Richard concludes a truce.

As the narrative jumps ahead one year, a mysterious robber-chief begins a campaign in Sherwood, and a peasant holding some coins proclaims, "Robin Hood!" Soon, the High Sheriff of Nottingham (William Lowery) is menaced by an arrow. Now Fairbanks really begins overacting, proving that his fear of being upstaged by the gargantuan castle (which was made to look even larger with well-executed glass shots) was pure balderdash: the bigger the set, the bigger the chew. And as the "robbing the rich to give to the poor" aspect comes into focus, his greenwood costume (including tunic, tights, cap with feather, and soft leather low-boots) and ebullient performance (skipping, hopping—off a concealed trampoline in one scene—and constantly signalling to his men with that arm thrust) make him look more like Peter Pan than Robin Hood.

Informed of Robin Hood's activities, the Lionheart plans to return to England. Continuing his altruistic campaign of redistributing the nation's wealth, Robin returns stolen relics to the Priory of St. Catherine's, where he is recognized by Marian, thus being reunited with his love. (Robin's meetings with each of the Merry Men are not shown. Instead of giving his audience cinematic depictions of these famous literary passages, Fairbanks chose to include the earlier 90 minutes of sleep–inducing spectacle.) When John learns that Robin is actually the Earl of Huntington and that Marian is alive, he orders the execution of the former and the capture of the latter.

In an attack on Nottingham apparently inspired by the Keystone Kops, Robin clubs John's troops, Will Scarlet (Maine Geary) lowers the visors on their helmets, and the Merry Men toss them into a well. Following Marian's incarceration, Richard arrives in Sherwood disguised as a stranger. Having entered the castle, Robin saves Marian after jumping from a window to escape Gisbourne, whom he subsequently strangles. Hearing a horn blast from the Merry Men, he surrenders and is prepared for execution, which is to occur upon John's personal command.

Soon after, the Merry Men secretly invade the castle, but when

John's men fire their crossbows, the bolts are stopped by the shield of a strange knight who reveals his identity as Richard the Lionheart, King of England. All of John's henchmen, including the Sheriff of Notting-ham, are rounded up and merrily abused as an orgy of celebration occurs. Once again, Richard calls for Huntington, who is wooing Marian.

That night, Robin and Marian are wed. As the revelry begins, they escape to their bedroom. In one last gasp of anachronistic humor, the lovers are interrupted by Richard's knock as they embrace on the bed. They do not answer—even for the King.

Considering the awe-inspiring production values, including the impressive art direction of Wilfred Buckland, Irvin J. Martin and Edward M. Langley, and Fairbanks' always amazing physical prowess, it is a shame that he did not entrust the writing of *Robin Hood* to some-one else. But all elements, including characterization, plot, production design, cinematography and, worst of all, acting, had to be centered on, or subordinated to, the Douglas Fairbanks persona. Therefore, as a Fair-banks film, *Robin Hood* is a classic, perhaps the best he ever made—and the fact that it was a smash at box offices across the nation proved that the combination of Doug and Robin was a popular one. However, as an adaptation of latter-day versions of the legend, it is a very mixed bag: visually impressive but dramatically ponderous during its first half and absurdly action-filled during its second; intended as a romantic depiction of the "Age of Faith," but filled with ludicrous 1920s comedy; including sets and costumes designed with a degree of historical accu-racy, but subordinating them to acrobatics that would be more at home in a film about a 20th-century circus (an element heightened by Fair-banks' playing for the hundreds of spectators who watched from grand-stands each day). Like all "historical" pictures, it is a product of its time, an uneasy combination of impressions about past epochs and pop-ular attitudes from the period of its making.

Discounting the over-the-top elements, half of the film is vastly entertaining (including a good performance by the reliable Alan Hale as Little John) and an interesting foray into the unique cinematic world of Douglas Fairbanks. He was a powerful screen presence and the great-est action star of the silent era. But by no means was he Robin Hood.

Fairbanks' outlaw antics did not end when the production wrapped, however. While attending the New York premiere of *Robin Hood* on October 18, 1922, Doug carried along the bow and arrows he used in the film. Never one to miss an opportunity for a publicity stunt, he again jumped into action when a reporter hinted that he had used a professional to perform Robin's feats of archery. Agreeing to give a demonstration of his true prowess with the bow, Doug led the reporter and a small group of people to the roof of the Ritz Hotel, where he aimed a shaft at a gargoyle on a building about 100 yards away. After hitting his mark he was asked to perform a more skillful feat, so, with characteristic bravado, he notched another arrow and let it fly with all the force he could muster.

Not long after, Fairbanks received a call from a reporter who had been present at the demonstration. Moments after Doug had fired his second shaft, a Polish immigrant was rushed to the hospital to have an arrow extracted from his rear end! Fairbanks, in an effort to avert any adverse publicity, immediately contacted his lawyer, Dennis F. O'Brien,

Lady Robin Hood (1925). **The nefarious Cabraza (Boris Karloff) menaces Catalina (Evelyn Brent), in the guise of "La Ortiga," a female hybrid of Robin Hood and Zorro.**

who visited the injured Pole, a furrier working in Manhattan, and gave him a $5,000 apology. (Here was a case of the rich *giving* to the poor after committing a thoughtless blunder!) The money wasn't quite enough, however, as the man demanded two tickets to *Robin Hood* and a meeting with Fairbanks, who attracted quite a local crowd when he arrived at the furrier's apartment.

The greatest box office success of Douglas Fairbanks' career, this first feature-length *Robin Hood* reached American screens at about the same time that Gaumont-Westminster's *Rob Roy* (1922) played in theaters on the opposite side of the Atlantic. The second film to feature the Scottish Robin Hood, this Alicia Ramsey adaptation of the Scott novel starred David Hawthorne as Rob, Gladys Jennings as Helen, and Sir Simeon Stewart as Montrose.

In 1923 a second-generation greenwood tale was told in the four-reeler *Robin Hood, Jr.*, directed by Clarence Bricker and featuring Frankie Lee, Peggy Cartwright, Stanley Bingham and Ashley Cooper. The following year Regent Films released *Robin Hood's Men*, a two-reeler starring Gerald Ames that was produced as the second episode of a British series called "Fights Through the Ages."

The outlaw's gender was changed for the first and only time in *Lady Robin Hood*, an American feature produced by R.C. Pictures and released through F.B.O. Filmed during the summer of 1925, the film is an interesting mixture of the English legends and the American Southwest directed by Ralph Ince and starring the popular silent actress Evelyn Brent. In one of his first noticeable roles, Boris Karloff plays Cabraza, a parallel of the Sheriff of Nottingham, while William Humphrey as the evil Governor represents Prince John. Brent's dual character of Catalina and La Ortiga, who rescues oppressed Californians from the two villains, is a clever female hybrid of Robin Hood and Zorro. Friar Tuck also is present in the form of D'Arcy Corrigan's Padre.

Nine

Fluent Treason: *The Adventures of Robin Hood* (1938)

L ong hailed as one of golden age Hollywood's true masterpieces, Warner Bros.' *The Adventures of Robin Hood* (1938) began as a remarkably absurd idea on July 19, 1935. Then working on the set of *Captain Blood*, period costume consultant Dwight Franklin wrote a memo to Jack Warner suggesting that the mogul cast "tough guy" James Cagney as the Prince of Thieves. Cagney recently had given a bizarre performance in Max Reinhardt's adaptation of Shakespeare's *A Midsummer Night's Dream* (1935), and now it seemed natural to feature him in another English extravaganza. And to support him, Franklin thought it best to cast fellow gangster cronies Frank McHugh, Allen Jenkins, Ross Alexander and Hugh Herbert as the Merry Men!

Warner bought the proposal for two reasons: romantic adventure epics were again in vogue, and Cagney consistently had been begging for non-criminal roles that would showcase his versatility. Surveying current Hollywood interest in the Robin Hood legends, Jack Warner discovered that several companies were preparing similar productions. Although producer Edward Small had dropped his plans to film *Robin Hood* as a follow-up to Reliance's *The Count of Monte Cristo* (1934), MGM had purchased all the working materials, including two script treatments of *Robin Hood and His Merrie Men* by Bernard McConville, and an outline and incomplete continuity script of a second version by Philip Dunne.

MGM was developing an operetta version of the legends for Jeanette MacDonald and Nelson Eddy, but, discovering that his own

Sir Guy (Basil Rathbone, left) and Robin (Errol Flynn) duel to the death at the climax of *The Adventures of Robin Hood* **(1938).**

studio possessed a controlling interest in the Reginald de Koven-Harry B. Smith light opera of 1890, Jack Warner went ahead with pre-production plans. In August 1935 producer Hal B. Wallis assigned the research to Herman Lissauer while hiring English screenwriter Rowland Leigh to prepare a script for Cagney as Robin and Guy Kibbee as

Friar Tuck. However, when the militant Cagney, then a vice-president of the recently formed Screen Actors Guild, walked out on the studio three months later, the production seemed in jeopardy.

Leigh was ordered to forge on with the treatment. Attempting to blend material from several of the ballads into a cohesive story, as well as create dialogue that sounded authentic yet would be understood by a modern audience, he turned over 40 pages to executive story editor Walter MacEwen in April 1936, when Warners announced that 27-year-old Errol Flynn, fresh from his overnight success in *Captain Blood*, would play Robin. And the following month Warners made a deal with MGM that left both studios free to pursue Robin Hood projects: the former would release a non-musical film titled *The Adventures of Robin Hood* prior to February 14, 1938, while the latter acquired all rights to the de Koven-Smith operetta, which would be filmed in 1939.

In the meantime, MGM released *Robin Hood of El Dorado* (1936), a south of the border Western starring Warner Baxter as a Mexican farmer who becomes the leader of a murderous outlaw gang. Ordered to vacate his land, Baxter's "Joaquin Murrieta" refuses and, after his young wife, Rosita (Margo), is murdered by four desperadoes, begins his reign of terror. Possessing no tangible connection to the Robin Hood legends, the film is a mixture of the Zorro tale and romanticized elements from the Mexican Revolution.

Rowland Leigh completed the first draft continuity script for the Warners *Robin Hood* in November 1936, but Hal Wallis let it languish on his desk for four months; and when he finally read it in March 1937, expressed his disappointment in a memo to associate producer Henry Blanke, noting the lack of character development and the stilted nature of the archaic dialogue. Leigh's version depicted the outlaw not as Sir Robin of Locksley, Saxon knight, but as the yeoman of the early ballads; and Maid Marian was not King Richard's ward but Sir Guy of Gisbourne's. The centerpiece of the script was the Robin-Marian-Gisbourne love triangle borrowed from the de Koven-Smith operetta.

The following month Wallis assigned the rewriting of the script to Norman Reilly Raine, whom Warners had on contract. A few weeks later, when Jack Warner decided to shoot the film in Technicolor, Walter MacEwen told Raine to re-fashion the screenplay to reflect this technical element. On July 6, however, Warner, in an effort to *decrease* the film's $1,185,000 budget, ordered Henry Blanke to have Raine eliminate the "huge mob scenes that were called for in the original script."[1]

An early sketch of "Robin's Men" produced by the Warner Bros. art department for the aborted 1935 film that later was re-worked as *The Adventures of Robin Hood* (from a rare original in the author's collection).

The next day Raine completed his draft, which featured modernized dialogue but retained several major incidents from the ballads and stories that Leigh had featured in his script: Robin and Little John's quarterstaff fight on the log over the stream; the Merry Men attacking Sir John's "ransom caravan" and the subsequent feast in Sherwood; Robin's capture and near-hanging from which he is rescued by the Merry Men; King Richard's incognito arrival in Sherwood; and Robin and Gisbourne's duel to the death. Also carried over were two key events inspired by *Ivanhoe*: the archery tournament at which Robin splits his opponent's arrow, and the siege of Nottingham Castle (Torquilstone Castle in Scott's novel).

At this point Wallis and Blanke met with staff director William Keighley to discuss the script. After several story conferences, Wallis asked Raine to write a second draft, which was still unfinished when the producer read it at the end of August. In this version Robin began to be depicted as the noble Sir Robin of Locksley, Will of Gamwell (Will Scarlet) became his squire, and Marian was a Saxon who, in the opening scene, already was in love with the outlaw.

Still unsatisfied with Raine's work, the production trio teamed him with successful Warners screenwriter Seton I. Miller for another revision. Managing to postpone the studio's commitment to the Technicolor company for about two weeks, Wallis asked for "at least two-thirds" of a complete script to be delivered by September 10.[2]

Apparently, William Keighley, regardless of budgetary restrictions, had suggested that they open the film with a lavish jousting tournament at which Robin and Sir Guy compete. An attempt to recapture the grand scale of the Fairbanks opus, this idea was not appreciated by Raine, who, in a heated memo peppered with profanity, justifiably voiced his criticism:

> The jousting tournament can never be anything but a prologue which, if done with the magnificence Mr. Keighley sees, will have the disastrous effect of putting the climax of the picture at the beginning — and I'll be goddamned if that is good construction dramatically in fiction, stage or screen, because the only way you could ever top it would be to have a slam-bang hell of a battle or something equally spectacular — and expensive — at the end....
>
> The Fairbanks picture, *in order to live up to its tournament fadein*, had to ring in the whole goddamned Crusades; and a light taste of the real Robin Hood story was dragged in as a tag at the end to justify the use of the name.[3]

On September 14 the script still did not contain a satisfactory conclusion. Wallis could not justify the expense of the *Ivanhoe*-inspired
siege, so he opted for another element adapted from the early ballads:
King Richard, accompanied by his retinue, and Robin and the Merry
Men disguise themselves as monks to secretly invade Nottingham Castle during the coronation of Prince John. Before the usurper can be
crowned, Robin hails his men and dispatches Sir Guy after a furious
duel. Richard banishes his brother, pardons the Sherwood outlaws and
gives the hand of Marian to Robin, whom he declares Baron of Locksley. For these scenes the Bishop of the Black Canons, a character extraneous to the ballads, was added by Rowland Leigh to provide the Saxon
band an entry into the castle. Held at dagger point by Robin, the bishop,
who intends to declare John "King of England," acts as if the "monks"
are accompanying him to the coronation.

While the script revisions continued, the cast was chosen and, on
one of the studio's large soundstages, 24 combat-able men were coached
in the use of broadsword and quarterstaff by Belgian fencing master Fred
Cavens and his son, Albert. And some of the extras cast as Prince John's
knights were padded underneath their tunics and taught how to take an
arrow in the chest from expert archer Howard Hill, who had been hired
primarily to tutor Flynn and perform Robin's feats in the close-up shots.
For each arrow taken on camera, Warners payed a handsome $150.

Stuntman and Flynn double Buster Wiles recalled Hill's talent and
tutelage of his movie-star friend:

> [O]n the Warner backlot, Errol introduced me to Howard Hill, a tall,
> firmly built fellow with dark, wavy hair and a warm smile.
> "Howard's the greatest archer around," said Flynn.
> Errol raised his bow and let fly an arrow aimed at a straw-filled
> target. Hill frowned as the arrow clipped the target's corner and sailed
> into the earth. He raised his own bow and instructed Flynn how to
> shoot. His arrow struck the bull's-eye dead center. Pretty soon, a small
> crowd had gathered to watch in awe as Howard's archery lesson
> became a demonstration of his remarkable skill. He lay on his back
> and, placing the bow between his legs, fired. Another arrow struck
> dead center. He stood up and pointed to a nearby telephone pole.
> "Well, I could hit that," I thought.
> But Hill pointed the bow skyward. The arrow sailed high in the
> air, then curved in a downward slope. It struck dead center—on top
> of the telephone pole ...
> Howard became a close friend of both Errol and me.... Howard

told me how he had come to Warners a few months earlier to audition for the archery work.... Although he enjoyed a superb reputation, he had been made to join an assembled group of professional archers, all vying for the coveted assignment.

On the studio lot, a gallows had been erected. Most of the archers were good enough to pin the noose to the wooden structure. Toward the end of the day, Howard's turn came. He declined to shoot, simply stating that he would return the following day.

"What's wrong?" asked the director of the competition.

"I would just rather shoot tomorrow," he said.

That evening, he took a hunting broadhead point, reversed it to where it was a V-shape, then sharpened the interior to a razor-fine edge. He practiced late into the night. The next morning, a snide voice greeted him.

"Well, Mr. Hill, are you any better today?"

Replied Howard: "How many times do you want me to cut it, and how much are you paying?"

He then shot an arrow that actually sliced the gallows' noose. He had won the job of supervising the archery in *The Adventures of Robin Hood*. Due to Howard's expert instructions, Flynn became a master with a bow and arrow....[4]

For the role of Maid Marian, the production team selected Olivia de Havilland, who had been paired so successfully with Flynn in *Captain Blood* and *The Charge of the Light Brigade* (1936), but Jack Warner opted for contract player Anita Louise, who was confirmed by Wallis in early September. However, by September 16, Wallis announced that de Havilland had been given the part. Joining the romantic leads were villain extraordinaire and accomplished fencer Basil Rathbone as Sir Guy, *Robin Hood* veteran Alan Hale as Little John, Melville Cooper as the Sheriff of Nottingham, and contract players Claude Rains and Ian Hunter as Prince John and King Richard, respectively. When David Niven proved unavailable, Flynn crony Patric Knowles was signed to portray Will Scarlet.

On September 27, 1937, filming began in Bidwell Park, a 2,400-acre preserve in Chico, California, that stretches nine miles up Chico Canyon along Big Chico Creek. To enhance the park's huge oak and sycamore trees, art director Carl Jules Weyl had his crew plant hundreds of bushes and flowers as well as adding artificial trees and stones to vary the landscape.

The first scene to be shot involved Flynn and Hale, who, for the first time on film, enacted Robin and Little John's rousing quarterstaff fight over the stream. But due to inclement weather and William Keighley's slow working methods and numerous camera set-ups, the filming of the sequence took more than three days. On October 6 Wallis wired the director, ordering him to speed up production and cut the scenes of the jousting tournament and the christening of the Merry Men in the greenwood. Raine had joined the company on location and continued to make revisions in the screenplay until October 13. Soon after, Wallis sent second-unit director H. Reeves ("Breezy") Eason to Chico to pick up Keighley's lagging pace, primarily by shooting some additional material for the scene involving the ambush of Sir Guy's "ransom" caravan.

While on location at Chico, Flynn spent much of his free time with Patric Knowles, who was one of his best drinking buddies until the end of his life. In 1990 Knowles recalled one of their after-hours pastimes, proving that they were as least as rebellious as their on-screen characters:

> It was our custom, every morning, on returning to our hotel from filming, to stop by the small airfield outside Chico.... I had a total of fifty hours flying time and Flynn had none—solo time, I mean. Well, I talked him into learning how to fly the [Piper] Cub and I'd like to mention ... that it took twelve hours of dual instruction to solo yours truly—Flynn made it in four hours. Our studio somehow found out about our flying every evening and we began to receive messages from various departments, warning us of the grave consequences should anything happen to us while flying. One note to me asked if I realized that I was endangering the life of the star of the picture and jeopardizing the investment of several millions of dollars. No one said anything about *my* life. We ignored all the notes and messages and continued to fly each evening until a telegram arrived. It was addressed to me and signed by the producer of the picture. It threatened me with some sort of legal action if I persisted in encouraging Flynn to fly.
>
> I asked the "old boy" what we should do about the threat and he laughed loud and long, as they say. "Don't get yourself in an uproar, old son. Just tear up the telegram and forget about it."
>
> I did, then we flipped a coin to see who would fly first. He won. "Why don't you have the driver put the car in the hangar, out of the way," he said. "Then the snoopers won't know whether we are here or not."
>
> We hid the car in the back of the hangar while Flynn "flewed." I mean *flewed*. We phooled all over the sky, showing off. Nothing really dangerous—just hammer stalls, tight turns and wing overs. After only four hours dual, he was a veritable Rickenbacker.

He didn't say a word as he climbed out of the cockpit and I got in. He simply leered at me with a let's-see-what-you-can-do look. Well, I did everything but fly through the hangar doors. Then, to finish off, climbed up to a thousand feet and did two loops, landing at the end of the second one.

You can imagine the smug grin I was wearing as I got out of the plane. I didn't wear it for long. Two men were approaching. One man I knew; he was the production manager from the studio, the other was a stranger … a Civil Aeronautics Authority man. They had arrived on the field just as I took off and had witnessed my performance. The studio manager informed me that they were going to lodge a complaint with the Screen Actors Guild. The C.A.A. man took away my license pending the outcome of the hearing on my case at a later date. The charges? Flying in a manner to endanger the lives and property of the public. Stunting without a parachute.

Later, in the car, on the way to our hotel, I asked Flynn where he was during the excitement. "Why, in the car having forty winks, old son," he said. "I started to learn my lines for tomorrow and simply dozed off."[5]

Flynn also joined Howard Hill on several hunting excursions that were captured on 16mm film by Rathbone, who had taken up home movie-making. Olivia de Havilland, who had been costarring in Warners' *Gold Is Where You Find It*, arrived at Chico on October 22 to appear in her set-ups with Flynn for the caravan and Sherwood feast scenes. On November 8 the company wrapped the Chico shooting and prepared to head back to Burbank, where the scenes set at the Kent Road Tavern, the Saracen's Head Inn and Marian's quarters in Nottingham Castle were to be filmed. Nine days behind schedule, Keighley continued his workmanlike direction, and one week later, moved his crew, principal actors, and scores of supporting players and extras to Busch Gardens in Pasadena to film the archery tournament scene.

On November 30 Keighley, having let the production slip 15 days behind schedule and considerably over the $1,440,000 revised budget, was replaced by Michael Curtiz, the versatile and dictatorial Hungarian who had directed Flynn in *Captain Blood* and *The Charge of the Light Brigade*. Although Keighley had been assigned to the project on the strength of his successful direction of Flynn in an earlier period drama, *The Prince and the Pauper* (1937), Wallis needed a taskmaster like Curtiz to power the lavish, action-filled scenes set at Nottingham castle, including Robin's defiant arrival with the "royal" deer carcass near the beginning of the film, and the coronation processional and furious melee that conclude it. Beating the retreat with Keighley was cinematographer Tony Gaudio, who was replaced by Curtiz' favorite, Sol Polito, who, under his direction, had just shot the Technicolor *Gold Is Where You Find It.*

Curtiz' original conception of the banquet, at which Robin defies Prince John and then singlehandedly fights off dozens of knights, had a distinct Douglas Fairbanks style that bothered Wallis, who later edited out ludicrous images of Flynn halting in mid-duel to drink a toast and then stopping a hail of arrows with a single shield. Before Curtiz began shooting the sequence, Wallis expressed his desire not to let the heroic romanticism get out of hand; referring to Robin's escape from the castle, he wrote, "The quicker he gets out of the room and up on the balcony the better, and don't let him [Curtiz] have Robin hold off a hundred men with a bow and arrow."[6]

Curtiz also directed the scene involving the Merry Men rescuing Robin from the Nottingham gallows. For the scene's most strenuous stunt, Flynn was doubled by Buster Wiles, who recalled:

> First, we filmed the scene where the hangman is toppled from the high ladder by a well-aimed arrow, fired by Howard Hill. Then I escaped from the gallows with my hands loosely tied behind my back. I leaped on a horse ... I galloped through the streets, with Prince John's men in hot pursuit. My scenes were filmed by a second unit crew, with Mike Curtiz directing the escape with his usual keen eye for excitement. When the time came to film Robin scrambling over the castle gate, Curtiz waved me over to his director's chair for instructions.
>
> "Singing Marie, you pretend to cut the rope, hold on, go up. Show lots of energy!"
>
> When "Action!" was yelled, I withdrew a sword from astride my horse, then chopped at a thick rope attached to the drawbridge. I grabbed the rope and held on, shooting upwards to the castle parapet. We got the shot in one take. On the other side, I lowered myself down a rope, then dropped about ten feet. Flynn stepped in for the closeup of Robin fleeing to freedom. "I'm sure bushed from that escape," said Errol.[7]

By December 4 unit manager Al Alleborn reported to Warner that Curtiz, Polito and the replacement technicians had the production right

Opposite top: The Adventures of Robin Hood (1938). **Robin (Errol Flynn) on the way to the gallows (frame enlargement).** *Opposite bottom:* **Sir Guy of Gisbourne (Basil Rathbone) eagerly awaits the execution (frame enlargement).**

on track, "100% better than the other crew."[8] In fact, Curtiz' work was so impressive that Warner and Wallis, easing up on their usual cost-effective approach, allowed the director to view all the footage shot by Keighley and then re-shoot or film additional footage to improve particular scenes. One of Curtiz' important contributions was expanding Robin and the Merry Men's ambush of the caravan, material that was shot at the very location where Fairbanks had filmed portions of his magnum opus 15 years earlier. (Located just outside Los Angeles, the woods and reservoir were now called Sherwood Forest and Lake Sherwood, respectively.) Retakes for other scenes included some additional archery tournament shots, filmed at the Midwick Country Club, and the sequence involving Crippen the Arrow Maker spreading the word about Robin's meeting at the Gallows Oak.

Curtiz finally wrapped the picture at 3:10 a.m. on January 15, 1938, after pushing his cast and crew for a solid 18 hours. The only mishap that occurred during his tenure on the film was an unfortunate tumble suffered by stuntman Fred Graham while doubling for Rathbone during his death scene. Taking a spectacular fall off a staircase ledge, Graham broke his ankle, adding a convincing bit of realism.

Other than a few inserts that were shot on January 22, the film, 38 days over schedule, was ready to be scored. During the production phase, editor Ralph Dawson had assembled the rough cut, but after shooting ended, Wallis tightened it further by removing bits and pieces to create the film's now-legendary, endlessly flowing rhythm (although the finished footage ran 193 minutes, the final cut was trimmed to 105). Knowing that it would not be completed by February 14, Wallis also re-negotiated the agreement with MGM, settling on a new release date of "before June 1."

Although Max Steiner had been chosen to compose the score, Wallis and Blanke preferred Austrian *wunderkind* Erich Wolfgang Korngold, who had been a Mozart-like child prodigy and composer of ballets and operas long before writing the music for *Captain Blood* and *The Prince and the Pauper*. At work on his opera *Die Kathrin* in Vienna, he had returned to Warners when his premiere was postponed for several months; but after viewing the black-and-white work print, he wrote to Wallis on February 11 to turn down the new assignment: *"Robin Hood is no picture for me ... I am a musician of the heart, of passions and psychology; I am not a musical illustrator for a 90% action picture."*[9]

On February 12 Warner, Wallis and Blanke sent music department head Leo Forbstein to Korngold's Toluca Lake house with a new, exclusive offer allowing him to work on a weekly basis, with the provision that he could leave at the end of any week and be replaced with another composer who would finish the score. So, while the Technicolor Company prepared the three-color dye transfer prints of the final cut, Korngold spent the next seven weeks composing and recording his majestic, rousing score.

Korngold wrote each selection as a detailed four-line piano piece which then was fully orchestrated by Hugo Friedhofer. With the Warner Orchestra assembled on Stage Nine, Korngold, listening to the dialogue through headphones as the work print played on a screen in front of him, conducted while recording engineer Dave Forrest captured the score. Curtiz and Blanke often dropped in to monitor Korngold's progress and enjoy the music, as did symphony aficionado Basil Rathbone, who was an ardent admirer of the composer. In fact, according to musical director Ray Heindorf, one recording session actually brought tears to the eyes of the implacable Curtiz.[10] A similar reaction no doubt played on Korngold's face two weeks after the score was completed, when Adolf Hitler's Nazi army invaded Austria and confiscated the composer's property in Vienna.

The final cost of *The Adventures of Robin Hood* totaled $2,033,000. Prior to the May 14, 1938, premiere it was previewed in Pomona, California, in early April. Much to Jack Warner's delight, this most expensive film in his studio's history was greeted with audience raves. On April 11 a second preview was held in Los Angeles, and a third followed at Warners' Hollywood theater two weeks later. Each showing generated enormous audience applause and enthusiastic reviews from the press.

A triumph in every department, *The Adventures of Robin Hood* is one of the Hollywood studio system's most impressive achievements, a collaborative work of art that thoroughly disproves the romanticized auteur theory so beholden to film scholars since the 1960s. The remarkable pace of the film—its images moving with a sustained rhythm; its scenes effortlessly segueing from one to the next—is, of course, attributable to directors Curtiz and Keighley, but also to the stunning editing skills of Hal Wallis, who worked very closely with Ralph Dawson. Even the great German expressionist William Dieterle made a small contribution by shooting the (beautifully photographed) Crippen the Arrowmaker montage. And all of this miraculously paced imagery,

showcasing the superb performances of a stellar cast, is further ener-
gized by Korngold's unforgettable music: like his other work in the film
medium, a complex, harmonic, pulsing score influenced by the great
European romantic composers of the late 19th century.

The extraordinary narrative economy that distinguishes all of the
film's 105 minutes begins immediately after the opening credits, as two
title cards set the historical stage:

> In the year of our Lord 1191, when Richard, the Lion-Heart, set forth
> to drive the infidels from the Holy Land, he gave the regency of his
> kingdom to his trusted friend, Longchamp, instead of to his treach-
> erous brother, Prince John.

> Bitterly resentful, John hoped for some disaster to befall Richard, so
> that he, with the help of the Norman barons, might seize the throne
> for himself. And then on a luckless day for the Saxons....

This text is followed by the appearance of a town crier who informs the
gathered villagers of Nottingham that their king is being held for ransom by Leopold of Austria—a scene that dissolves into the castle, where
Prince John and Sir Guy are plotting to raise the Saxons' taxes. Here,
the conflict is established within seconds, the scene ending with John
knocking over a goblet that trickles blood-red wine onto the stone
floor—the first of many transitions that enhance the film's consistent
flow.

A montage scene of Norman depredations follows, then leads to
Much the Miller's Son (Herbert Mundin) being harassed by Sir Guy and
his retinue for killing a royal deer in Sherwood. Here, as Guy raises his
mace to threaten Much, Robin (who has ridden into the scene with Will
Scarlet) "announces" himself to the villain (and the viewer) by shooting one of his black arrows, which knocks the weapon to the ground.
Raine and Miller simply could not have devised a better way of intro-
ducing Robin, immediately establishing three essential components of
the legend: his prowess with a bow, his challenge to Sir Guy, and his
protection of the poor and starving peasants.

Planting the seed of outlawry, Robin becomes the topic of discussion at "the great cold hall of Nottingham," where Prince John is feast-
ing with his knights, Sir Guy, the Sheriff, and Maid Marian. Soon, Robin
comes boldly into the hall with a deer carcass, brazenly fights off two
men-at-arms, and then plops the hairy meat down on the table in front

of John. Raine and Miller's masterful screenplay really begins to shine in this scene when Robin makes known his rebellious intentions:

> SHERIFF: You think you're overtaxed, eh?
> ROBIN: Overtaxed, overworked and paid off
>   with a knife, a club or a rope.
> MARIAN: Why—you speak treason.
> ROBIN: Fluently.

The scene is played beautifully by all concerned, particularly Flynn, whose natural acting talent and disregard for authority combine to create one of cinema's most memorable and entertaining acts of defiance, the first interpretation in the history of the legend that depicts Robin's revolt as a personal, *individual* choice. Challenged by the Normans, he threatens to rebel on his own terms and then single-handedly battles his way from the castle. As Stephen Knight writes, "Robin is an identity in fully modern terms, an epitome of the personalizing of resistance in recent times."[11]

Now proclaimed an outlaw, Robin, accompanied by Will, roams Sherwood, looking for stout men to join his cause. The lively and humorous meeting with Little John—brilliantly choreographed to allow the underrated Alan Hale to alternate each word of dialogue with a blow of his staff—is followed by the gathering at the Gallows Oak, where Robin recites the key tenet of the outlaw legend, including for good measure one of the cardinal components of chivalry:

> Do you, the freemen of the forest, take oath to despoil the rich only
> to feed the hungry, clothe the naked, and shelter the old and the sick;
> to protect all women, Norman or Saxon, rich or poor?

During the ensuing montage depicting the guerrilla activities of Robin against the Norman tax collectors, the outlaw's black arrows speed into the frame like magic, stopping the marauding villains dead in their tracks. In one shot, the arrow strikes out a candle after piercing the back of a vicious molester, and another impales the top of a table standing between Sir Guy and his knights (recalling a similar event in Robert Louis Stevenson's 1883 novel *The Black Arrow*). This scene contains another choice bit of dialogue, laced with ironic gallows humor, spoken by Sir Geoffrey (Robert Warwick) to Sir Guy: "Our men can't even lay a hot iron to the eyes of a tax dodger without getting a black arrow in the throat! It's an outrage."

Like Robin's meeting with Little John, the next scene adapted from the ballads (the encounter with Friar Tuck) continues the playful dueling spirit established in the earlier vignette—a style considerably different than that used in the serious combat scenes pitting the outlaw against Sir Guy and his knights. When Tuck (Eugene Pallette) objects to Robin's theft of his leg of mutton, emphasizing that he is "sworn to poverty," the outlaw counters, "If this is poverty, I'll gladly share it with you"; and after Robin forces the friar to carry him, piggy-back, across the stream (another adapted event), Tuck twists Robin's nose during their broadsword duel (an echo of Little John's earlier thumping of Robin's foot with his staff, sending him splashing into the water). The gravel-voiced Pallette plays Tuck as a lovable crank, a man of the cloth who is also a deadly swordsman with a terrible temper.

The ambush of Sir Guy's caravan is a cinematic tour-de-force of performance, choreography, stage combat, composition, color, editing, art direction and costume design. Milo Anderson's costumes for Rathbone and de Havilland, in particular, are absolutely stunning, only two of several gorgeous ensembles each of them wears in the film. Curtiz' shots of the Merry Men scaling the trees like huge insects effectively foreshadow the attack, and the long shots of Sir Guy's party overarched by Bidwell Park's gargantuan oaks are breathtaking.

After Marian has supped reluctantly with Robin, he introduces her to some of the dispossessed and tortured Saxons who are grateful for the outlaw's kindness. Imbued with a somber mood that recurs only briefly later in the film (during Marian's "trial" and sentencing to death), this scene is rendered even more poignant by the celebratory events that bracket it (the feast, and the Merry Men sending Sir Guy and the Sheriff packing, respectively). Flynn and de Havilland both play the scene with great conviction, culminating with a remark from Robin that emphasizes his "right over might" philosophy. This outlaw is not a revenge-seeking racial separatist, but an egalitarian freedom fighter: when Marian asks why a Saxon knight should risk his own well being, he replies, "Saxon or Norman, what does it matter? It's injustice I hate, not the Normans."

This scene is a trademark Warner Bros. vignette, much in line with their "social problem" films focusing on the unfortunates, the poor, the lowlifes and the criminals abandoned by the American system during the Great Depression. The studio had only begun producing adventure films in 1935, but even *Captain Blood* contains elements of this

Lady Marian Fitzwalter (Olivia de Havilland) fears for Robin's safety (frame enlargement).

fundamental Warners theme, as do all the prime Flynn vehicles, particularly those directed by Curtiz, who worked in all genres but specialized in gritty, expressionistic dramas such as *20,000 Years in Sing Sing* (1933), *The Walking Dead* (1936) and *Angels with Dirty Faces* (1938).

Robin's prowess with a bow is demonstrated further in the spectacular tournament sequence, in which Korngold's regal music, Anderson's costumes (particularly the exquisite white and light-blue gown worn by de Havilland), Howard Hill's amazing feats of archery, and Flynn's electric performance merge to create an unforgettable cinematic experience. Referred to with the medieval term "wolf's head" twice in the film, Robin literally acts like one of the canine creatures as a close-up shows Flynn peering like a hungry wolf over the shoulder of another potential contestant before banging on his steel helmet to motion him aside. He then cockily walks onto the field and into the archers' line.

Although the Warners publicity department released a story claiming that Howard Hill accomplished Robin's feat of splitting the bull's-eyed
arrow of Philip of Arras, this famous bit of cinematic archery actually
was a trick performed by Buster Wiles, who later admitted:

> Howard Hill had a role in the picture, as Captain of the Archers....
> But as great as Howard was, the publicity story was off the mark by
> a long shot. Howard was indeed able to strike another arrow, but the
> notch deflected a direct split, and it didn't photograph well. A wire
> was rigged in front of the Administration Building, and I fired the
> arrow down the wire. Now it can be revealed—Buster Wiles split the
> arrow![12]

After winning the golden arrow, Robin is captured by Gisbourne's
men and told that he will be hanged for treason. When Sir Guy com-
ments that "there may be some who will regret that a man of your pecu-
liar talents should be cut off so early in life; but personally...," Robin
interrupts him, adding, "you think the sentence extremely lenient." This
excellent dialogue is also historically accurate, considering that the standard English sentence for treason was hanging, drawing and quartering
(a punishment that would have been far too realistic for a 1938 audience and the Production Code Administration).

Robin and Marian's moonlit encounter at the maiden's window is
one of golden age Hollywood's most memorable love scenes. Having
been rescued from the gallows by the Merry Men, the outlaw risks his
neck by climbing the castle wall to eavesdrop on Marian as she tells
her servant Bess (Una O'Connor) that she is in love with Robin. After
entering through the window (much to the dismay of the ever-proper
Bess), Robin attempts to get a true romantic declaration from Marian,
who, denying it, briefly sends the outlaw back out into the night. Playing up the fact that he is being exposed to his enemies, Robin (finessed
by Flynn in his best devil-may-care style) then re-enters for the
inevitable embrace. Now Marian also vows to aid him and the Merry
Men by "watching for treachery" at the castle while they work from the
outside.

Soon after, King Richard and his retinue arrive back in the area,
where they accidentally cross paths at the Kent Road Tavern with the
Bishop of the Black Canons (Montagu Love). Discerning the monarch's
identity, the bishop rushes to Nottingham to inform Prince John and Sir
Guy. Overhearing their murderous plans, Marian then sneaks out to

King Richard the Lionheart (Ian Hunter) and Robin devise a plan to outwit the treacherous Prince John (frame enlargement).

warn the king. In this scene, Curtiz created one of his most powerful compositions: a long shot showing John, Sir Guy and the bishop in the foreground, while Marian creeps down the enormous stone staircase in the background. Featuring two planes of action, the shot, having a deep focus effect, is visual storytelling at its finest.

The remainder of the film contains similarly stunning images, all tied together by Curtiz' direction, the superb performances of the entire cast, and Dawson and Wallis' masterful editing. The beautiful matte shot of the procession to Nottingham Castle provides a lavish introduction to the climactic scene showcasing the conflict-resolving duel, executed with unsurpassable power by Flynn and the incomparable Rathbone (who, at 45, would have skewered his 28-year-old opponent had the fight been real). Able to incorporate his trademark expressionistic style into even a bright Technicolor film, Curtiz created one of cinema's most memorable images by throwing huge shadows of the duelists against a stone pillar on the castle set; this shot, elegantly blending the ballet-like movements of Flynn and Rathbone with the shadows (which

Director Michael Curtiz' famous expressionistic shadow shot of the dueling Robin and Gisbourne (frame enlargement).

seem to have a life of their own) and Sol Polito's fluid camera, is simply the best of its kind.

Not only is *The Adventures of Robin Hood* a great film in its own right, but it is also the best cinematic adaptation of material from the ballads, an unsurpassed, timeless evocation of the storybook Saxon versus Norman version of the legend. Although the film is outstanding in every department, its reputation among the masses rests primarily on the lincoln green–clad shoulders of Errol Leslie Flynn, who is at the height of his powers and still several years away from being remembered mainly for his legendarily debauched personal life (a reputation created, in part, by his own personal propaganda, including his posthumously published, ghost-written 1959 "autobiography" *My Wicked, Wicked Ways*, in which he barely mentions *Robin Hood*). Even though his public persona was damaged seriously by a 1943 statutory rape trial (he was acquitted on evidence proving that he was framed by the father of his alleged "victim") and the biographical travesty *Errol Flynn: The*

Untold Story, Charles Higham's 1979 account slanderously accusing Flynn of being a Nazi spy,* his status as cinema's greatest swashbuckler remains intact, due in large part to his Robin Hood characterization.

Perhaps the Flynn persona is best represented by one of his lines in *The Adventures of Robin Hood*, when the incognito Richard the Lionheart asks Robin who is to blame for the current state of England. Quickly responding, the outlaw places responsibility, not with Prince John, but with Richard, "whose job was here at home, protecting his people instead of deserting them to fight in foreign lands." When Richard asks him if he condemns "Holy Crusades," Robin replies, "Aye, I'd condemn anything that left the task of holding England for Richard to outlaws like me!" Matching Flynn's appeal, although playing his mortal enemy, the great Basil Rathbone strikes quite a dashing figure as the finest villain of his long career. Then the most expensive freelance character actor in Hollywood, he made Sir Guy his most memorable rogue, using his precise diction, vast Shakespearean training, and prowess in stage combat to out-evil his previous arch-villains, including Levasseur in *Captain Blood* (who also dies at Flynn's swordpoint), Mr. Murdstone in *David Copperfield* (1935) and Pontius Pilate in *The Last Days of Pompeii* (1935). And his Shakespearean countryman Claude Rains is the ideal Prince John, the perfect scheming complement to Sir Guy's devilish man of action.

Immediately upon its release, *The Adventures of Robin Hood* created a standard of cinematic excellence that no filmmaker in his right mind could (or would attempt to) equal. But the formidable shadow of this great film did not prevent B-filmmakers from attaching the name of the outlaw to programmers featuring similar themes of establishment oppression.

In 1941 Republic brought the English legend back to the American West in *Robin Hood of the Pecos*, in which Roy Rogers, in a reversal of roles, plays sidekick to George ("Gabby") Hayes' outlaw leader. In post–Civil War Texas, Hayes' "Gabby" Hornaday is a resourceful fellow who rallies his comrades to stave off the depradations of marauding

---

In his excellent 1990 book Errol Flynn: The Spy Who Never Was, *Flynn scholar Tony Thomas proves that Higham, in order to "assassinate" the deceased actor, went so far as to falsify copies of FBI documents obtained from the National Archives and Records Administration. Flynn was no Nazi spy, but actually worked for the British O.S.S. during World War II. Other authors and investigators subsequently have "cleared" Flynn of the ridiculous Nazi charge.*

Northern carpetbaggers. However, the spotlight on Hayes does not prevent Rogers from warbling his usual quota of songs, in this case to lovely Marjorie Reynolds.

Two years later Columbia contributed its "medieval" Western, *Robin Hood of the Range* (1943), starring B-stalwart Charles Starrett as the foster son of a railway manager who aids local homesteaders in their fight against his pop's capitalistic company. Though this film was yet another programmer using the Robin Hood tale to attract an audience, it provides further proof that the outlaw legend is one of the most pervasive and effective in the popular culture of the Western world.

Ten

A Round of Robins: Variations on the Legend (1946–54)

Eight years after the success of *The Adventures of Robin Hood*, Hollywood blessed the outlaw and his Marian with a son, fully grown and versed in the rebellious ways of the greenwood. Based on the novel *The Son of Robin Hood* by Paul A. Castleton, Columbia's *The Bandit of Sherwood Forest* (1946) cast Cornel Wilde as "Robert of Nottingham," who returns to Sherwood, not to rob the rich to give to the poor, but to save young King Henry III and the Magna Carta from the evil machinations of the Regent of England, William Pembroke (Henry Daniell), and the ever-nasty Sheriff (Lloyd Corrigan).

Plotted and paced like a B-western, *Bandit*, like its famous predecessor, was helmed by two directors, George Sherman and Henry Levin, and utilized the expertise of three cinematographers (including *Adventures of Robin Hood* veteran Tony Gaudio) to lend a Technicolor gloss to the predictable proceedings. The elder Robin (Russell Hicks) is also on hand to save the great charter, aided by stalwarts Little John (Ray Teal), Friar Tuck (Edgar Buchanan),Will Scarlet (John Abbott) and Allen-a-Dale (Leslie Denison), who, according to a contemporary critic, "aren't given enough opportunity for comedy."[1]

Loaded with chases and "shoot 'em ups" (using arrows rather than bullets), *Bandit* is long on action at 85 minutes, but its dramatic deficiencies are alleviated somewhat by the impressive camerawork of Gaudio, William Snyder and George Meehan, Jr., and the editing of Richard Fantl. Cornel Wilde, with his toothy smile, is reminiscent of Douglas Fairbanks, but his characterization holds interest as the first cinematic

Robin Hood to champion a sitting monarch rather than the poor masses or a struggling king such as Richard I.

Familiar tenets of the Western also permeate Columbia's *The Prince of Thieves* (1948), Charles H. Schneer and Maurice Tombragel's adaptation of Alexandre Dumas' 1872 Robin Hood novel which had been translated into English in 1903. Shot in Cinecolor by Fred Jackman, Jr., this Howard Bretherton-directed potboiler features good production values let down by Jon Hall's tongue-in-cheek Robin and Alan Mowbray's over-the-top Tuck.

The all-too-familiar "evil knight lusting after the maiden" premise dominates the film, although here it is transformed into a subplot involving Lady Christabel's (Adele Jergens) efforts to rebuff Baron Tristram (Gavin Muir), her father's favorite whom she loathes. Robin, who of course has his own "Lady" Marian (Patricia Morison), and his men, including Tuck, Little John (Walter Sands) and Will Scarlet (Syd Saylor), come to the rescue, delivering the maiden to her own true love, Sir Allan Claire (Michael Duane).

Relegated to a supporting position in this film, Robin and the men of Sherwood do nothing more than set aright a romance, rather than saving England from an iniquitous usurper. By the time *The Prince of Thieves* was released, the cinematic impression of the Robin Hood legends had been reduced to a generic strategy, one that would "find its best market in the juvenile trade on Saturday matinees."[2] This film could have substituted any locale, including early California, the jungles of Africa or the lawless Wild West, and inserted the appropriate action hero: Zorro, Tarzan of the Apes or the Lone Ranger.

The same can be said for the next low-budget offering, Columbia's *Rogues of Sherwood Forest* (1950), which features beefcake heartthrob John Derek as Robin, Earl of Huntington, another son of old Robin. Tramping back over familiar greenwood ground, George Bruce's script is set during the actual reign of King John (George Macready), whose oppressive taxes incite the young Hood's rebellion, resulting in the monarch's signing of the Magna Carta. In his final film role, Alan Hale played Little John for the third time, supported by the corpulent Billy House as Friar Tuck, Lester Matthews as Allen-a-Dale and Billy Bevan as Will Scarlet.

Released the same week, Warner Bros.' *The Flame and the Arrow* (1950) transplanted the Robin Hood plot to medieval Italy, blending representative situations with the scenery-chewing acrobatics of former circus performer and would-be actor Burt Lancaster (as "Lombard Mountain Man" Dardo) and his partner, Nick Cravat, here playing his mute sidekick Piccolo. Eighty-nine of the most bombastic minutes of film ever released (surpassed two years later by the 104-minute, excruciatingly tongue-in-cheek Lancaster follow-up *The Crimson Pirate*), *The Flame and the Arrow* is rendered almost listenable by the typically rousing musical score of the legendary Max Steiner.

1950 also witnessed *The Trail of Robin Hood*, another Roy Rogers Western, but this time offering a creative twist on the familiar tale. Reluctantly coming out of retirement to act in the film, former low-budget star Jack Holt agreed to portray an altruistic man who sells Christmas trees to destitute families. When his humanitarian ways are threatened by a corporate villain, Roy and his band of faithful followers set things right. An upbeat programmer, *The Trail* proved a Yuletide box-office winner in small towns across the U.S.

A feature resembling a television episode, Hal Roach's 60-minute *Tales of Robin Hood* (1952) surprisingly includes some good performances and the fine cinematography of Hollywood veteran George Robinson. Although Robert Clarke and Broadway musical star Mary Hatcher make a lackluster Robin and Marian, Wade Crosby, Paul Cavanagh, and Robert Bice add some color as Little John, Sir "Gui" and Will Scarlet, respectively. Leroy H. Zehren's screenplay follows the familiar Saxon versus Norman tale, highlighting all the prominent clichés: robbing the rich to give to the poor, the climactic duel, the regaining of the outlaw's noble title, and the marriage of Robin and Marian.

Ivanhoe (MGM, 1952)

During 1950, producer Pandro S. Berman began making preparations for the most expensive epic film ever shot in Great Britain, screenwriter Noel Langley's remarkably faithful adaptation of Sir Walter Scott's *Ivanhoe*. Prevented from taking its British profits out of the country, MGM had millions to spend on the film, and for the next two years a formidable crew of technicians, including art director Alfred Junge and costume designer Roger Furse, painstakingly re-created the architecture, weaponry and fashions of the late 12th century on 120 acres at Boreham Wood Studios outside London.

Ivanhoe (1952). **Robert Taylor as Sir Wilfred of Ivanhoe in MGM's outstanding adaptation (frame enlargement).**

Working with Junge, advisers from the London Museum helped design Torquilstone Castle, which was built full scale and surrounded by a moat 20 feet wide and 10 feet deep. Military advisers also were on hand to design authentic yet safe weapons, including 12- and 15-foot lances with hollow centers and rubber tips. Colonel Linden White recalled:

> We had to design special saddles so that a falling rider wouldn't be trampled by a horse, and we had one of the hardest jobs teaching players how to charge at full speed with a 40-to-60 pound suit of armor. We had some accidents, but luckily nothing too serious.[3]

One of Berman's biggest challenges was capturing his choices for the film's two lead roles. Neither Robert Taylor nor Elizabeth Taylor wanted to appear in *Ivanhoe*, but MGM, in an effort to break Liz's affair with director Stanley Donen, ordered her to portray Rebecca, a

Locksley (Harold Warrender) prepares for the thunderous siege of Torquil-stone Castle in *Ivanhoe* (frame enlargement).

move that also secured Robert, who was in love with her, too. He later said:

> When I was told to do *Ivanhoe* much against my wishes, it wasn't as boring as I had expected. I had Elizabeth Taylor in that one, and when I knew she was going to be my leading lady I kind of hoped this time I might get "somewhere" with her. She was in full bloom then, but to my disappointment she was head over heels in love with Michael Wilding, and if it hadn't been for that, I would have tried my luck with her.[4]

The film is billed as "Sir Walter Scott's *Ivanhoe*," and for once this credit is deserved. Although it runs a brisk 107 minutes, most of Scott's dense and, at times, interminable novel is represented in Langley's script. Here, as in the novel, Locksley is a small supporting character, yet the film emphasizes his role, perhaps due to the cinematic popularity of Robin Hood. Five minutes into the film, Sherwood Forest appears on a map as Sir Wilfred of Ivanhoe returns to England to seek out his estranged father, Cedric the Saxon (Finlay Currie), and beloved Rowena (Joan Fontaine). As a group of Norman knights, including Brian de Bois Guilbert (George Sanders), discuss the fact that there may be "a cutthroat behind every tree," Locksley (Harold Warrender) and his Little John-like associate, the Clerk of Copmanhurst (Sebastian Cabot), survey the situation from behind a nearby hedge.

Always accompanied by the Clerk, Locksley continually shadows Ivanhoe, and after the knight crowns Rowena "Queen of Love and Beauty" at the jousting tournament, the outlaw pledges to aid him in defeating the arrogant Normans, including Prince John (portrayed by Guy Rolfe as a vinegar-faced weasel). As in the novel, Locksley is not an independent outlawed rebel but a soldier who leads his Merry Men in a nationalist cause. During the beautifully staged attack on Torquilstone Castle, the Merry Men literally become a siege army and, at one point, Locksley saves Ivanhoe's life when he shoots Front de Boeuf (Francis De Wolff) off one of the battlements. Shades of the Maid Marian-Guy of Gisbourne relationship are also present in De Bois Guilbert's lusting after Rebecca.

The seige of Torquilstone is one of the most impressive battle scenes ever filmed. Berman's selection of action director Richard Thorpe was a brilliant move, as were cinematographer Freddie Young and editor Frank Clarke, who contributed stunning images and a powerful tempo to this 30-minute sequence. One thousand extras were assembled for the battle, and the potentially dangerous siege maneuvers, including high falls from the castle battlements, were monitored by members of the British army. Many of the images, particularly those featuring hails of arrows, are unforgettable, and anticipate similar effects created by Mel Gibson 43 years later for *Braveheart*. The musical score by epic master Miklos Rozsa provides a perfect aural backdrop for the visual kinetics; interestingly, some of the melodies, which the composer based on 12th-century pieces, also prefigure *Braveheart*, which was scored with ethnic realism by James Horner. The climactic joust between Ivanhoe and de Bois Guilbert is also a remarkable scene, in which Rozsa's use of a heartbeat-like drum pulse dramatically increases the suspense.

But *Ivanhoe* is not just an epic spectacle. Like Scott's novel, its content also reaches a grand scale, intelligently and powerfully exploring the religious, social, political and military aspects of the era. On hand to provide insightful commentary is Wamba (Emlyn Williams), the jester who is freed by Ivanhoe in a poignant scene.

Felix Aylmer is superb as Isaac of York, lending a great dignity to Scott's Semitic subplot. When de Bois Guilbert objects to Isaac's presence at Cedric's dinner table, Wambaugh observes, "For every Jew who is not a Christian, I'll show you a Christian who is not a Christian."

Later, when Isaac tells Ivanhoe that King Richard "was no friend to my people," referring to the looting of synagogues to help finance the crusade, the knight replies that, upon his return, the Lionheart will create religious equality. Knowing this to be impossible, Isaac counters, "Let Richard promise this instead. Let him promise *justice* to each man, whether he be Saxon or Norman, or Christian or Jew. For justice belongs to all men, or it belongs to none."

Rebecca (Elizabeth Taylor) experiences remorse at the mortal wounding of Sir Brian de Bois-Gilbert (George Sanders) in this frame enlargement from *Ivanhoe.*

Ivanhoe. George Sanders gives one of his most complex performances, as the Norman knight Brian De Bois Guilbert (frame enlargement).

"But that is a Christian teaching," Ivanhoe responds.

"Strange as it may be, Sir," says Isaac, "we are taught it, too."

The entire cast is excellent, including the American Robert Taylor, who is stoic yet sincere and thoroughly believable as Sir Wilfred. Joan Fontaine is her usual elegant but warm self, combining strength with vulnerability, much as her sister, Olivia de Havilland, does in *The Adventures of Robin Hood*. Felix Aylmer and Emlyn Williams both give dignified and touching performances as the downtrodden characters, and Elizabeth Taylor, contrary to her own opinion of the role, does much more than lend extraordinary beauty to the lavish visuals.

George Sanders offers the finest performance, one of the best he gave in a career distinguished by great portrayals. His Brian de Bois Guilbert possesses much more depth than Scott's literary version: although he lusts after Rebecca, who is repelled by his advances, Sanders plays the role with such complex yet subtle emotions that the viewer must feel sympathy for him. Guilbert is a villain capable of hatred and

Ivanhoe. As the honorable Issac of York, Felix Aylmer brilliantly conveys Scott's Semitic subplot (frame enlargement).

evil, yet he also possesses qualities of chivalry, grace and occasional gentleness.

Robert Douglas, who appears as Sir Hugh De Bracy in the film, recalled that "as an actor [Sanders'] range was intense, possessing a magnificent voice, great poise, and above all an unusual intelligence and approach to any part he undertook.... We had adjoining rooms during *Ivanhoe*, and he preferred to dine with my wife and me in his robe rather than dress and go out. I liked him so much."[5]

But Sanders' participation in the film also brought an unexpected turn of events in his personal life. Prior to leaving for England during the summer of 1951, he insisted that his then-wife Zsa Zsa Gabor remain in Los Angeles. "You would just be bored and would make it impossible for me to work," he told her.

Seeking sympathy from her mother, Gabor wept, "I cannot live without him. I will kill myself." But soon her despair turned to joy when she began a show business career to rival that of her insecure husband. Accepting an offer from Sanders' brother, actor Tom Conway, to join him on the television show *Bachelor's Haven,* she so impressed and entertained both the studio audience and home viewers that *Variety* dubbed her an "instant star." By the time Sanders returned four months later, she had hired a manager, a dramatic coach and a public relations organization to help her handle the 10 film offers she had received. At the Los Angeles airport, George surveyed a newsstand, only to be floored by the visage of his beloved wife staring at him from the October 13, 1951 issue of *Life* magazine! Perhaps his rising jealousy reminded him of De Bois Guilbert's feelings for Rebecca in *Ivanhoe.*[6]

Nominated for three Academy Awards (Best Picture, Cinematography and Musical Score), *Ivanhoe* also was praised by many contemporary critics, Noting that "a remarkable forcefulness is achieved not customary in spectacle films," the *New York Times* placed it in the same class with Sir Laurence Olivier's *Henry V* (1944).[7]

Although Robin Hood is a subordinate character in the film, his legendary code of justice for those unprotected by the law is well represented by the Ivanhoe-Isaac relationship. And though Locksley appears on-screen only for a few minutes, he is an important element in *Ivanhoe.* A fine literary adaptation and an exciting, monumental yet intimate adventure epic, *Ivanhoe* is one of the most impressive productions to include Robin Hood.

The Story of Robin Hood and His Merrie Men (Walt Disney, 1952)

Following the success of his adaptation of Robert Louis Stevenson's *Treasure Island* in 1950, Walt Disney decided to produce new versions of classic British Isles tales, shot entirely in the United Kingdom and released through RKO-Walt Disney British Productions Ltd. Again relying on *Treasure Island* producer Perce Pearce and screenwriter Lawrence Edward Watkin, Disney hired Ken Annakin to direct the exterior scenes for *The Story of Robin Hood* at Denham Studios, while two additional units, helmed by Alex Bryce and Basil Keys, were assigned to shoot location footage.

During the summer of 1951 Disney diligently researched the legends while on a working holiday in England. Ken Annakin frequently joined him for lengthy discussions about the content of the film:

> I remember talking about the original Errol Flynn *Robin Hood*, and I
> looked at it, just to get an idea what had been done before, because I
> never like to do anything twice. Walt didn't seem very worried about
> seeing the original, and in fact, I doubt if he ever did. His approach
> is always that the film is a Disney picture, and therefore, because of
> his attitudes and his approach, the picture is bound to be different
> from anything else made on that subject before.[8]

The first major cinematic re-telling of the legends since *The Adventures of Robin Hood*, Disney's film is quite different than its predecessors. Although it does not possess the symphonic style and pacing and the stellar cast of the Flynn epic, it features a superb cast, finely wrought characterizations, beautiful art direction and costume design, and several ballad-oriented elements eschewed by earlier versions. Two particularly memorable inclusions are the use of Allan-a-Dale (Elton Haytes) as the narrator of the tale, a wandering minstrel who sings to the peasants about the outlaw's exploits, thus providing a colorful connection to the original ballads; and Robin and the Merry Men's use of whistling arrows, each having a different pitch to indicate a particular event, as a greenwood communication device.

While incorporating the ballad incidents involving Robin's quarterstaff fight with Little John and his subsequent piggyback ride on Friar Tuck at the stream, as well as the archery tournament from *Ivanhoe*, Watkin focused on Anthony Munday's 1598 depiction of the outlaw as the dispossessed Earl of Huntington, who, in 1190, rallies his countrymen to fight Prince John after King Richard leaves on the crusade and Robin's father, Hugh Fitzooth, is murdered by one of the Sheriff of Nottingham's henchmen. Prior to being outlawed for avenging his father's death, the lord of the greenwood is young Robert Fitzooth (Richard Todd), who enjoys archery and the company of Maid Marian (Joan Rice), a companion since childhood who now is the ward of King Richard and his mother, Eleanor of Aquitaine (Martita Hunt), a historical figure who made her cinematic debut in this film. Later, after Marian realizes that Robin Hood is actually her old friend, she suggests to the Merry Men that they combine the fruits of their robberies to ransom Richard from Leopold of Austria. In an exciting original scene, Robin and the men arrive in Nottingham during a presentation by the Sheriff (Peter Finch), who claims to the peasant populace that he has donated all his personal riches to help raise the ransom of 100,000 marks. Discovering a treasure chest loaded with coins and priceless jewelry in

The Story of Robin Hood and His Merrie Men (1952). Robin Fitzooth (Richard Todd) and his father, the Earl of Huntington (Clement McCallin, right) at the archery tournament in Walt Disney's admirable version of the legend.

the villain's quarters, the outlaws then drag it into the town square and add it to the collection as Robin shouts, "Three cheers for the Sheriff!"

The Story of Robin Hood may be Disney's best live-action film, simultaneously a visually stunning spectacle and a convincing narrative rooted in realistic performances by Todd, Rice, James Robertson Justice (as Little John), and particularly the superb Peter Finch as the Sheriff, a fine counterpart to Rathbone's Guy of Gisbourne in *The Adventures of Robin Hood*.

But Hubert Gregg is the acting standout. Choosing a quieter, more subtle approach, rather than the controlled pomposity of Claude Rains, Gregg interprets perhaps the finest Prince John ever to grace the screen, a gently conniving, thoroughly believable would-be monarch who carries out much of his own dirty work, personally incarcerating Maid Marian in a dank dungeon instead of relegating the deed to an underling while basking in the warmth of his fireplace at Nottingham Castle. Gregg's approach echoes that of Todd, who portrays Robin as a calmly in-command, articulate and wily outlaw while avoiding Errol Flynn's archetypal cockiness and bravado.

Throughout the film Watkin's screenplay includes interesting variations on familiar events. The archery tournament features an appearance by Hugh Fitzooth, who proves himself to be England's finest bowman. During the final round, the elder Huntington splits *Robin's* arrow, yet asks Prince John and the Sheriff to present his son with the golden trophy because his shaft was the first to hit the bull's-eye. "Midge" the Miller's poaching of a royal deer is also given a clever twist, being combined with the traditional "rescue from the gallows" incident: arrested by the Sheriff, the hapless peasant is dressed in the animal's hide and strung up as several mounted knights ride in a circle and beat him with cudgels before Robin and the Merry Men save him. The duel between Robin and the Sheriff is also sufficiently different than earlier versions, with the outlaw escaping over the Nottingham drawbridge as the dishonorable officer is crushed to death by the closing mechanism.

Perhaps most satisfying is the relationship between Robin and Marian, which is far less stilted than the Flynn–de Havilland coupling of 14 years earlier. From the beginning the screenplay suggests that these two characters have a special affinity for each other, and the later scene involving the outlaw carrying his love across a stream even features a (very brief) tinge of passion (a rarity for an early 1950s Disney adventure). Following Richard's return to England, the couple is "ordered" to marry, as in *The Adventures of Robin Hood*, and the outlaw is knighted with the title "Earl of Locksley."

Although his songs often feature anachronistic, post-medieval elements, Allan-a-Dale is a pleasant presence throughout, actually meeting up with Robin, Little John and Will Scarlet in Sherwood Forest, where he eventually joins the outlaw band and participates in their climactic battle with the Sheriff's forces. The only minor flaw in the performances is contributed by James Hayter, whose "typically Disney" Friar Tuck goes over the top at times, particularly during a bizarre "duet" in which he sings two parts, one in his own voice and the other as a chaste, tinny-voiced maiden!

Rob Roy: The Highland Rogue
(Walt Disney, 1954)

In 1953, inspired by the success of *The Story of Robin Hood* and *The Sword and the Rose*, Perce Pearce, Lawrence Edward Watkin and Ken Annakin began working on a third Disney collaboration, *Rob Roy: the Highland Rogue*, the first sound film based on the legend of the Robin Hood of the Highlands. Adapting their material from the historical Rob's exploits rather than Scott's novel, the trio began preparing for a lavish location shoot in Scotland when the J. Arthur Rank Corporation, to whom Annakin was under contract, refused to let him direct another film for Walt Disney.

Replacing Annakin with Harold French, Pearce became so involved in creating an "authentic" atmosphere for the film that Disney's target juvenile audience was forgotten along the way. Watkin's screenplay is dark, convoluted and extremely violent for the period, and his plot focusing on Rob Roy's *organization* of a rebellion against King George, although conveying the spirit of the outlaw's life and times, is an ahistorical fabrication. Rather than exacting revenge against Rob and his family as repayment for a £1000 loan, Watkin's Duke of Montrose (Michael Gough) is a direct aide to German Geordie (Eric Pohlmann) who personally attempts to capture the outlaw. Montrose becomes Secretary of State for Scotland after deposing the Duke of Argyll (James Robertson Justice), who is not the Campbell of history but a MacGregor who tries to convince Rob (Richard Todd) to lay down his arms and strike a bargain with the king. In the film's most absurd scene, Rob manages the historically impossible feat of obtaining Geordie's amnesty for himself and his clan, including the reinstatement of the MacGregor surname, during a summit in London!

"You are a great rogue," the Teutonic king praises.

"And you, sir, are a great king!" Rob admonishes.

The film compresses Rob's life and legend into a single fictionalized rebellion, ambiguously noting only "the 18th century" as the date of the event. Watkin presumably used the 1715 Jacobite Rebellion as his reference material, but his screenplay incongruously mentions Highland revolts that occurred "in '48 and '78 and '93," dates that do not correspond to even aborted risings by the clans against the Hanoverian government.

However, the stunning locations chosen by Pearce and French are the true highlight of the film, and are used to far greater advantage than in Disney's 1960 adaptation of Robert Louis Stevenson's *Kidnapped*. (Interestingly, some of the events in *Rob Roy* seem to have been inspired by several of Stevenson's novels, including *Kidnapped*, *Catriona* and *St. Ives*.) Equally impressive is the accurate weaponry wielded by the MacGregors, particularly the 18th-century basket hilt swords and the five-foot claymores similar to the famous blade used by William Wallace. Production designer Carmen Dillon's sets also lend an air of authenticity, as does a herd of Scottish blackface sheep used by the MacGregors to waylay Montrose's coach.

Although Richard Todd does not manage a very convincing Scots accent and is too well groomed and attired, he does resemble Rob Roy in one respect: he is very short (a physical characteristic that aided him in playing Robin Hood two years earlier). However, he

Rob Roy: The Highland Rogue (1954). Robert Roy MacGregor, the Robin Hood of the Highlands (Richard Todd), and his wife, Helen Mary (Glynis Johns), in Walt Disney's dark, uneven fictionalization.

does not possess the enormous chest and arms for which Rob was famous.

Curiously, whereas Rob's wife, Helen Mary, played a large part as the strong female influence in his life, the film focuses on his mother, who prevails upon Argyll to intercede with Montrose and King George. Watkin's version of Helen Mary, as played by the fetching but wooden and whiny Glynis Johns (whose accent is anything but a Scots one), is merely a weak female character appearing from time to time to add some romantic interest. Mother MacGregor is a tough old crone who, when shot by the redcoats, hides her pain from Rob, even when her house is set aflame (one of several events in which the historical Helen Mary was involved that the film transfers to the older woman). The film treads a bit closer to the Rob Roy legend when the redcoats attempt to molest Helen Mary, although the Disney version never suggests actual rape and includes Rob appearing miraculously to fight off the lecherous Englishmen.

Some of Rob's actions are based on fact, including his daring escape from the redcoats after he is arrested during the wedding ceilidh thrown for him and Helen Mary at Inversnaid. Diving into a river, he eludes the English fire as he tumbles over a roaring waterfall. Later, Rob makes more harrowing escapes, and his confrontation with Killearn (Geoffrey Keen), who is extorting double rents from the MacGregors, is also patterned on an historical incident.

Finlay Currie (who, during the 1950s and early 1960s, appeared in nearly every film set in Scotland) plays Hamish MacPherson, who adds some Jacobite flavor by mentioning "Bonnie Dundee's" efforts at the Battle of Killiecrankie, but also contributes the film's most obnoxious moment by furiously blowing on a bagpipe reed while Rob is trying to converse with his wife. This unnecessary potshot at the bagpipes mars an otherwise respectable musical score incorporating several traditional Scottish melodies and some effective a cappella Gaelic "mouth music." Composed by Clifton Parker, the music benefitted from Muir Matheson's direction of the Royal Philharmonic Orchestra.

As Montrose, Michael Gough gives one of his finest performances, combining intensity and subtlety as he imbues the Duke with concentrated ambition and evil, making the character a fine Hanoverian Sheriff of Nottingham to Todd's Jacobite Robin Hood. Although the plot is primarily fictitious, Gough's portrayal adds to the film's respectful depiction of Highland culture, including accurate representations of the language, music and customs. When Rob spurs the MacGregors to battle, they unleash their clan cry of "Gregolach!" to frighten the English. Some of the scenes set in London also feature historical references, including a shot of street hawkers selling printed ballads about Rob, showing that the Highland rogue is becoming a legend in his own time.

Though Disney's *Rob Roy* is certainly a mixed sporran, blending an historical setting with an outlandish story and unnecessary humor and character distortion, French and Watkin's dark, grim and violent approach sets the film apart from the studio's other primarily light-hearted costume dramas. And while it joins Scott's novel in creating false impressions about the real Robert Roy MacGregor, it serves as an adequate introduction to the legend of the Robin Hood of the Highlands.

Eleven

Low-Budget Brigands:
The Hammer Hoods
(1957–73)

Following the release of Disney's *The Story of Robin Hood*, the outlaw disappeared from theaters for the next five years, only to be revived on the small screen in a television series, *The Adventures of Robin Hood*, from 1956–60. Starring Richard Greene, these four seasons of episodes were shot in England by the Sapphire company and became hugely popular on both sides of the Atlantic. Gleaning much of its content from the Flynn classic and combining cramped studio interiors with bits of location footage, the claustrophobic series also featured Alan Wheatley as the Sheriff and Leo McKern (in a hammy pastiche of Claude Rains' Prince John) as Sir Roger de Liel.

From 1957 to 1973, five features about Robin Hood were made in Great Britain, four of them by Hammer Film Productions, Ltd., who seemed nearly as interested in their own national legend as they were by the assorted monsters, vampires and mummies that had been inspired by American films of the 1930s. Work on the amateurish *Men of Sherwood Forest* (1957) began the previous year, with Michael Carreras producing, Val Guest directing, and future Hammer ace screenwriter Jimmy Sangster acting as production manager. Set in 1194, with King Richard imprisoned in Germany, the film opens as John Fitzroy, a Lionheart envoy, is killed by agents of Prince John and the Sheriff of Nottingham, who have disguised themselves as Merry Men. In an attempt to capture Robin Hood (Don Taylor), whom the Sheriff (Leonard Sachs) has been trying to waylay for 10 years, two unscrupulous noblemen meet with the outlaw in Sherwood and, lying that Richard is already on his way back to England, persuade him to stop Hobb and Dickon, two hench-men who have been ordered to kill the King. After Robin outwits the pair of rogues by getting them drunk, he learns they were hired by Sir Guy Belton (David King-Wood), whose castle the outlaw visits in the guise of Gilbert of Lancaster, a lute-strumming troubadour. Due to his own investigative and athletic prowess—and a bit of help from Little John (Leslie Linder) and Friar Tuck (Reginald Beckwith)—he eventually recovers a Saracen icon containing a note from the King, looted from the corpse of Fitzroy. When Richard (Patrick Holt) finally arrives in England, Robin and the Merry Men, aided by the luscious Lady Alys (Eileen Moore), a resident of Sir Guy's castle, save him from assassination.

Allan MacKinnon's screenplay, the first to include a mention of Barnesdale as well as Sherwood, is interesting and somewhat original, but would have benefitted from a larger budget and a more capable action director. Val Guest's handling of the dueling scenes is so inept that one wonders how any of this footage survived in the final cut. The production values are so poor that a number of very good performances, particularly that of Reginald Beckwith as Tuck, are wasted. Unfortunately, Beckwith's portrayal is marred by one of MacKinnon's few anachronistic absurdities: the Friar's obsession with gambling devices such as the shell game, roulette and poker. (Is this medieval England or modern Las Vegas?) The card game eventually metamorphoses into strip poker, sinking the content to an even lower level.

Indeed, all of the ridiculous comic relief could have been elimi-nated. Even more annoying was Guest's insistence that Robin and the Merry Men literally *be merry* throughout all 77 minutes of the film, even when threatened with violent death and chained in a foul dungeon. A scene of Robin and Tuck happily singing a terrible, off-key ballad while Lady Alys files through their chains is excruciatingly bad.

Don Taylor's interpretation of the outlaw is the Robin Hood cin-ema's only blatant Errol Flynn rip-off. Not only are his costume and facial hair modeled on the Flynn look, but so are his delivery, manner-isms and facial expressions. While it is true that the wicked Tasmanian is the archetypal Robin, filmdom did not need a pallid pastiche. And although Eileen Moore is breathtakingly beautiful, Lady Alys' fascina-tion with the outlaw and desire to hear "Gilbert of Lancaster's" rendi-tions of the Robin Hood ballads is terribly contrived, regardless of the slight connection her request makes with historical reality. She is merely a pale, yet mouth-watering, substitute for the familiar Marian.

Another blatant borrowing from *The Adventures of Robin Hood* is the character of Alys' servant Elvira, a faint shade of Una O'Connor's Bess. And the film also borrows a character name from *Ivanhoe*, Wamba, which is assigned to an insignificant jailer at Sir Guy's castle.

All told, *Men of Sherwood Forest* may be the worst Robin Hood film of the sound era. The title itself is misleading. Though several of the legendary Merry Men appear, Robin and Tuck are the only forest outlaws who are actual characters. Will Scarlet appears very briefly, and Little John figures into little of the action. Nothing from the early ballads or other Robin Hood tales is used, although the songs and Allen-a-Dale are mentioned by Lady Alys. But the visual style is the film's biggest flaw, a lackluster atmosphere made worse by badly staged battles, inferior weapons and costumes, and embarrassing art direction that awkwardly combines exterior shots of a real castle with interior scenes featuring plaster sets of a different color. Perhaps the film would have been an arrow's length better if Michael Carreras had robbed more from rich investors to give to the poor filmmakers.

Though shot in England, *The Son of Robin Hood* (1959) was the only non–Hammer film about the outlaw released during this period. Made on a tight budget for 20th Century–Fox by producer-director George Sherman, the film benefited from the Cinemascope lensing of Arthur Grant and the capable period art direction of Norman Arnold, both of whom contributed to a colorful and exciting pace that appealed to young filmgoers.

Al [David] Hedison stars as Jamie, a young rebel who rises to the fore after Deering Hood, the "son" of Robin Hood, proves to be a girl (June Laverick), in yet another second-generation twist on the old tales. Together, Deering, who was sent for by her father's old followers, and Jamie save England from a familiar pair of villains, an evil regent called Chester (Marius Goring) and his officer, Des Roches (David Farrar). Misleadingly titled, *The Son of Robin Hood* is notable for its gender-bending premise, but its impact is eroded by the Merry Men's eventual need for a male leader. The only connection to the ballads is Little John (who appears, in some form, in every major Robin Hood film), though Robin himself does not make an appearance. Heavy on action, with a lessening of the pace during the scenes involving Deering and Jamie, the film appealed almost exclusively to the youth market.

Two years later, Hammer was back in the greenwood, creating its own widescreen opus (in "Megascope"), *The Sword of Sherwood*

The Son of Robin Hood (1959). Title lobby card for 20th Century–Fox's Saturday matinee depiction of a second-generation Hood.

Forest, starring Richard Greene (who had graduated from playing Robin on television) and studio horror stalwart Peter Cushing (as the Sheriff of Nottingham). Co-produced by Greene for a Columbia release, the film was directed by Terence Fisher, who had worked with Cushing on many occasions, notably pairing him with Christopher Lee in *The Curse of Frankenstein* (1957), *Horror of Dracula* (1958) and a violent adaptation of Conan Doyle's *The Hound of the Baskervilles* (1959), among others.

In *Variety*'s January 11, 1961, review, the critic "Tube" observed that, though little from the early legends is included, the timeless nature of the subject remains: "Although the lyrical charm and cultural strain of the anonymous original ballads have virtually vanished through commercial erosion, there's plenty of life left in the characters, whose conflicts are communicable to the modern mind."[1]

Though Fisher shot much of the film on location in Ireland, his usual stodgy style, including a leaden pace, unimaginative compositions and bright, even lighting, create a general mood of *un*excitement. This time around (the aging) Robin, supported by Little John (Nigel Green) and Friar Tuck (Niall MacGinnis), rescues Marian (Sarah Branch, a typically buxom Hammer beauty) and Hubert Walter, the Archbishop of Canterbury (Jack Gwillim), from the evil clutches of the Sheriff and his benefactor, the Earl of Newark (Richard Pasco).

Material from the original "A Gest of Robin Hood" is included early in the film when Robin and Little John aid a traveler who has been pursued by the Sheriff. Marian then lures Robin to the Sheriff, who, wanting to capture the stranger, offers to pardon the outlaw. Refusing, Robin is chased back to Sherwood, where, in a poorly directed sequence, the soldiers are ambushed by the Merry Men.

For the majority of the film, Robin and the men attempt to discover the identity of the strange visitor, who unfortunately dies with these words on his lips: "Danger at Bawtry." Soon they ride hell bent for Bawtry Castle, which Nottingham is attempting to seize from the Archbishop, whom the Earl of Newark wants assassinated. Incredibly, when the Sheriff displays some conscience and refuses to support Newark, he is killed. Then Robin engages the Earl and his men in a laughably inept sword fight that miraculously culminates with the rescue of Canterbury. The entire pedestrian business closes when the Archbishop, acting as the King's Chancellor during Richard's absence "fighting the French," pardons Robin and orders Tuck to perform the marriage of the outlaw and his beloved.

The following year, Hammer produced an even lower-budgeted Sherwood installment, *A Challenge for Robin Hood* (1962), scripted by Peter Bryan and directed by C. M. Pennington-Richards. Always a studio quick to churn out endless sequels for films that had proven even mildly successful at the box office, Hammer really went on the cheap this time, providing 20th Century–Fox with what *Variety* referred to as a "reprise of the Robin Hood legend [that] seems to have been produced 20 years ago, even down to its poor, mushy color qualities."[2]

In Bryan's script the usual "robbing the rich to give to the poor" premise is intact, but the villains are changed once again, this time appearing as Roger de Courtenay (Peter Blythe), an evil cousin of Robin's who has established himself as a dictator over the serfs in his fiefdom, and the Sheriff (John Arnatt), who waits until the last minute to join the fray, slyly observing de Courtenay's unsuccessful attempts to capture the outlaw. When Robin (Barrie Ingham) and the Merry Men,

THE EPIC STORY

OF THE MIGHTIEST ARCHER
OF THEM ALL...AND
THE FURY OF THE
SAXON WAR THAT
TURNED INTO...

SEE!

The Seige of
Sherwood Forest!

The Rescue of
Maid Marion!

The Gallows of
Courtney Fair!

The Terror
Torture
by Fire!

The Villainy
of the Norman
Traitor!

A Challenge for Robin Hood

STARRING
BARRIE INGHAM · JAMES HAYTER · LEON GREENE · PETER BLYTHE · GAY HAMILTON

PRODUCED BY CLIFFORD PARKES · DIRECTED BY C. M. PENNINGTON-RICHARDS
SCREENPLAY BY PETER BRYAN · COLOR by DE LUXE · A SEVEN ARTS-HAMMER PRODUCTION · RELEASED BY 20th CENTURY-FOX

A Challenge for Robin Hood (1962). Original advertisement for Hammer's low-budget retelling of the legend.

including Little John (Leon Greene) and Friar Tuck (James Hayter), obligatorily attack Nottingham Castle to rescue Marian (Gay Hamilton) and her little brother, the Sheriff fights long enough to meet his predictable fate.

By the time *A Challenge for Robin Hood* was released, the legends apparently had been mined for all their cinematic worth, and a major

A Challenge for Robin Hood. Using a ridiculously cheap, historically inaccurate sword, Robin (Barrie Ingham) engages in an uninspired bit of derring-do.

passage of time would be required before they again would seem fresh on the screen. Too many adventure films about the outlaw had been made, and far too many fabricated absurdities had been invented to replace the tediously familiar events from the ballads. The low-budget, programmer status of *A Challenge* proved that Hammer's jaunt in the greenwood should come to an end (although perhaps it should never have begun with *Men of Sherwood Forest*!). *Variety*'s "Tony" continued:

> What may irk traditionalists is the meeting with the giant wrestler, Little John. Gone is the famous quarterstaff fight on a log bridge. In its place, Little John already knows Robin. This version may simply draw laughing disbelief as it did when the audience saw Robin shoot an arrow through a ribbon carried aloft by a pigeon, while the great marksman was blindfolded.[3]

Eleven years after the release of *A Challenge for Robin Hood*, Hammer tried its hand at one last Robin Hood film, *Wolfshead* (1973), an aptly titled but turgid production made during its final decline, a period when films like *The Satanic Rites of Dracula* (1973) tolled a sad death knell for the once successful studio. That same year, Disney released *Robin Hood*, an animated feature for children that cast all the legendary characters as talking animals: Robin (voice of Brian Bedford) became a wily and merry fox, Little John (voice of Phil Harris) a friendly bear, Prince John (voice of Peter Ustinov) an effeminate lion with a mother fixation. The minstrel character from the earlier Disney film was transformed into a musical rooster (voice of Roger Miller), who travels about, performing anachronistic but charming songs with an American folk twist.

Several of the anthropomorphic characters are Americanized, including Little John, who uses slang terms from the 1960s, Friar Tuck (voice of Andy Devine), the Sheriff of Nottingham (voice of Pat Buttram), and two of the sheriff's vulture henchmen (Ken Curtis and George Lindsay). And adding to the Yankee atmosphere, legendary Tin Pan Alley tunesmith Johnny Mercer contributed one of the songs, "The Phony King of England," performed by several of the characters as they deride Prince John while celebrating in Sherwood.

Interestingly, some of the content, including fairly sophisticated dialogue and scenes of the heroes in drag, is quite unusual for a Disney animated feature, sailing straight over the heads of its targeted age group. Although children invariably laugh at the antics of Prince John, who is little better than a feline moron, his infantile thumb sucking is perhaps a wee bit too psychoanalytical for them to understand.

When *Robin Hood* was made in 1973, each Disney cartoon still had its own individual charm, unlike the late 1980s and 1990s features that have stuck to the same formula, endlessly recycling the same character types (beefcake heroes, lithe young heroines and seriocomic animal sidekicks) and bombastic Broadway songs that have no connection to the depicted cultures and historical eras.

Except for some of the major characters, nothing from the ballads is used in the film, but a few incidents from *The Adventures of Robin Hood* and *The Story of Robin Hood* are interspersed with predominantly original material. *Ivanhoe*'s archery tournament is adapted once more, with the Sheriff actually taking part in the contest. Perhaps the greediest Nottingham ever, this wolf in noble's clothing collects a little bunny's birthday present (a single farthing, which required long-term saving by his family) and a blind beggar's (actually Robin incognito) alms for Prince John's tax coffers! One of the most clever elements is the depiction of King Richard, who appears, respendent in crusader's surcoat, as a courageous, robust, hugely maned lion, providing quite a contrast to his cowering brother (who, having no mane, is really a *lioness*).

The Chairman of the Board as the Prince of Thieves: *Robin and the Seven Hoods* (1964)

W̶h̶o could have guessed that one of the most interesting visual-izations of the Robin Hood character would be a Prohibition-era mobster version portrayed by Frank Sinatra? Proving the timelessness of the outlaw, Sinatra's "reincarnation" of the character, who presents a humorous yet thought-provoking view of social realities and police corruption in late 1920s Chicago, does not need to adhere to the period "sanctity" of the legend to be effective (or acceptable).

Subsequent films inspired by the Robin Hood legends have retained the popularly accepted late-12th century setting while awkwardly adding anachronistic characters (*Robin Hood: Prince of Thieves* [1991]) and content (*Time Bandits* [1981], *Robin Hood: Men in Tights* [1993]), but *Robin and the Seven Hoods* (1964) is successful because the entire pro-duction is updated while retaining the social message, albeit in a satir-ical style. Unlike these other films, Sinatra's approach utilizes history as a referent rather than a point of departure.

Robin and the Seven Hoods takes the Western world's most leg-endary populist hero and places him simultaneously within two of the United States' most traumatic historical events: the gangland wars of 1920s Chicago and the early days of the Great Depression. Set during a time when government at the local level was corrupt and the federal bureaucracy seemed uninterested in the average Joe, the film offers its own updated version of the classic Saxon versus Norman motif. While

Robin and the Seven Hoods (1964). Frank Sinatra as "Robbo" in a publicity still that also appears in the film.

the gang-influenced Sheriff of Chicago is the parallel of the Prince John–controlled Sheriff of Nottingham, the (unmentioned) President Herbert Hoover, whom many came to view as an absentee leader, could be the parallel of King Richard the Lionheart.

Sinatra and pals Dean Martin and Sammy Davis, Jr. (along with sometime members Joey Bishop and Peter Lawford, whom Frank ousted in 1962), preferred to call their collaboration "the Summit" rather than the more popular "Rat Pack." The original Holmby Hills Rat Pack had been created as a "living room drinking club" in Los Angeles by Humphrey Bogart and Lauren Bacall, who, when not partying in their own home, joined other nonconformist friends for meetings at Mike Romanoff's Restaurant in Beverly Hills. Sinatra, who was a friend of Bogie's and, later, a fiancé to Bacall, had been closely associated with the Holmby Hills gang, but his own group of performers and business associates had little in common with this earlier, philosophically anarchistic club. His Summit celebrated the carousing, self-deprecating, improvisational comedy, crooning and hip swing music of the Vegas nightclub scene, a far cry from Bogie's bohemian get-togethers. And Sinatra hated the term "Rat Pack," which was attached to his group by the press but originally coined by Bacall upon her observing the extremely dissipated state of the Holmby Hills mob during a Frank-sponsored week-long binge in Vegas.

While the first Summit film, the vastly entertaining *Ocean's Eleven* (1960), also starring Martin, Davis, Lawford and Bishop, actually is set in the top casinos of Vegas, Sinatra, as producer, wanted to do something substantially different in the subsequent "Rat Pack" entries. But while *Sergeants Three* (1962) is merely a passable Western parody of Kipling's "Gunga Din," *Robin and the Seven Hoods*, which adds Bing Crosby to the potent mix of Sinatra, Martin and Davis, reaches the level of smart social satire, simultaneously a wittily written parody of the gangster genre (including appearances by legendary Warner Bros. bad guys Edward G. Robinson and Allen Jenkins [who, nearly 30 years earlier, had been named as one of the potential Merry Men in Warner Bros.' aborted James Cagney Robin Hood project]), a musical with memorable songs and dynamic dancing, and a bizarre Prohibition twist on the Robin Hood legend.

Sinatra and his pals had enormous fun making the film, which began shooting in Chicago on October 31, 1963, despite two extremely traumatic events that occurred during production. The first incident began very ironically on the morning of November 22, 1963, during the filming of Big Jim's (Robinson) funeral at a Burbank cemetery, where Sinatra comically commented on a headstone marking the grave of a man named John Kennedy (whose dates read 1802–1884). A few hours later, around noon, word was passed around the set that Frank's friend President John F. Kennedy had been shot in Dallas.

"Get me the White House," Sinatra ordered an assistant. After speaking briefly with a presidential aide, he returned to the set and said, "Let's shoot this thing, 'cause I don't want to come back here any more."[1] After the cast and crew recovered from the shock, filming continued.

Less than three weeks later, on December 8, 1963, Sinatra scrapped a scheduled kidnapping scene after his son, 19-year-old Frank, Jr., was abducted from a Lake Tahoe hotel and held by three men for a $240,000 ransom. Having planned the crime well in advance, the kidnappers were paid by Sinatra three days later, but rather than delivering Frank, Jr., at the appointed time, one of them eventually released him at the drop off point along the San Diego Freeway. Picked up by a security officer of the Bel Air Patrol, the terrified young man was then taken to the Los Angeles home of his mother, Nancy. Within 48 hours, the inept kidnappers were in police custody. The incident understandably hit Sinatra very hard, but he maintained an outwardly calm appearance, giving a fine performance in the film. He particularly enjoyed working with director Gordon Douglas, who always came to the set well prepared, often shooting scenes in a single take. Frank hated wasting time while making films, and had a reputation of walking off sets when directors insisted on unnecessary preparation or re-takes.

David Schwartz's witty and wacky script includes Chicago versions of several characters from the legends: Sinatra's "Robbo" (also called Robin Hood at times); Little John (Dean Martin); Will [Scarlet] (Sammy Davis, Jr.); Marian (Barbara Rush), the daughter of "Big Jim" (Edward G. Robinson); Allen A. Dale (Bing Crosby); and Guy Gisborne (Peter Falk). The Sheriff of Nottingham character also is present in the form of Sheriff Octavius Glick (Robert Foulk), described as a "schmendrick" (by gangsters and the public) on several occasions.

Sinatra's Robbo is one of the very few characters, perhaps the *only* mob leader, in the history of the gangster genre to refuse to commit murder to achieve his ends. When Marian offers to pay him $50,000 to eliminate Sheriff Glick, the man responsible for her father's

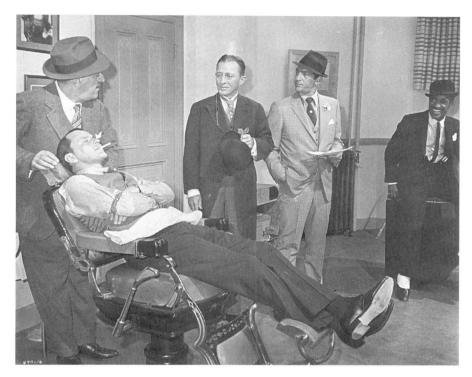

Robin and the Seven Hoods. **Robbo, Allen A. Dale (Bing Crosby), Little John (Dean Martin), and Will (Sammy Davis, Jr.) discuss the publicity surrounding the "dumping" of $50,000 at the Blessed Shelter Orphans Home.**

assassination, he turns her down; but when Gisborne has the untrustworthy lawman encased in concrete, Marian pays Robbo anyway. This act precipitates the Robin Hood angle when Robbo orders Little John and Will to "dump" the $50,000 at "an old ladies' home" or "orphanage." The following morning, the newspapers herald, "Robin Hood in Chicago," and a radio announcer declares that the well-known gang boss is using "the gaming table and bootleg beer to aid the unfortunate." The only person Robbo and his men actually "take for a ride" is Gisborne, but the script intimates that the killing was committed in self-defense.

When all the Robin Hood publicity ensues, Robbo tells the press that the $50,000 gift to the Blessed Shelter Orphans Home was a one-time beneficence and that his "name is Robbo, not Rockefeller"; but soon, Little John, inundated with letters from unfortunates asking for assistance, informs his boss of the fall-out. "How do you know they ain't chiselers?" John asks. Giving his fellow man the benefit of a doubt, Robbo replies, "How do you know they are?" and orders Little John to send each of them "a couple hundred." Soon, the gang is visited by Allen A. Dale, an amanuensis from the orphanage versed in literature, who reveals that he made "the Robin Hood comparison." Robbo then appoints Allen head of charities, declaring, "Start this bum off with a c-note a week." "Oh, gee. I'm a hood. I'm a hood!" the sheltered ex-waif joyously declares.

After the gang opens a free soup kitchen, a "project of the Robbo Foundation" (a parody of the actual fronts run in Chicago by Al Capone, who became a folk hero to many down-and-outers in the Windy City), they accept further charity donations during the debut of their new, elaborate speakeasy casino (built to replace Robbo's earlier joint that was "hit" by Gisborne's boys). As comely waitresses in Lincoln Green leotards and feathered forest caps collect the money, Allen and Little John count it, sitting beneath a large banner advertising the "Robin Hood Foundation." Earlier, when one of the men is confused about who Robin Hood was, Little John replies, "He was some Englishman who wore long, green underwear and had an operation going for him in the forest."

As head of charities, Allen opens a Robin Hood club at the orphanage, outfitting the boys with feathered caps and bows and arrows. And, apparently, they take the "robbing the rich to give to the poor" concept to heart; later, one of Gisborne's "mugs" complains, "I caught a kid stealin' a tire off my car the other day, and he pulled a bow and arrow on me!"

Interestingly, the film avoids a romantic interest for Robbo, who is not duped by Marian's attempt to regain her father's position as mob boss of Chicago. In its depiction of Marian, *Robin and the Seven Hoods* ranks as the only film to cast the traditional lover of Robin in a villainous light. After she is unsuccessful in seducing Robbo, she manages to manipulate the less cautious and very amorous Little John, who eventually dumps her when he cannot betray his boss and friend. But Marian never deviates from her plan, and before film's end, leads both Gisborne and Deputy Sheriff Potts (Victor Buono) to their demises in concrete cornerstones for new Chicago buildings.

When Robbo is framed by Guy and his mugs for the murder of Sheriff Glick, he is forced to listen to the "testimony" of a literal parade of liars. (Meanwhile, a Chicago headline reveals, "Robin Hood's a Hood!") During his time on the stand, Gisborne offers his alibi: Glick's murder occurred on a Tuesday afternoon, and each week at that time he always plays mah jongg quietly with some companions at the *Nottingham* Hotel! Later, while trying to explain the public support Robbo has achieved, Guy tells Marian, "The fact that the man [Robin Hood] has been dead for six-hundred years—it don't mean nothin'."

In a career distinguished by many outstanding film performances, Sinatra is truly in his element in *Robin and the Seven Hoods*, always in control, backing down to no one, entering rooms with the self-assured swagger he learned from his idol Humphrey Bogart. In his only portrayal of a gangster (he previously had played a cold-blooded killer in *Suddenly* [1954] and a gambler in *Guys and Dolls* [1955] he is able to combine his "tough guy" persona with his considerable comic talent, not to mention the two opportunities to flex his legendary "reed," as he preferred to call it. And the Robin Hood angle also reflects his own personality, as he was both somewhat of an outlaw (a self-professed "outsider") and a life-long contributor to various charities across the globe. This tailor-made characterization is not surprising; after all, he produced the film. (Sixteen years earlier, Sinatra twice referred to Robin and Marian in what he later called the most embarrassing film of his career, MGM's 1948 musical fiasco, *The Kissing Bandit*. Two years after making *Robin and the Seven Hoods*, he mentioned the outlaw again, in the Rod Serling-scripted *Assault on a Queen* [1966]; while charming the exquisite Virna Lisi, he refers to her as "a blonde, Italian Robin Hood.")

Composed by Sammy Cahn and James Van Heusen, two of Sinatra's favorite tunesmiths, and arranged by long-time associate Nelson Riddle, the eight songs provide potent musical punctuation to Schwartz's script. Not surprisingly, Dean warmly solos on a sentimental crooner ballad, "Any Man Who Loves His Mother," while the multi-talented Sammy flies alone, tapdancing across a bartop and shooting up Gisborne's casino, as he belts out "Bang, Bang." Bing, instructing a group of orphans, warbles the charming, laid-back "Don't Be a Do-Badder," and Frank swings "My Kind of Town," the Chicago anthem that became one of his signature songs. The Cahn-Van Heusen contribution also includes collaborations between Bing, Dean, Frank and Sammy (the hilarious "Mr. Booze," performed during the "mission casino" scene) and Bing, Dean and Frank (the excellent soft-shoe number "Style"), as

well as a number sung by Peter Falk ("All for One"). This last, the most
utterly odd musical moment, occurs at the beginning of the film, when
the Chicago mobsters (including Allen Jenkins as "Vermin"!) become
backing vocalists for Guy, who, in the wake of Big Jim's "demise,"
declares himself the new boss of the Windy City.

The "Mr. Booze" sequence, during which Robbo's joint is auto-
matically transformed into an austere Skid Row mission adorned with
temperance slogans, is a musical and comic highlight, with Crosby
becoming "the Reverend Allen A. Dale." That the entire Summit had a
marvelous time shooting the scene is openly apparent: when Davis blew
a line, testifying that "sin," rather than "gin," overtook him, Martin,
attempting to mask his mirth, added, "Yeah, a little of that, too," before
returning to character. (Gordon Douglas and editor Sam O'Steen left it
in the final cut.) In fact, Crosby appears to be enjoying himself
immensely throughout the film, giving a splendid performance. However, his offscreen relationship with Sinatra apparently was not as pleasant; although Frank was a life-long fan of Bing's musicianship, still
photographer Ted Allan later recalled that Ol' Blue Eyes, a very gentle
father, repeatedly chastised his hero for the abusive way he treated the
Crosby children.[2]

Other than the vocal performances (patterned after those in *Guys
and Dolls*, which pairs Sinatra with a [barely] singing Marlon Brando),
the gangster scenes are played straight, with only a layer of expertly
integrated comic exaggeration added for good measure (particularly
served up by Peter Falk, who demonstrates keen timing in his turn as
the ambitious yet intellectually challenged Gisborne). Like Warner
Bros.' "golden age" gangster parodies *The Little Giant* (1933), *A Slight
Case of Murder* (1938) and *Larceny, Inc.* (1942), all starring Edward G.
Robinson (who displays the same ineptly self-reliant quality — albeit in
a more subtle style), *Robin and the Seven Hoods* (unlike the later parodies of Mel Brooks and others) eschews buffoonery, slapstick and sight
gags for a more sophisticated style in which the comedy arises *naturally* from the absurd counterculture of gangsterism. The very nature
of Robbo and Guy Gisborne's competing operations, not to mention the
corruption of the Chicago police, provides the springboard for situations that are hilarious yet grounded in an historical milieu. Even the
violence, a staple element in gangster films, is downplayed. The only
violent action visualized is committed by the mobsters against inani-
mate objects, namely the two casinos owned by Robbo and Guy. And

though Sheriff Glick and Deputy Sheriff Potts both get taken for rides, these crimes occur off-screen; when the officers are again mentioned, they have become part of the cornerstones. The only on-screen murder is that of Big Jim, who is gunned down by the singing mugs at his birthday party!

The entire "gang war" is a game pitting Robbo against Guy, who commits all the actual crimes usually associated with mobsters. Of course, the film does exactly what the early Warners gangster classics were accused of doing—romanticizing and glamorizing the ruggedly individualist criminal lifestyle—but these gang members are humorous, likable lugs whose violent acts are the adult equivalent of children breaking each others' toys.

Some of the humor is downright bizarre, including two running gags involving Potts' love of cocoa and one of Robbo's men who has a passion for knitting. In one scene late in the film, just before irate women break into the free soup kitchen (which Marian has transformed into a counterfeiting operation), the obsessive knitter is seen demonstrating his craft for Little John. The only truly weak comic element in the film is the ending, which depicts Robbo, Little John and Will reduced to working as bell-ringing Santa Clauses at Christmas, an abrupt and unsatisfying conclusion to a clever and funny story combining two seemingly incompatible genres.

Though noting the disappointing denouement and the "threadbare story," *Variety*'s "Whit" was enthusiastic about the film:

> Warner Bros. has a solid money entry ... sparked by the names of Frank Sinatra, Dean Martin and Bing Crosby to give marquee power.... Hefty laugh situations are afforded as pic unreels....
>
> Performance-wise, Falk comes out best. His comic gangster is a pure gem and he should get plenty of offers after this. Sinatra, of course, is smooth and Crosby in a "different" type of role rates a big hand.... A lovely assortment of hood types back them effectively.[3]

Purists of the legend may have a difficult time acquiring a taste for *Robin and the Seven Hoods*, but this particular updating could not make more sense, particularly in a satirical film. What better period in which to set a new version of the story than the early Great Depression? The film merges the legendary populist hero of the 14th century with the legendary 20th century celebratory figure of the gangster who represented the "pull himself up by the bootstraps" individualist embodying the American dream. And the film is a visual treat, with formidable cinematographer William H. Daniels' stunning Cinemascope compositions creating the best-looking Robin Hood film since the 1952 *Ivanhoe*. A unique viewing experience, it is one of the strangest Hollywood films ever made.

Thirteen

The Revised Robin: *Robin and Marian* (1976)

Nineteen seventy-six was a year during which England's most beloved literary legends received a less romanticized, more "realistic" treatment by filmmakers. First, Sir Arthur Conan Doyle's Sherlock Holmes was revealed to be a neurotic, troubled drug addict in *The Seven-Per-Cent Solution*, Nicholas Meyer's adaptation of his bestselling 1974 novel. One of old Blighty's most enduring legends, Holmes had been depicted by revisionists before—as in Billy Wilder's *The Private Life of Sherlock Holmes* (1970)—but never in such an unflattering and vulnerable light.

England's most potent and indestructable cultural symbol, Robin Hood had been depicted as an older man in films focusing on the exploits of his equally rebellious offspring, but never in the way screenwriter James Goldman and director Richard Lester chose for *Robin and Marian*, a film set in the Middle Ages but reflecting then-current post–Watergate attitudes about authority and society.

During 1974 Lester, fresh from the huge box-office success of *The Three Musketeers*, had been approached at his Twickenham office in London by Peter Gruber (then an assistant to Columbia's David Begelman), who placed seven 3 × 5 note cards on the director's desk.

"On each of them is a story idea that Columbia owns," Gruber told him. "Pick the one you want and make it for us. I'm not going to leave this office until you agree."

Surveying the cards, Lester passed on six of them, but his eyes fixed on the seventh, which read, "Robin Hood as an older man." "*That*'s what I'd like to do," he said.[1]

Soon after this brief meeting, a dinner was held at the Berkley

For

Robin and Marian

Love is the greatest adventure of all.

COLUMBIA PICTURES and RASTAR PICTURES present

AUDREY HEPBURN

SEAN CONNERY

ROBERT SHAW

IN

"ROBIN AND MARIAN"

A RICHARD LESTER FILM

NICOL WILLIAMSON

DENHOLM ELLIOTT   RONNIE BARKER

KENNETH HAIGH   IAN HOLM

and RICHARD HARRIS as Richard the Lionheart

ROBERT SHAW
as The Sheriff of Nottingham
NICOL WILLIAMSON
as Little John
DENHOLM ELLIOTT
as Will Scarlet
RONNIE BARKER
as Friar Tuck
KENNETH HAIGH
as Sir Ranulf
IAN HOLM
as King John
and RICHARD HARRIS
as King Richard The Lionheart

A RAY STARK-RICHARD SHEPHERD Production • Music by JOHN BARRY

Executive Producer RICHARD SHEPHERD • Written by JAMES GOLDMAN

Produced by DENIS O'DELL • Directed by RICHARD LESTER

PG PARENTAL GUIDANCE SUGGESTED
SOME MATERIAL MAY NOT BE SUITABLE FOR PRE-TEENAGERS

Columbia
Pictures

THEATRE

Hotel, where Lester met with his agent, Judy Fox-Scott, Begelman, James Goldman and others to discuss and determine a preliminary budget for *The Death of Robin Hood*, which he would direct and produce. A handshake from Begelman ended the affair.

Six months later, Lester, with no more word about the Robin Hood film and unable to reach Begelman in Hollywood, was not only confused but also a wee bit angry. While meeting with independent producer Ray Stark at Columbia Studios in Burbank, Fox-Scott spied a script titled "*The Death of Robin Hood*, a Ray Stark production" lying on his desk. Laying Begelman by the heels, the infuriated agent reminded him of his handshake with her client in London.

After Begelman denied he had ever been at the Berkley Hotel, Lester set about reclaiming his project. One year later, having made a deal with Ray Stark and his associate, producer Richard Shepherd, Lester, under protest, had to accept two things if he wanted to direct the film: a bloated budget and a title change to *Robin and Marian*.

Promoted as an "adventurous love story," *Robin and Marian* stars Sean Connery as the first Robin Hood with a Scottish burr and Audrey Hepburn as a Marian who, after her earlier relationship with the outlaw, became Abbess of Kirklees Abbey . But now Robin, middle-aged and tired, returns to England disgusted with his comrades' behavior on the Third Crusade and the senseless folly of King Richard's recent death.

Lester initially wanted Connery to play Little John, but then gave him the starring role, going so far as to fly to the actor's home in Marbella, Spain, to sign him. Although he had just returned from Morocco, where he had endured a grueling schedule for John Huston's adaptation of Kipling's *The Man Who Would Be King* (1975), Connery accepted the part of the aging outlaw. Then 45 years old, Connery begrudgingly submitted to a full physical to satisfy the insurance company covering the actors in the film.

Hepburn, who had not acted in seven years, agreed to a "comeback" because she admired Goldman's *The Lion in Winter* and thought that the new film downplayed violence in favor of romance. Frail and underweight, the 46-year-old actress had a difficult time during the location shoot near Pamplona, Spain, where she was troubled by Lester's tendency to film everything in one take while using several cameras to

Opposite: **Original advertisement for James Goldman and Richard Lester's revisionist version of the legend.**

A middle-aged Robin (Sean Connery) leans on his longbow in *Robin and Marian* (frame enlargement).

capture different angles. Falling ill, she was unable to hide her sickness from the unforgiving lenses. Known for her reclusiveness, she did not interact with her colleagues off camera, and flew to Rome every weekend to stay with her husband and 14-year-old son, Sean. She had brought her five-year-old daughter, Luca, with her to Spain, but grew worried when the little girl's fascination with one of the broadsword replicas flew in the face of her pacifist beliefs.

Lester wrapped the film after shooting in Spain for six weeks, often working his cast and crew to the breaking point. While Connery, who had requested a hiatus in the shooting, was so tired that he bowed out of the cast party and drove straight home, Lester was perturbed that the producers had wasted an enormous amount of money on unnecessary trips from Hollywood to the location, driving the budget from $1.5 to $5 million.

Robin and Marian opens with King Richard's (Richard Harris) fatal folly at Chalus-Chabrol, where the crossbowman using a frying pan for a shield mortally wounds him. Just before the bow-less archer *throws* the bolt at Richard, striking him in the shoulder, Robin and Little John (Nicol Williamson) arrive to advise the king that "there is no treasure!" Of course, the Lionheart pays no heed, and rather than wasting away in a field tent after the incident (as did the historical Richard), Harris' version is allowed to masticate the medieval scenery, resorting to the trademark shouting that so often has marred his performances. But the scene provides an interesting variation on the usual Richard-Robin relationship, showing them disagreeing and quarrelling rather than praising each other's actions.

From the outset Lester and Goldman inject the film with a realistic atmosphere, showing Robin and Little John discussing their middle age and laboriously hacking their way through the forest when they reach Sherwood. Sitting down with Will Scarlet (Denholm Elliott), who mentions the popular ballads that have been circulating, Robin admits that he and the men "didn't do" the events celebrated in them. Another "realistic" element is a mention of Barnesdale, one of the few times this Robin Hood location is referred to in a film. Reunited with Marian, Robin's revisionist nature (or "political correctness" in current terminology) is revealed when he discusses the horror of massacring helpless women and children at Acre during the Crusade. (Marian's political conscience in this scene must have pleased Hepburn.)

Lester re-creates medieval England with a great degree of historical accuracy, making *Robin and Marian* the first film about the outlaw to depict the squalor, dinginess and unsanitary lifestyles of the period. Though earlier films often focused on the romance, pageantry and derring-do of the legends while including bits of historical reality, this revisionist version clearly defines the difference between the legends and the "real" Robin Hood. It was also the first film since Fairbanks' *Robin Hood* to depict the outlaw actually joining Richard on the crusade. The costumes and weaponry, too, add to the historical ambience, eschewing brightly colored clothing for earthy tones and leather, and costume swords for heavy steel hand-and-a-half and two-handed broadswords.

Goldman's script also addresses the power of myth and how the ballads have created a persona for the outlaw that has increased his effectiveness against the Norman usurpers. At one point, one of Prince John's (Ian Holm) men tells him, "Have you ever tried to fight a legend?"

Incidents adapted from the ballads include a scene from "Robin

Robin musters enough strength to fight the Sheriff of Nottingham (Robert Shaw) in *Robin and Marian*.

Hood and the Potter," in which Robin and Little John steal a cart loaded with household wares, and the scene depicting the outlaw's death at Kirklees Abbey, which originated in the "Gest" and was transformed further in later ballads, stories and plays. Seriously injured during his sword duel with the Sheriff of Nottingham (Robert Shaw), Robin is spared from further suffering by Marian, who offers him poison. The scene concludes with the poignant image of Robin shooting one last arrow out the window to mark the spot of his grave. The touching, well-acted relationship between Robin and Marian, reaching a high point when she reveals that she attempted to commit suicide after he left on the crusade, is often undermined by John Barry's heavy-handed and syrupy score, a generic 1970s work that easily could be from a typical Western of the period. Only a few scenes featuring authentic medieval music save it from total disaster.

While Hepburn makes a frail and somewhat anachronistic Marian, Connery is fine as the slightly broken down but still effective Robin, going so far in one shot to reveal that, indeed, men wore no undergarments beneath their 12th-century tunics. (At one point in the filming, a crewman had to usher away onlookers who were gawking at the actor's bared buttocks.) The rest of the cast is also excellent, particularly Williamson as the sensitive Scottish Little John, and the formidable Shaw (in one of his last roles) as the wily Sheriff.

But overall, the revised Robin is also a depressing one. The focus on "realism" makes *Robin and Marian* strikingly different from earlier films about the outlaw, but its dispelling of the core of the myth is unsettling. The film emphasizes obsolescence, its bright spot being the depiction of Marian's love for, and Little John's loyalty to, Robin. Opening with the death of a raving Richard, the screenplay dissects the legends before finally killing off an all-too-human hero. The inclusion of the ballad-inspired death at Kirklees is admirable; but filtering down the legends into a simple love story, depicting the outlaw as just a man, rather than a "great man," may bring the audience closer to the character, but we also lose something more significant. In our current age so devoid of heroes, we can always appreciate the undying spirit of Robin Hood.

Earning only $4 million at the box office, *Robin and Marian* was judged a failed experiment by its makers. Lester said:

> The title should have been left as "The Death of Robin Hood." In changing it we were inviting the kind of mindless technique many critics have of evaluating the movie by the last one you made [*The Three Musketeers*]. To me the movie was not a "comedy adventure," but people kept asking me where the jokes were. Sean is an actor who looks for humor in his parts, to humanize his character, which is quite right. But Robin was straight. I always saw it like that, and because

of the connotations of the changed title, it prompted the wrong reaction.[2]

Connery agreed with the director:

> That's what it was about, and people were disappointed because from the new title they expected some stirring adventures. The whole thing was very much anti-mythic. This guy comes back after eighteen years in the Crusades and he shouts, "Hey, I'm back." And of course no one much cares any more. And he's getting up each morning in the forest, creaking and groaning and coughing and having a leak in the bushes and it's all too much for a man of his age. They hated that idea in the States. They can't take the idea that their hero might be over the hill and falling apart. Also, we never anticipated the resistance from the Catholics. They protested about Marian being a nun, and helping me to die and then committing suicide.[3]

Of the film's content, Connery concluded, "Maybe you just can't tamper with myths that way."[4]

The universal mythical nature of the outlaw spirit was interpreted by Russian filmmakers two years later in a Communist production titled *Arrows of Robin Hood* (1978), released by Moscow's Sovfilm organization. However, a far more lighthearted impression was offered by English director Terry Gilliam, who was joined by his former Monty Python mates John Cleese and Michael Palin for *Time Bandits* (1981), a whimsical fantasy ride through various eras of European history.

Temporarily shelving his screenplay for *Brazil* (then called *The Ministry*), Gilliam decided to make an original film for children. After receiving the financial support of Denis O'Brien and George Harrison, whose Handmade Films had produced the Python feature *Life of Brian* in 1978, he began filming on location in Morocco with Sean Connery, who plays the Greek King Agamemnon. He also cast an entire array of international stars including Sir Ralph Richardson (as the Supreme Being), Shelly Duvall, Katherine Helmond, Ian Holm (as Napoleon), David Warner and Kenny Baker (*Star Wars'* R2-D2). Michael Palin, who appears in several scenes, also co-wrote the script with Gilliam.

A scene set during the late 13th century features John Cleese as an upper-crust Robin Hood who runs his Sherwood camp like a twisted Victorian charity organization where handouts are offered to individuals who simultaneously are physically abused by the Merry Men. When the young time traveler, Kevin (Craig Warnock), and his dwarfish hosts land in Sherwood, they insist on talking to the man the outlaw band refers to as "the boss." John Cleese recalled:

> Apparently, the role of Robin Hood had originally been written for Michael Palin. Denis O'Brien was keen for me to be in the film, though Terry didn't want me—I only learned that eighteen months later—but Denis felt I would help sell the film in America, so he insisted that I be in it. I was sent the script, pointed at Robin Hood, and read the stage directions—"to be played like the Duke of Kent"—and I thought it was very funny, and said I would love to do it. I enjoyed doing *Time Bandits* enormously, despite the fact that Terry made me shave my beard off. I did it the morning of the shooting, seven a.m. in the forest![5]

Though the Robin Hood episode is a brief segment in a somewhat overlong film that awes the viewer with visual splendor, a mind-boggling mixture of historical parodies, dazzling special effects, and an ever-brilliant Ralph Richardson (in one of his last performances), it provides perhaps the best comic take on the outlaw legends, a far better satire in its brevity than the interminably unfunny feature-length version another filmmaker would offer a decade later.

In 1982 Columbia Pictures Television produced the first small-screen feature-length film to include Robin Hood, a lavish two-part version of *Ivanhoe* closely adapted from Scott's novel and shot on location in England. Starring Anthony Andrews as Ivanhoe and James Mason as Isaac of York, John Gay's teleplay curiously opens in somewhat confusing fashion, skipping over Scott's establishing section set at Rotherwood and merely showing Ivanhoe warning Isaac about a Norman ambush before speeding directly into the tournament at Ashby. Here, all the major characters are introduced: Cedric the Saxon (Michael Hordern, who also appeared in the 1952 *Ivanhoe*), Rowena (Lysette Anthony), Rebecca (Olivia Hussey), Prince John (Ronald Pickup) and the three Norman knights—Brian de Bois-Gilbert (Sam Neill), Reginald Front-de Beouf (John Rhys-Davies) and Maurice de Bracy (Stuart Wilson), all of whom Sir Wilfred defeats in the jousting. The following day the tournament is continued, with the Black Knight arriving to help Ivanhoe, known as "the Disinherited One," during the mass battle with the Normans. When Ivanhoe is injured, no one but Rebecca comes forward to tend to his wounds.

As in the novel, Ivanhoe lies wounded on a litter and in Torquilstone

Castle for much of the film. (Noel Langley's screenplay for the 1952 epic actually increased his recuperative powers to give Robert Taylor more screen time.) An hour into the narrative, Locksley (David Robb) makes his first appearance, after Wamba becomes lost in Sherwood during the Normans' capture of Isaac, Rebecca, Ivanhoe and the party of Cedric (including "the noble" Athelstane [Michael Gothard], a character that does not appear in the 1952 film). Discovered by the Black Knight (whom the audience now recognizes as the Lionheart [Julian Glover]), the fool and the king are then ambushed by the Merry Men. Addressing his prisoners (and not knowing the identity of the Black Knight), Locksley does not introduce himself, but refers to his top three associates, Little John, Will Scarlet and Friar Tuck (Tony Haygarth)— the only Merry Man to receive screen time. Later, when Front-de Beouf is discussing the impending siege of Torquilstone, the Norman warrior reveals, "In the forest, they call him Robin Hood."

Robin and his men sign on with the Black Knight and take part in the siege, during which the King gets into the very thick of it (as did the real Lionheart during battle). Although the lengthy scene does not match the 1952 version for sheer visual and dramatic power, it is exceptionally well staged, directed and edited (though, regrettably, only one "hail of arrows" shot is included). During the violence of the siege, a tender sequence involving Ivanhoe and Rebecca provides a fine dramatic counterpoint.

After the successful storming of the castle, the outlaw, still not knowing the identity of his commander, tells the King that he is "Robert Locksley" but is "known as Robin Hood." Of course, the Lionheart already knew full well the tales of the Sherwood man in Lincoln Green.

Aside from the clumsy beginning, this *Ivanhoe* is a first-rate production beautifully photographed by John Coquillon and effectively punctuated by Allyn Ferguson's musical score incorporating traditional medieval melodies and instrumentation. The acting is superb across the board, aside from James Mason's occasional whinyness as Isaac, whose role is enlarged considerably from the supporting position the character holds in the novel. Gay and director Douglas Camfield focus on Isaac as the most important character, bringing the Semitic subplot to the fore, an admirable yet somewhat heavy-handed attempt to enlarge Scott's presentation of racial and religious prejudice in medieval England. The narrative would have been far more balanced had some of Isaac's scenes been deleted in favor of additional Locksley footage,

Ivanhoe (1982). David Robb's excellent Robin of Locksley in Columbia TV's admirable version of Scott's epic novel (frame enlargement).

such as the archery tournament—another major chapter that was omitted. (Of course, another tournament would have increased the already considerable budget.) Aside from the Torquilstone scenes, Robin appears again only at the end, when he and Tuck arrive to view the Ivanhoe-Gilbert duel from afar.

John Rhys-Davies contributes his usual blustery villain, while Stuart Wilson is nobly and subtly menacing as de Bracy. Sam Neill is outstanding, incorporating a convincing accent as de Bois-Gilbert but playing him as a far more evil villain than George Sanders' 1952 version. Rebecca's threat to throw herself from a battlement at Torquilstone is thoroughly understandable when he expresses only carnal lust, without a trace of love or understanding. However, later in the film, he begins to temper his selfishness with moments of decency, particularly during the climactic duel with Ivanhoe. Having beaten Sir Wilfred to the ground, he is about to deliver the *coup de grace* but, upon gazing at the doomed Jewess, hesitates long enough to allow his foe to run him through.

Olivia Hussey is beautiful, humble, caring and strong, giving great complexity to the faithful Rebecca, while Lysette Anthony brings all her innocent, doe-eyed exquisiteness to Rowena, Ivanhoe's true love. Though he is King Richard's right-hand man, David Robb's Locksley still expresses the independent spirit of the outlaw, creating the best portrayal of Robin since Richard Todd's in the 1952 Disney film. And the great character actor Julian Glover (who later would play Dr. Livesey in Fraser Heston's superb 1990 adaptation of Stevenson's *Treasure Island*) interprets perhaps the best Lionheart ever filmed.

Sadly, the only other 1980s cinematic referral to the outlaw of Sherwood was spoken by Catherine Hicks in *Star Trek IV: The Voyage Home* (1986). Attempting to waylay Captain Kirk (William Shatner) and Mr. Spock (Leonard Nimoy) to achieve her own politically correct ends, she calls them "Robin Hood and Friar Tuck" (while the two *Star Trek* stalwarts are innocently attempting to escape molestation simply by walking down a San Francisco street).

Fourteen

Beverly Hills or Barnesdale? *Robin Hood: Prince of Thieves* and *Robin Hood* (1991)

During the 1980s John Cleese's comic turn as Robin was the outlaw's only silver-screen incarnation, while David Robb's Locksley was his only appearance in a feature-length television film. Perhaps, with Margaret Thatcher and Ronald Reagan at the respective helms of the United Kingdom and the United States, viewers might have welcomed a bit of a sociopolitical balance. (But then, audiences were far too busy watching the likes of Rocky and Rambo. And we can only be thankful that no one hired Sylvester Stallone to play Robin. "Yo, Marian!" would not have been beneath '80s Hollywood standards.)

But Robin did appear in various television series and specials in Great Britain. Sean Connery's son Jason followed in his father's footsteps for Goldcrest's *Robin of Sherwood* (1984–86), taking over from Michael Praed, the series' original star. The interesting musical score was provided by the Irish group Clannad, who began their careers playing traditional Celtic music but eventually drifted into the more commercial, musically tedious New Age genre. The BBC also produced some Robin offerings, a one-season series titled *Maid Marian* (1988–89), this time switching the gender focus, and a program called *Fellow Traveler* that was broadcast by HBO in the United States.

169

Robin Hood: Prince of Thieves (Warner Bros., 1991)

Two ambitious Robin Hood feature films went into production during 1990; both were intended for theatrical release the following year, but only one actually reached American screens. Fearing that Morgan Creek Productions' *Robin Hood: Prince of Thieves*, a $50-million action extravaganza starring Kevin Costner, would totally overshadow the more modestly budgeted, historically respectful *Robin Hood*, 20th Century–Fox Chairman Joe Roth accused his rivals of "acting unjustly, if not immorally" by attempting to beat his company to the marketplace.[1] Having signed John McTiernan to begin directing Mark Allen Smith's screenplay *The Adventures of Robin Hood* in October 1990, Roth was appalled when Morgan Creek announced they would start shooting a month earlier. (To make matters worse, a third company, TriStar, briefly flirted with making a Robin Hood film, tentatively slated to begin production in September.) Eventually, Roth, squeezed out by Morgan Creek, opted for a May 13, 1991, broadcast on the Fox network.

When the role of Robin Hood was offered to Kevin Costner, he viewed it as a chance to participate in a lengthy athletic event. "I am physical in my acting," he said. "So the chance of shooting bows and arrows and fighting with staves and swords is terrific. It is like being in a sports situation every day."[2]

Commenting further on his Americanized approach to the character, Costner hit the bull's-eye when he explained, "We are not offering a repeat of the old Robin Hood story."[3] Giving themselves license to do anything with the outlaw hero, producer-screenwriters John Watson and Pen Densham admitted, "We wanted today's generation to be inspired by a fresh incarnation of the Sherwood rebel.... [We] want[ed] to add some new characters, some fresh twists and some real surprises!"[4]

Having more in common with the 1990s than the 1190s, Watson and Densham's "surprising" screenplay—which adds a ridiculous New Age sorcery element to the conflict between Robin and the Sheriff of Nottingham—seethes with political correctness, most obviously represented by the feminist-tinged portrayal of Maid Marian (Mary Elizabeth Mastrantonio) and the inclusion of the Moor Azeem (Morgan Freeman), Robin's sidekick, a character completely extraneous to the legend. Ironically, Freeman, while playing a fabricated character, is the only actor in a major role who is not badly miscast, unlike Costner, Mastrantonio, Christian Slater, and even Alan Rickman, whose Richter-scale

American-accented Robin is as stiff as his staff as he fights an incredibly hirsute Little John (Nick Brimble) in Warner Bros.' politically correct travesty of the legend, *Robin Hood: Prince of Thieves* (1991).

scenery chewing as the cartoonish Sheriff of Nottingham is one of the most obnoxious examples of overacting in cinema history.

A remark by Mastrantonio proves that the principal players were proud that *Prince of Thieves* would be an MTV-generation effort championing historical amnesia. Her facetiousness shows that she and her cohorts did not recognize the magnificence of the 1938 *Adventures of Robin Hood*, particularly Flynn's incomparable performance and Olivia de Havilland's strong-willed Marian:

> The story was new—Robin Hood to me was just Errol Flynn in tights—so there was much to learn and absorb.... Once I realized that this Maid Marian has plenty of guts I was into the part. She is not just someone to hang on the arm of Robin, so I thought, "Count me in."[5]

Beyond the 1990s feminist updating of Marian, the script's most ridiculous anachronism is a dysfunctional family angle involving Slater's

Will Scarlet and Costner's Robin that is awkwardly inserted near the
end. Possessing no conception of the Will of the ballads, Slater said:

> Several things were put into the script after I was cast. For instance,
> the fact that Robin Hood really screwed up my life when I was
> younger. His father dated my mother and I was the result. I came forth
> into the world as Robin's half-brother. There is one point in the film
> where I have to tell Robin the truth. So it adds an edge to the whole
> movie for me.[6]

(Perhaps Slater could set straight a few medieval historians, who surely
do not realize that "dating" was popular during the 12th and 13th centuries.)

David Nicksay, President of Morgan Creek Productions, first read
Watson and Densham's screenplay on February 13, 1990. After convincing his colleagues to make the film, company owner James G.
Robinson focused on signing an actor to play Robin. "We had the three
top star actors in mind," he later said, proving that box office receipts
were the main concern, not casting a performer who was right for the
role.[7] One of the "top three" was Mel Gibson, who, having just completed Franco Zefferelli's *Hamlet* (1990), turned it down.

Hired just 10 weeks before production began, director Kevin
Reynolds, a longtime friend of Costner's, started shooting on location
at Burnham Beeches in Buckinghamshire on October 8, 1990, keeping
in mind that the film had to be completed in 100 days (before Fox could
release its *Robin Hood*). As each day passed, autumn continued to lessen
the amount of usable light, and Reynolds assembled his cast and crew
at 5:00 every morning. When darkness fell, he then viewed the day's
footage, which invariably kept him up until midnight. When asked about
his approach to the material, he revealed that, by creating a facade of
realism, he could mask Watson and Densham's ahistorical and anachronistic additions to the script: "I wanted to make it look realistic. I can
relate to something much more strongly if it feels real. That gives us
the chance to cross the line of making something realistic—and take
that occasional fantastic step."[8]

Of all the "occasional fantastic steps" in the film, none is more fantastical than expecting audiences to accept the wooden, mumbling,
stoop-shouldered, blow-dried, non-English accented Costner as Robin,
a miscasting move that rivals Clark Gable's King of Hollywood turn as
Irish political leader Charles Stewart Parnell (in MGM's *Parnell* [1937])

and a pasty-faced Laurence Olivier's absurd attempt to play General Douglas MacArthur (in the Moonie flop *Inchon* [1981])! It simply is one of the most luckluster lead performances ever filmed.

James Robinson, too, had envisioned a believable version of the legends: "We thought we would get a more accurate observation by making this production with a British crew on British soil. After all, Robin Hood is the very essence of England."[9] But why shoot the film in England and hire a "British crew" if an all-American actor incapable of speaking with an accent has been cast in the title role? Michael Curtiz and William Keighley shot *The Adventures of Robin Hood* entirely in California, and that film's setting is far more convincing. At least Errol Flynn was Australian (and many people in 1938 thought he was Irish).

Production designer John Graysmark also attempted to create a realistic setting, closely studying the architecture and lifestyles of England during the late 12th century. He wanted to suggest the squalor of medievalism, rather than emulate the romanticized and "clean" look of earlier costume epics: "The truth is that it was a filthy time of dark days, freezing castles, colorless clothes, limited food and no hygiene. We have tried to get as close to what we now research as 'the truth,' without making the film a history lesson."[10] Graysmark need not have been so concerned with taking his "realism" too far, for *Prince of Thieves* has little in common with actual history. In his account of the production, author Garth Pearce writes, "Graysmark ... would not even let a sheep or goat be used which did not comply with what would have been seen in the 1190s."[11] Why, then, did the producers not apply this requirement to the film's characters and the actors who played them?

Joining in Graysmark's meticulous attempts to inject realism into the film, set dresser Peter Young took great care in providing accurate yet safe weapons for the various types of characters: Robin and his greenwood companions, the Norman rulers, and the imported Celts who attack the Sherwood camp. Young created both actual replicas of swords and arrows, and fiberglass and rubber versions to be used in potentially dangerous maneuvers. He made 10 different versions of the sword stolen from Robin's father by the Sheriff of Nottingham, including lightweight models; two with retractable blades; a larger, cumbersome model to suggest the Sheriff's difficulty in wielding it; and a smaller one that allowed Robin to handle it with ease.

Stunt coordinator Paul Weston assembled a complement of 80 stunt men, including Simon Crane, who doubled Costner in several scenes.

However, Costner was so enamored with the physicality of the film that Weston occasionally found it difficult to rein in the star's enthusiasm:

> I had to stop him doing quite a few things that would have put him at risk. Even so, he still pushed everything to its boundaries. I would be watching as he would lean out a little too far to give the best possible shot for the director…. Stunt men would honestly like the actors to act—then go away and leave the stunts to us.[12]

As Howard Hill had done for Errol Flynn in 1938, archery expert Gabe Cronnelly performed all of Robin's amazing feats with the bow and arrows, although 1990 film and sports technology did not require him to match his predecessor's prowess. Like Hill, Cronnelly was required to cut a hangman's noose in a scene in which Robin saves some of his cohorts:

> Robin might have just done it at fifty yards distance if he had used a broadhead arrow—and was very lucky. But I needed spot-on accuracy. So I was in a kneeling position so I would not be seen on camera, about seven or eight yards from the rope, using a modern compound bow. Fortunately we needed only two takes and I split the rope on both occasions.[13]

To accomplish the remainder of the off-camera archery feats, Cronnelly used the period longbow replicas fashioned from yew for Costner and his on-screen colleagues.

The single greatest defect of *Robin Hood: Prince of Thieves* is not the awful acting, but Densham and Watson's screenplay, which merely grafts the Robin Hood story onto the ever-popular post–*Star Wars* action-adventure plot. As with most examples of this current genre, the film relegates its characters to a position secondary to the violent action scenes, which feature rapid montage editing and breakneck pacing that seldom allow the viewer to witness what is happening. As David Denby writes in his *New York* review,

> Kevin Reynolds is half faker, half rousing action director. The faker shoots much of the violence in tight close-up with many cuts in the middle of the action; one sees limbs thrashing about, a blade slicing the air, and then someone landing on the floor with a thump. In other words, one sees nothing at all.[14]

Right on target, the *Christian Science Monitor*'s David Sterritt identifies the real rationale behind the film:

> Members of the production team reportedly joked about their project by calling it "Raiders of the Lost Sherwood Forest" while it was being made—and sure enough, the movie is dominated less by the spirit of Merrie Olde England than by the shade of Indiana Jones and his big-budget shenanigans. It's a lively picture, and there's every chance it will become one of the year's biggest hits. But this won't mean 1990s audiences want to explore the historical byways of days long past. It will simply mean the Age of Spielberg is more solidly in place than ever.[15]

No Herculean stretch of the imagination could make Kevin Costner a believable Robin Hood. Although Hollywood producers have

Robin Hood: Prince of Thieves. **The horse gives a more impressive performance than its rider—a wooden, somniferous Kevin Costner as the worst Locksley ever filmed.**

always had dollar signs in their eyes, a more blatantly commercial casting decision can barely be imagined. (In fact, Warner Bros. made *Star
Wars*–level merchandising deals that produced *Prince of Thieves* nov-
elizations, video games, sleeping bags, clothing, trading cards, party
supplies, mugs, buttons, and a tie-in with a fast-food chain.) Costner is
so bad that literally no one liked him in the role. Every major critic who
reviewed the film came to the same conclusion, that the casting of Costner was intended to rob from audiences who were forced to suffer
through a very poor script. Following are some excerpts reflecting the
consensus on Kevin.

Marcia Magill, *Films in Review*:

> What do we have for fifty million dollars, seven of which goes
> to Costner? Well, to paraphrase Shakespeare's Julius Caesar: "The
> fault, dear Brutus, is in our star." Costner, currently Hollywood's dar-
> ling ... turns in a curiously listless and passive portrayal as the dash-
> ing rogue.[16]

Kenneth Turan, *Los Angeles Times*:

> The ads have got it wrong. Kevin Costner very definitely *isn't* "Robin
> Hood: Prince of Thieves," and his noticeable awkwardness in that
> rebel's role underlines the problems this muddled, fitfully effective ver-
> sion of the most durable English legend has in deciding which face it
> wants to present to the world at large....
>
> [Costner's] Robin is the doofiest yet put on film; it is almost impos-
> sible to accept him as a leader of men. Costner plays the dread des-
> perado of Sherwood Forest like a deadhead on a spiritual quest.[17]

David Denby, *New York*:

> Kevin Costner ... may look the part, but he's about as outgoing as a
> marmot. Quiet and self-contained, with a flat, toneless American
> voice, Costner is not believable (or entertaining) as a leader of En-
> glish yeomen. What is there about this dull fellow that could inspire
> dispossessed peasants to live in the woods with him and take up arms
> against tremendous odds? Costner is joyless and matter-of-fact, a
> speaker at a marketing seminar.... He's a handsome but inert block at
> the center of a huge, roistering production that is trying very hard—
> too hard—to take the romance out of the old legend.... What harm is
> the Robin Hood legend doing that it needs to be so rudely modern-
> ized?[18]

Jami Bernard, *New York Post*:

The accent problem—Costner's voice coach fled the set faster than a speeding arrow—leaves our hero with a bland surfer-speak that has trouble straddling some of the windy Olde English dialogue he is given. (How come in all these $50 million movies nobody shells out a few bucks for a decent script?)

But the real problem ... is that [the film] is hog-tied by its own good intentions churning out a static morality lesson for the '90s rather than an exciting romp in the woods with a hero for the ages.... There is no merriment among the Merry Men of Sherwood Forest as they go about taking from the rich and giving to the poor. This economic redistribution plan sits heavy on the shoulders of our Robin, who rarely smiles, often seems hapless, and almost never swings from vines. Where is Errol Flynn when you need him?...[19]

Jack Mathews, *Newsday*:

To appreciate the full grain of the wooden performance Costner carves out of Sherwood Forest, you have to hear his flat, high school delivery of the line, "Do you yield?" This is the great Robin of Locksley? No way; more like Robin the Dude, far out and California dreamin' in 12th-century England.... No, Kevin Costner is not up to playing the brash, charming, athletic Robin Hood....[20]

Richard Corliss, *Time*:

In Costner's ... take on the legend, the only green power is at the box office.... The leads ... are all American, intoning flat varieties of American English. They sound like tourists stranded in Sherwood Forest. And they inadvertently give a new meaning to the story: now Robin and his band are vagrant colonials who save England from those who can actually speak the language.

Dull speaking, in Costner's case, is an emblem of miscasting. The character of Robin Hood demands emotional exuberance—not Costner's forte. He does not spring; he is coiled. He is a reactive actor; audiences enjoy watching him think.... But Nottinghamshire is no place for California dreamin'....[21]

J. Hoberman, *Village Voice*:

Like *Dances with Wolves*, *Robin Hood* is distractedly pictorial and tepidly revisionist.... The star's langorous mumbling adds a good 10 minutes to the movie's running time, but the controversy about his accent (or rather, lack of one) seems a displacement. The problem is less diction than attitude. For Americans, the Robin Hood story is one more version of our own revolution and Hollywood's two most celebrated Robins, hyperactive Douglas Fairbanks and pathologically swashbuckling Errol Flynn were both jaunty colonials. Not exactly insouciant, Costner's Robin is more of a doggedly righteous dude.[22]

Only in Hollywood could a man be paid $7 million for such inferior work; but then, Jim Carrey has far surpassed Costner's atrocity, time and again being paid $20 million for his set-devouring, ultra-obnoxious travesties—comic equivalents of Alan Rickman's out of control Sheriff. Why do audiences—and some performers—confuse *more* acting with good acting? And why did the aforementioned critics, who all panned Costner, praise Rickman? Perhaps because he provided such a contrast to Costner's *nothing*; but he could have given a performance of subtle villainy (as do Basil Rathbone in *The Adventures of Robin Hood* and Peter Finch in *The Story of Robin Hood*) and accomplished the same feat. While all the critics admitted that Rickman was unabashedly over the top, only Kenneth Turan had enough taste to criticize him:

> Alan Rickman [is] a comic-relief Sheriff of Nottingham who oozes toxicity like a barrel of sludge from Three Mile Island. Rickman is funny enough, but his clowning has the regrettable effect of making him useless as a creditable villain, severely crippling that side of the film.[23]

Rickman's dialogue is so outrageous ("I'm going to cut his heart out—*with a spoon*!) and wildly tongue in cheek ("It's amazing I'm sane!") that one wonders how such a talented actor could deliver it, even in an over-the-top style and for a large check. But the flaws in the Sheriff of Nottingham depiction go far beyond Rickman's unbearable performance; Densham and Watson's premise of the character controlling England in King Richard's absence is the most ludicrous element in the history of Robin Hood films. Where in the name of the Normans is Prince John?

But there are no Normans or Saxons in the film; only Englishmen who either side with Richard or with Nottingham, a shire (county) sheriff whom the screenwriters absurdly assume wields enough power and influence to take over the entire nation. Although the historical Norman-Saxon conflict had ended by 1194 and the Third Crusade, the fictionalized version is the bedrock upon which the popular Richard the Lionheart version of the outlaw legend is built. Densham and Watson's elimination of Prince John merely increased the importance of the Sheriff character, which in turn allowed for even more megalomaniacal scenery mangling. When one of his underlings refers to his domain as "The House of Nottingham," the screenwriters' ignorance of English medieval history becomes staggeringly apparent. And even the Sheriff's traditional colleagues in tyranny have been altered to increase his hegemony: Sir Guy of Gisbourne (Michael Wincott) is now his "cousin" who, after disappointing his evil relative, receives a fatal (and gratuitous) sword thrust to the abdomen.

Other needless embarrassments include Robin getting kicked in the crotch by the macho Marian, who later lingers over him bathing in a waterfall in a gratuitous Costner nude scene (the California tan lines are another nice surfer-dude touch); Will Scarlet using anachronistic profanity after Robin and Azeem catapult over a castle wall and land in a fortuitously abandoned hay cart; and a *Star Wars*–like shot from the point of view of an *arrow* shot by Robin! But the most inane moment in this thoroughly insipid film is the 1990s dysfunctional family scene. After Will shouts, "You ruined my life!" Robin exhorts (via Costner's unbelievably block-headed delivery), "I have a brother! I have a brother!" Unconnected to any previous footage, this overwrought incident is abruptly and awkwardly inserted into the plot and is the nadir of Pensham and Watson's deconstruction of the Will Scarlet character, who has absolutely nothing in common with Robin's poetical companion in the ballads, stories or earlier films.

The sole well-cast actor in a major role, Morgan Freeman was given some of the best dialogue in the film. Being an outsider to England (and the Robin Hood canon), Azeem often makes witty observations about the nation and its society: "The hospitality in this country is as warm as the weather." However, since the screenwriters saw fit to ahistorically insert him into the story, they also made him the inventor of several anachronistic devices, including the spyglass and gunpowder (which Robin and his men subsequently use in their successful assault on Nottingham). Azeem also delivers the baby of Little John's wife, who already had given birth to seven children (making this Little John the only such patriarch in the history of the legends; these weary outlaws definitely are *not* the Merry Men!).

After production wrapped, Costner admitted that "it was not a

great professional experience."[24] Kevin Reynolds, preferring to change
dialogue and shoot additional angles of many scenes, allowed little
time for adequate rehearsals. Unwilling to listen to the suggestions
of others, he grew to resent Costner's attempts to direct some sequences, and eventually their friendship suffered. (Later, Reynolds was furious when the executive producers chose to re-edit the film without his
input.)

To perform the concluding wedding ceremony of Robin and Marian, Reynolds hired Sean Connery for a brief cameo as King Richard,
who, for the first time in Robin Hood cinema, speaks with a thick Scottish burr. (Connery seemed better able to mask the accent when he was
younger—in *Robin and Marian*, for instance. Paid $400,000 for this
walk-through, he donated his fee to the Scottish Educational Trust.)
And while his noble presence raises the quality of the film a wee bit, it
is also a further absurdity, though not the final one. As the closing credits fade in, Canadian rock singer Bryan Adams and his band arrive in
Sherwood Forest to perform their syrupy power ballad "Everything I
Do, I Do for You," a song having nothing in common with the historical era, culture or events depicted in the film, lending one last note of
insipidity to a mindless viewing experience. But the greatest artistic sin
of the offensively commercial *Robin Hood: Prince of Thieves* is that it
usurped the theatrical throne from a far more entertaining, intelligent,
historically accurate and *deserving* motion picture.

Robin Hood
(20th Century–Fox, 1991)

While *The Adventures of Robin Hood* is the finest work of cinema
showcasing the legends, Fox's 1991 film, unfortunately relegated to television (except for some European theatrical screenings), is the most
historically authentic screen interpretation. But with Sir James Clarke
Holt (Professor Emeritus of Medieval History at Cambridge, former
president of the Royal Historical Society, expert on the Magna Carta
and the reign of King John, and author of the best book on the "real"
Robin Hood) acting as adviser, how could it be anything less? *Robin
Hood* evokes the Middle Ages by eschewing the Technicolor of previous epics for muted earth tones, misty moorlands and mud, and presents an accurate picture of feudalism and why those in power wanted

Robin Hood (1991). Little John (David Morrisey), Robin (Patrick Bergin), and Will Scarlet (Owen Teale) discuss plans for their band of Sherwood outlaws in Fox's entertaining and authentic version of the Saxon versus Norman legend.

to maintain it. Anchored by Patrick Bergin's excellent performance, it is also a vastly entertaining film.

Like the Flynn classic, it opens with the Much the Miller's Son incident, but rather than prefacing it with an on-screen set-up (written titles and a town crier), Sam Resnick and John McGrath's screenplay begins with the serenity of the autumn greenwood (which is *brown* at this time of year). Just after a fox, a badger and a deer are shown in their natural habitat, the silence is rent by a patrol of nasty Normans chasing poor Much, who has killed a royal deer to stave off starvation.

Soon we are introduced to Sir Robert Hode, Earl of Huntington (a name, undoubtedly suggested by Holt, that links the character to one of the possible real Robins), Sir Miles Falconet (Jurgen Prochnow), a repulsively arrogant Norman hybrid of Sir Guy of Gisbourne and the Sheriff of Nottingham, and Baron Roger Daguerre (Jeroen Krabbe),

Maid Marian's uncle and a past friend of Robin's. When Robin is arrested for interfering in the Much incident, he privately strikes a deal with Daguerre, but after Falconet complicates matters at the public hearing, his old pal must levy a harsher sentence. Here, the scene offers the most detailed depiction of a declaration of outlawry ever included in a Robin Hood film.

Also for the first time, Barnesdale is used as an actual location — during the quarterstaff fight scene involving Robin and Little John (David Morrissey). When describing the ensuing duel, John informs Robin, "Barnesdale rules. You're in Yorkshire now." Filmed at a stunning location replete with a rushing waterfall, it is the most realistic of all the Robin–Little John contests (a most welcome element, considering that the fight had been filmed so many times before). The revelation from Will Scarlet (Owen Teale) that Robin cannot swim also casts a very human light on the legendarily invincible outlaw. After running downstream and pulling him out of the water, Little John takes Robin and Will to an outlaw camp in the forest, where he welcomes them into the community. Rather than depicting Robin as the founder of the commune (as do earlier films), this version shows him eventually taking over and better organizing a resistance force established by the capable Little John.

Further references to a Northern origin for "Hode" include Little John's mention of the Great North Road and Daguerre's identification of Barnesdale as Robin's base of operations, along with the "forests of Doncaster, Blythe and Sherwood." This blending of history with the ballads is also well represented by Friar Tuck (Jeff Nuttall), who not only possesses his usual hearty appetite (for both food and battle), but also is a representative of the corrupt and hypocritical Medieval Church. When first accosted by the Merry Men in the forest, Tuck reveals that he is a seller of holy relics (actually chicken bones passed off as those of the saints). During the Middle Ages, clerics persuaded individuals to "buy their way to Heaven" through the ownership of "pieces of wood from the holy cross," bones such as those peddled by Tuck, or an "indulgence" (a type of insurance policy that *might* allow a sinful relative passage into the Lord's domain). Referring to the indulgences sold by the Church, Robin calls the friars "bloodsuckers" who always are loaded with money. Later, the men enter a church, and as Robin holds a dagger under the preacher's cassock, they relieve the premises and some of the wealthy parishioners of ill-gotten gold. Advising that the sermon continue as planned, the outlaw threatens to make him "more nun than abbot."

After Robin, during a bold rescue mission, saves a group of peasants from hanging, he is endeared to the other outlaws and their families. Resnick and McGrath's screenplay brilliantly integrates the romanticized "robbing the rich to give to the poor" motif by depicting it as an afterthought by the outlaws, who originally steal out of vengeance against the Normans. During a discussion about the fate of the loot, Will Scarlet proposes the practical concept that, since much of it is tax money collected from the Saxon peasants, then it should be distributed among them. "It's not right to keep it," he remarks. Rather than merely supporting the 19th-century romanticization of the outlaw's robbery, the film offers a far simpler and more realistic interpretation. (Here again is J. C. Holt's influence.)

Another welcome bit of historical detail is a subplot involving the development of the Welsh longbow, discovered by Robin and the incognito Marian as they meet Emlyn (Anthony O'Donnell), a diminuitive Welshman delivering a load of bows to Daguerre's castle. Offering twice as much money to Emlyn (who is angered by the Normans' reference to him as "Taffy"), Robin persuades him to outfit the army of the greenwood instead, and soon he is piercing armor with broadhead arrows.

The ballads also are mentioned in their proper historical context. Upon meeting Robin, Emlyn reveals, "They're making songs about you and your Merry Men." A short time later Prince John (Edward Fox), having arrived to chastise Daguerre for allowing his taxes to be stolen by the outlaws, expresses his concern that the singing of the ballads is proof of the peasants' support for Robin Hood. When Daguerre opines that the people only wish Saxons and Normans to be treated with equal consideration, John intimates that such tolerance would violate the divinely inspired hierarchy and lead to a toppling of the feudal order.

Another connection to early Robin Hood entertainments is the Fools' Parade that leads to the climactic confrontation between the outlaw and Falconet. With Friar Tuck posing as the Lord of Misrule, the Merry Men gain entrance to Daguerre's domain while dressed as fantastical woodland characters. Soon they attack and send hails of arrows over the castle wall in an attempt to stop the forced marriage of Falconet and Marian (Uma Thurman). After commenting on the sinfulness of the proceedings, the poor cleric (Richard Moore) who was molested by Robin is again threatened when Falconet seethes, "Abbot, your opinion was not asked for, nor, for that matter, was your version of God's opinion. We'll answer as man and wife now, or you will be consulting God direct!" Providing additional evidence of her "masculine" abilities (she earlier posed as a boy to enter the greenwood camp), Marian dispatches a guard with Robin's sword before tossing it to him—just in time for Falconet to be skewered.

Having been shrouded in semi-darkness, mist and muted tones throughout the film, the victorious Merry Men now are bathed in bright sunlight as spring triumphantly arrives during the wedding ceremony of Robin and Marian. The end of winter and the promise of spring bodes well for the English people, who finally get a glimpse of color in their lives. Unlike earlier literary and cinematic versions, King Richard does not return in the nick of time to witness these events; instead, this *Robin Hood* offers a more realistic conclusion to an admirably authentic narrative. The success of the Merry Men against Daguerre, who promises to treat his own people and the Saxons equally, is a *regional* one, not the national revolution of earlier dramatizations. Prince John, who appears briefly in only one scene, is concerned with matters other than the Barnesdale-Sherwood tax revolt, and King Richard presumably is still in the Holy Land or held captive at Durnstein. Like history and reality, the film offers no tidy, simplistic conclusions, only the promise of a brighter future should Robin's success hold forth.

Filmed on location at Peckforton Castle in Cheshire, Tatton Park and Betws-Y-Coed in Wales, *Robin Hood*, although presented in muted colors, is a visually impressive work distinguished by a uniformly superb supporting cast (particularly the incomparable Jeroen Krabbe as Daguerre and Uma Thurman, who looks like a medieval artwork brought to life, as arguably the best Maid Marian in film history) and an atmospheric musical score by Geoffrey Burgon (which incorporates period instruments and arrangements—including a group of minstrels in the Fools Parade scene). The swords used in the film are the most historically accurate—in design, size and materials—to appear in a Robin Hood production: when a duel occurs, the viewer hears, not the metallic whack of costume weaponry, but the clash of real steel.

Like MGM's suppression of Rouben Mamoulian's masterful *Dr. Jekyll and Mr. Hyde* (1931) ten years after its release (which allowed the studio to rob from it to make its own travesty starring the all–American Spencer Tracy as the British Jekyll and Hyde) *Robin Hood*'s relegation to obscurity by the equally inferior Costner opus is a sad cinematic irony.

In an attempt to capitalize on the hype surrounding *Robin Hood: Prince of Thieves*, Goodtimes Video, a company that markets affordable copies of public domain film titles, released *Robin Hood: The Movie*, a 60-minute "feature" compiled from the 1956–60 Richard Greene series and following the basic plot of the Flynn film (although the packaging ironically touted Greene as the "original Robin Hood!"). Colorized "to appeal to modern audiences" (which only transforms black and white into bad pastel shades of blue and brown), this pathetic attempt to assault the wallets of an impressionable public was made even worse by the addition of a repetitive and syrupy synthesizer score.

A very medieval-looking Uma Thurman as arguably the screen's finest Maid Marian in Fox's *Robin Hood* (frame enlargement)

Robin Hood: Men in Tights (Fox 1993)

During the 1970s, Mel Brooks directed several effective parodies of popular film genres, reaching his apex by collaborating with Gene Wilder on the masterful *Young Frankenstein* (1974). But by the time he made *History of the World, Part I* in 1980, he had run out of fresh ideas, and his films became unfunny, relying too much on tasteless sexual innuendoes and obvious, tongue-in-cheek humor.

Although it is not as bad as the appalling *Spaceballs* (1987), *Robin Hood: Men in Tights* is among Brooks' worst work. Whereas he had created clever parodies of popular genres in the past, this film shows him using tired *shtick* in an attempt to wring some box-office dollars from a resurgence of interest in the outlaw. While *Men in Tights* does include references to earlier films, particularly the Errol Flynn classic, it primarily is a labored send-up of *Robin Hood: Prince of Thieves*. Although Brooks should receive some credit for poking fun at Costner's travesty, he should have made a better film. But after all, since *Prince of Thieves* already raises enough laughs, was a parody necessary?

The level of Brooks' humor in *Men in Tights* is immediately apparent in the opening scene, when a group of blacks in Robin Hood tunics
perform a ridiculously anachronistic "medieval" rap number, taking a
timeless legend and reducing it to 1990s popular youth culture. In a nod
to Mark Twain's *A Connecticut Yankee in King Arthur's Court*, Brooks
then adds one anachronism after another, including tennis shoes, Larry
King, martial arts, the National Guard, Vincent Price, Abraham Lincoln
and Mississippi. Mixing sex with sheer offensiveness, he then depicts
a blind man (a parody of a character in *Prince of Thieves*) feeling a cen-
terfold in the braille edition of *Playboy*. (This type of humor was
offensive 50 years ago and has no place in a 1990s film.)

While most of the parodies of Costner elements are insipid—here,
for example Azeem is called "Ahchoo"—there are a few genuinely funny
scenes, particularly the quarterstaff fight between Robin (Cary Elwes)
and Little John (Allan Kramer), who operates a proper *toll* footbridge.
During the battle, their staffs keep breaking in two until they are reduced
to about a foot in length, and then Robin knocks Little John into a barely
trickling stream; afraid of drowning, the Merry Man admits that he cannot swim.

Another pleasant moment occurs in a scene based on Flynn's swaggering entry into Nottingham Castle in *The Adventures of Robin Hood*.
Giving forth his best Flynn laugh and carrying a pig on his shoulders,
Elwes' Robin confronts Prince John (the ever-neurotic Richard Lewis)
with his plans for a rebellion.

"And why should the people listen to you?" John asks.

"Unlike some other Robin Hoods, I can speak with an English
accent," Robin replies. (The fact that the language of the period was
Anglo-Norman is beside the point!)

Not content with just a few dozen anachronisms, Brooks never lets
up, working in references to Winston Churchill, Malcolm X, Marlon
Brando and Clint Eastwood; but he alternates these with more sex jokes
(particularly phallic imagery) and his usual quota of Jewish humor,
including his own appearance as "Rabbi Tuckman."

Although the quarterstaff scene is a highlight, the archery tournament is another of Brooks' unfunny misfires. Robin loses the contest
when his arrow is split by another archer, but he receives a second
chance after the actors fall out of character (as if they are ever *in*) to
check their scripts. Not satisfied with taking shots at blacks, the blind
and women, Brooks now swipes Native Americans by having the crowd

do the Atlanta Braves' "tomahawk chop" as Robin fires; after the shaft "gooses" several people, the "patriot arrow" (an anachronistic reference to the Persian Gulf War) hits the bull's-eye.

There are also plenty of self-conscious references to Brooks' earlier films. Marian has a *German* maidservant, à la *Young Frankenstein* (in which the character actually made sense) and *High Anxiety* (1977); Prince John has a mole that keeps moving from one spot to another (like Igor's hump in *Young Frankenstein*); Rottingham asks Robin and others to "walk this way," and all the characters literally mimic his gait (a ubiquitous and *very* tired gag in the director's work); and, after Rottingham is defeated, Robin appoints Ahchoo (Dave Chapelle) as the new sheriff. In this last gag, Brooks even mentions the film's title: when the crowd asks, "A black sheriff?" Ahchoo replies, "It worked in *Blazing Saddles*!" It is unfortunate when a director deliberately recycles the same material, but Brooks' smug references to his own work are not only unfunny but downright egocentric.

The film's infantile level of humor reaches its absolute nadir at the very end, when Patrick Stewart affects his best Sean Connery lisp as Richard the Lionheart, who interrupts the wedding of Robin and Marian, kisses the bride and gives his blessing. Stewart should have been ashamed to accept a role that, in a reference to the king's defeated brother, required him to declare, "From this day forth, all the toilets in this kingdom will be known as 'johns'!" Many previous Robin Hood films had included very entertaining moments of lightheartedness and humor. Did the legend actually need to be degraded by humor of such an offensive nature? (This "irreverent" approach was much more successful in the hands of Monty Python in their final two feature films, which are just as offensive but much funnier.)

Fifteen

Robin's Caledonian Renaissance: *Rob Roy* and *Braveheart* (1995)

Rob Roy *(United Artists, 1995)*

Although a "movie tie-in" paperback edition of Sir Walter Scott's novel was marketed during the theatrical release of *Rob Roy* in 1995, the film bears no resemblance to it. In fact, barring a few major liberties, Alan Sharp's screenplay is closely based on a specific period in the life of the historical Robert Roy MacGregor.

Deciding to produce a film about Scotland "that would also work for a wide international audience,"[1] Peter Broughan of Talisman Films pitched the idea of a Rob Roy story to his partner, Richard Jackson, an Englishman who was unfamiliar with Scottish history but interested in its dramatic possibilities. Approached by the production duo to script the project, Alan Sharp accepted with alacrity:

> The character had plenty to offer in the way of catching my interest. Rob Roy was a man of honor caught up in circumstances which were way beyond his power to control. The really intriguing part came in exploring how a man of action reacts when his actions cannot ultimately affect the outcome.[2]

After accepting Sharp's first draft of the screenplay, Broughan and Jackson offered it to Scottish filmmaker Michael Caton-Jones, who had

Opposite: *Rob Roy* (1995). Original poster art for United Artists' powerful and historically authentic visualization of the life and legend of Robert Roy MacGregor.

directed several successful Hollywood films but had not set foot in his
native land for 17 years. At first too busy to accept the assignment,
Caton-Jones reconsidered after he attended the Edinburgh Film Festival,
a trip that "awakened a desire ... to do a movie" in Scotland.[3]

Impressed with Sharp's draft, Caton-Jones showed it to United
Artists President John Calley, who sent the director back to Scotland to
scout possible locations. Caton-Jones also began to cast the picture, and
immediately chose Liam Neeson, a long-time friend who had acted for
him in film school, to play Rob. Neeson loved the screenplay, particularly the romantic subplot:

> What actually drew me to the script was the romance in the story. It
> wasn't just a swashbuckling adventure all about guys, numerous
> swordfights and stuff. At the heart of this story is this genuine love
> bond between Rob Roy and his wife, Mary ... they grew up together
> as children, and it was ... a bonding of two people that was ordained
> in heaven. These two people *have* to be with each other....They laugh
> at the same jokes, the same things upset them.[4]

Indeed, Sharp had emphasized Rob's strong relationship with Mary
as well as focusing on his outlaw-making struggle with the Marquis of
Montrose and Graham of Killearn. To bring the writer's excellent portrait of Mary MacGregor to cinematic life, Caton-Jones cast Jessica
Lange, who instantly viewed it as a golden opportunity:

> My initial reaction was how rare it is to find a script so beautifully
> written, with a female role as multi-dimensional as Mary. What struck
> me—and what I think I liked best about it—was how purely male and
> female it was, full of love and lust, trust and honor, sexuality and sen-
> suality.[5]

Offered the role of Montrose—"the nastiest man in Scotland," as
Caton-Jones described him—John Hurt accepted without even reading
the script, but he soon realized that the Marquis was far from a one-
dimensional villain:

> He's a salon animal, a sophisticate of the Scottish court. He's described
> as having twenty faces, none of which is human. But, really, he's just
> a great believer that everyone should know and keep their place. That
> in itself is a code of honor ... as opposed to his henchman, Cunning-
> ham, who is the picture of amorality.[6]

Based on the dandy duelist Henry Cunningham of Boquhan, Archibald ("Archie") Cunningham was created by Sharp as a wicked fop, outwardly effeminate but absolutely lethal with a rapier in his hand. For this scene-stealing role, Caton-Jones cast Tim Roth, who spent many long hours studying and practicing fencing to match his character's razor-sharp wit with equally adept swordplay.

One day during pre-production, while walking down a Los Angeles street, Caton-Jones bumped into Eric Stoltz, who previously had acted for him in *Memphis Belle* (1990). Learning that he had no work lined up for the summer of 1994, Caton-Jones asked Stoltz if he would like to join him in Scotland. "Sure," the young actor replied, accepting the role of Alan McDonald, Rob's trusted but ultimately tragic right-hand clansman. In the remaining supporting roles, the director cast cinematic neophyte Brian McCardie as Alasdair (Rob's younger brother) Brian Cox as Killearn and veteran Scottish character actor Andrew Keir as the Duke of Argyll, all of whom were thrilled to interpret Alan Sharp's accurate period dialogue.

Keir, who has spoken the words of a legion of fine screenwriters, said:

> The essence of good scripting ... gives you what you need.... I think [Sharp] must say the lines before he writes them, because the rhythms, the way you would say something, are absolutely right.... In fact, if you change Alan's dialogue, it throws you. That's how much is perfect.[7]

Cox expanded his colleague's impression:

> The great strength of this whole project is the script ... I think that's really why I did it, because it's the best script I've read in a long, long time. [Referring to Killearn] Scumbag or no scumbag, it's a wonderful script, and Alan Sharp is a man who really knows his craft, and it's a joy just to be given a script like this. You don't get them too often.....
> Killearn ... is horrible. He's the villain of the villains, a totally reprehensible individual....[8]

Young McCardie, having had a distinguished apprenticeship on the stage and television, also noted Sharp's contribution:

> I think it's the best script I've ever read. I think it's fantastic. It reads like a novel, and the way he describes scenes is unique, and he doesn't

use cliched language, and therefore it conjures up an image clearly in your head.[9]

With his cast assembled, Caton-Jones set up production head-quarters at Fort William in the Western Highlands, planning to shoot much of the location footage in nearby Glencoe and Glen Nevis. On July 25, 1994, Caton-Jones and cinematographer Karl Walter Linden-laub began shooting the opening scene of the film in the mountains, where the beauty and grandeur of the area almost overwhelmed the director:

> I remember standing on top of hillsides saying, "My God, look at that." The vast panorama of nature is unsurpassable. The actors were working against this fantastic backdrop that could never have been duplicated with special effects. It could not have been thought up in its detail and beauty. It's a wondrous gift.[10]

Steeped in the lore of the period, Neeson, who appeared in the scene with McCardie, Stoltz and others portraying Rob's clansmen, noted that the setting enhanced the believability of his performance:

> It's wonderful to stand there, dressed in the period, and know that these hills and mountains haven't changed in millennia—that Rob Roy and his clan actually trudged those hills and would have seen those views and marvelled at those sunsets. You don't have to act that; it's all there for you.[11]

But filming in the rugged Highlands can be treacherous, particu-larly at Glencoe, the sight of the infamous massacre of the Jacobite MacDonald clan in 1692. Constantly threatened by imminent thunder-storms, the cast and crew often had to rush to capture whatever set-ups they could before rain began to fall. But over the following 13 weeks of principal photography, only three days were lost to inclement weather. The greatest technical challenge for Lindenlaub was his attempt to match shots while contending with the incessant shift from heavy cloud cover to bright sunlight. During the location filming, Brian Cox com-mented:

> Well, I think there's a lot of nonsense about our inclement weather. It is *the weather*, and if you're going to make a film about Scotland, you've got to understand the weather. I mean, I think its all *balls*, all

Liam Neeson, garbed in the tartan of an eighteenth century Highlander, as the honorable title character in *Rob Roy*.

this waiting for the sun to shine or not the sun to shine. I think you shoot, no matter what. Our cameras are pretty well developed these days, and I think we're getting a wee bit too spoiled about what kind of weather we're shooting in. All you have to do is take a couple shots of the scenery, because it's devastating; and its particularly devastating and changeable, when you see the kind of clouds lowering over the hills, exactly as you see over the camera at the moment. It's very effective, and it looks wonderful.[12]

Access to some locations presented periodic problems, particularly when Caton-Jones had chosen a site inaccessible to motor vehicles. To reach one of these untamed areas, the cast and crew had to climb out of their four-wheel-drive trucks and tramp the hills and heather, much as Rob and his men did three centuries earlier. To transport the heavy equipment, workers laid temporary metal roads on which vehicles, dubbed "Scot-Track Tanks," carried the cameras and lighting gear. In order to film the closing scenes set at the home Rob shares with Mary and his two sons, Caton-Jones had to make arrangements with the British Army to borrow military helicopters. Since the site was a National Trust for Scotland property, no metal tracks or other potentially damaging materials could be used on the land.

At Loch Morar, Scotland's deepest lake, production designer Assheton Gordon and his crew constructed Rob and Mary's stone house at Craigrostan, which is invaded and burned by Killearn's men, including Cunningham, who first brutalizes then rapes Mary. In the event that nature failed to provide enough early-morning loch vapor, Caton-Jones had two fog machines brought to the site, although his drivers had to transport them over a 15-mile single-lane road while simultaneously contending with local fishery trucks.

Inspired by the natural environment, Neeson and Lange developed a warm working relationship that made Rob and Mary's love seem even more believable. At first, Neeson was a bit awed by Lange's reputation, but quickly overcame any anxiety to join her in depicting the couple's deep, very passionate bond. Lange said:

The script ... carried with it none of the neurotic love of the twentieth century; it was clear, it was pure, it was male and female, man and woman. It was full of love and trust and honor and lust and sexuality and sensuality, and to me it was great because those relationships are so rare on film. Having known nothing beforehand ... I was immediately caught up in the story....

There isn't a day ... that I didn't walk outdoors to take one of my five-mile walks ... I was awestruck by everything about the place, about the land—really made a huge difference in playing this character. The spirit of the place seemed somehow to enter into the portrayal of Mary....

I felt right from the beginning that there was an ease and a kind of naturalness between [Liam and me] that made playing this character and playing this relationship very easy. Liam embodies all of Rob's physicality and rage, tempered with tenderness, sweetness, and sensuality—all those things that make Mary love him so much. I never had to strive to find those characteristics in Liam, so it was very easy to play a woman in love with him, a partner to him.[13]

With the Highland scenes in the can, Caton-Jones moved the entire company east to Perth, where the sequences involving the Scottish aristocracy were filmed. The set for the village scenes was constructed near Megginch Castle, which provided the perfect period atmosphere, while Drummond Castle and its lavish sculpted garden served as the elegant residence of Montrose.

The contrast between the rugged Highlands and genteel Perth suggested the division between the poor rural clansmen and the wealthy landowners—a dichotomy further represented by the differences in Sandy Powell's costumes for the two social classes. While Powell based the clothes worn by Montrose, Argyll and Cunningham on paintings he had viewed in Scotland's museums, he found very little reference material on the early tartan garb worn by the MacGregors—a dearth of information created in large part by the outlawed status of the dress following the 1745 Jacobite Rebellion.

Having trained with swordmaster William Hobbs whenever each of them had any spare time, Neeson and Roth now prepared to shoot the climactic duel between Rob and Cunningham, an integral narrative and dramatic element. Although Roth had never fenced in a film, he worked tirelessly to perfect the physically demanding combat choreography that he described as "like learning a ballet."[14] Using a thin fencing rapier against Neeson's more rugged Scottish basket-hilt claymore, he helped to realize Caton-Jones' intention to create the screen's most realistic, historically accurate sword duel.

While editor Peter Honess began assembling a rough cut of the film, composer Carter Burwell worked on his score, incorporating traditional Scottish material such as the tunes "Morag's Lament" and "The

High Road to Linton," which were performed by the Scots group Caper-caillie, whose lead vocalist, Karen Matheson, appears in the film as a ceilidh singer. Her three vocal contributions—on the traditional songs "Ailein Duinn" and "Theid Mi Dhachaigh," and Burwell's own "Hard Earth"—added an authentic Gaelic ambience to the soundtrack. The composer also included historical pieces performed by the Chieftains and the Musicians of Swann Alley, an early music group. Legendary uilleann bagpiper Davy Spillane also lent his period expertise to the project.

When the final cut was completed, Caton-Jones realized that he had contributed something unique to the annals of adventure dramas:

> It was great going back home. I had forgotten how beautiful Scotland is and I've never seen the country captured on film like this before. I look back on it now and think, "We did it, we really did it."
>
> I had a terrific time ... with *Rob Roy*, I was not only able to direct a magnificent story, but I was doing something that allowed me to present my heritage to the rest of the world.[15]

Producer Peter Broughan offered this summation:

> I think it's a grace-under-pressure story. I think it's become the story of a noble, moral, principled man who is carrying the responsibility of his people, of his clan—and, in having that responsibility, is put into jeopardy, has his name taken from him ... has his land taken from him ... who has his wife violated.... So he's a man who loses everything, but who has to survive without turning into the kind of monster ... that his enemies are.[16]

Before *Rob Roy* opens with an extreme long shot of a great Highland glen and a loch receding into the distance, a title card explains:

> At the dawn of the 1700s, famine, disease and the greed of great noblemen were changing Scotland forever. With many emigrating to the Americas, the centuries-old clan system was slowly being extinguished.
>
> This story symbolizes the attempt of the individual to withstand these processes and, even in defeat, retain respect and honor.

Although the film runs 139 minutes, Alan Sharp's story is fairly simple, focusing on Rob's attempt to help his clan by borrowing £1000 from Montrose and the subsequent conflict brought about by the theft of the money and the outlaw's refusal to malign the Duke of Argyll. Only one scene of cattle reaving is included—the opening sequence depicting Rob and the Gregorach reclaiming one of Montrose's herds from a scurvy band of "ragged arsed tinker cur-thieves" led by Tam Sibbald (David Hayman)—although Rob later vows to reave the Duke's stock after his home at Craigrostan is burned and, unbeknownst to him, Mary is raped by Cunningham. When Mary visits Argyll to ask for his help in extricating her husband from Montrose's snare, the Duke mentions the harrying of his rival's cattle and the collecting of blackmail by Rob and his men.

The film remains remarkably faithful to the locations and period, designated as "The Scottish Highlands, 1713" at the beginning of the second scene, but adds certain dramatic elements to Rob's personality and actions to give the narrative a slightly more violent, action-adventure atmosphere. While the historical Rob never killed an opponent, but only fought until "first cut" (a tradition depicted in one scene, when the arrogant Will Guthrie [Gilbert Martin] challenges him in a tavern), he does dispatch three knaves during the course of the film: Tam Sibbald, Guthrie (in a later tavern sequence), and finally, after nearly being slain himself, Cunningham (in the climactic duel scene). Killearn (referred to as "a greasy capon" by Montrose) is also killed (by Mary and Alasdair), although the historical henchman was eventually set free by Rob.

The Whig-Jacobite conflict is mentioned at various times, and plays a role in Rob's difficulties with Montrose, but this material is undoubtedly confusing to most viewers, who have no knowledge of 18th-century British politics. In particular, Montrose's political ramblings and taunting of Argyll during the duel between Cunningham and Guthrie (seen early in the film) will prove indecipherable to nearly anyone not versed in Scottish history. While the realism added by this historically accurate material is admirable, it does bog down the narrative a wee bit.

Several detailed touches suggest the rugged and difficult life of the Highland clansmen, including the opening scene depicting Alan MacDonald stooping down to sniff and then taste a fairly fresh pile of cow dung in order to estimate the location of the band of tinkers. (Here, Lindenlaub performs a flawless 180-degree pan, showing a sweeping, breathtaking Highland panorama.) Other realistic material includes the weapons used by the different "classes" of Highlanders (while the Gregorach wield quality basket-hilt swords crafted by professional smiths, the tinkers have only jagged blades with homemade iron baskets), Rob's biting of Cunningham while he is tied up and taunted by the fop, and the great cattle reaver's use of a carcass for a hiding place after his heroic escape from the Bridge of Glen Orchy (another event based on the historical incident).

Powell's costume designs for the aristocrats closely resemble the styles depicted in period paintings, and the colors are beautifully rendered by Lindenlaub. The scene in which Rob visits Argyll to plan the duel with Cunningham is a particular highlight: Lindenlaub's lighting of one composition—a long shot depicting Rob (in the right foreground, with his back to the camera) speaking to the Duke (seated in the left background) as sunlight filters in through a window (at right)—makes it appear as if an 18th-century etching has sprung to life.

Caton-Jones uses two distinct visual styles to reinforce the social dichotomy between the poor Highlanders and the opulent aristocrats. While Rob's world is one of vast, green exteriors sometimes enhanced by sunlight, the environment in which Montrose and Cunningham exist is a dark, claustrophobic interior world that rarely benefits from a breath of fresh air. One juxtaposition, in particular, drives this point home: a slow dissolve from a standing stone against which Rob and Mary make passionate love (one of the film's most powerful moments) to the confines of Montrose's office, where the stern Duke reprimands the philandering fop.

Another scene, this time involving quick cross-cutting, juxtaposes the two worlds. As the MacGregors throw a ceilidh to celebrate Rob's impending success at the stockyards of Carlisle, Alan MacDonald is pursued and murdered by Cunningham, who steals the £1000 (while Rob expected a signed note, Alan was given a large bag of coins by the treacherous Killearn). In a beautifully edited sequence set to the rhythm of a rousing Scottish reel, shots of the chase are alternated with close-ups of the musician's instruments (including a fiddle and uilleann pipes) until the horses halt. Then the ceilidh singer performs a beautiful Gaelic lament as Alan is stabbed to death and his horse slowly saunters into the MacGregor's encampment, drawing the two opposing worlds tragically together.

Caton-Jones and Lindenlaub consistently make the most of their remote locations, simultaneously recreating the Highlands of the early 18th century and proving that little has changed in some desolate parts of the area in nearly 300 years. Whether or not it was done intentionally— one shot, framed from within Rob and Mary's dwelling and showing him (background, screen center to left) walking off toward Argyll's men and his impending duel with Cunningham, while she (right foreground, with her back to the camera) sadly watches him go—is a re-working of one of John Ford's famous compositions in *The Searchers* (1956).

However, there is one shot that unfortunately mars the visual style, albeit briefly, when the director includes an obtrusive slow-motion close-up of Alasdair dying after being shot by Cunningham's troopers a second time. This unnecessary depiction of agony is superfluous and interrupts the film's admirable tempo.

Sharp's screenplay, aside from a few murky political inclusions and Scots terms some viewers may not understand, consistently captures the ambience of the era, particularly the way in which his dialogue mingles dialects and poetical prose with realistic emotions. The relationship between Rob and Mary, superbly enacted by Neeson and Lange, provides a welcome, warm, equally powerful contrast to the outlaw's cold and violent conflicts with the aristocrats and their henchmen. The script is leavened with sporadic, subtle humor that balances the narrative; and there is only one example of the gallows humor that is often a very tongue-in-cheek element in action-adventure films: just before Mary discovers the body of Betty Sturrick (Vicki Masson), an unfortunate young woman who hangs herself after being impregnated by the iniquitous Cunningham, she tells Alasdair that the poor lass is "near the end of her tether."

Neeson is much taller than the historical Rob, but he was the ideal choice for the role, both physically and ethnically. Throughout the film, he combines a powerful heroic quality with an engaging vulnerability, displaying great pain when abused by Cunningham and wrenching mental anguish when learning of his wronged wife's travails at the hands of his enemies. And Lange, in one of the best female roles of the 1990s, is at least Neeson's equal, giving a thoroughly convincing and transcendent performance that should have earned her an Oscar (although she was not even nominated; only Tim Roth was recognized by the short-sighted Academy). Most critics praised her majestic portrayal, including Jack Garner of the Gannett News Service, who also noted that the historical characterization is strong yet does not pander to the current political flavor of the day:

> Unlike most women in period adventures, Jessica Lange's Mary is no mere appendage. Thanks to the power of Lange's performance and the

Jessica Lange in an unforgettably beautiful performance as Rob's capable wife, Mary MacGregor, in *Rob Roy*.

ingenuity of Alan Sharp's screenplay, Mary also is a person of heroic strength and character. Without resorting to politically correct feminist revisionism, Sharp has conceived ways to make Mary an equal partner in Rob Roy's endeavors.[17]

(Now, if Sharp had written *Robin Hood: Prince of Thieves*, and if Lange had been substituted for Mary Elizabeth Mastrantonio, just imagine what *could have been* if Kevin Costner had been relegated to the woodpile.)

Rob Roy includes several elements that depict the historical outlaw's similarities to Robin Hood. Of course, the way in which the Gregorach support him suggests the Merry Men; but more specifically, a scene showing Rob returning to Craigrostan is a more direct reference: observing the squalor around him, he tells his brother that he is tired of seeing his clan and kin going cold and hungry. Rob then develops the plan to borrow the £1000 to drive cattle to the profitable stock yards of Carlisle. Later, when Montrose asks him how many people he is master over, Rob informs the Duke that he is "master of none," but instead has "200 souls in his care." (This later reference is also a link to a scene in *The Adventures of Robin Hood,* in which Robin tells Maid Marian that he aids his fellow countrymen, not for a reward, but because it is the right thing to do. And the climactic duel between Rob and Cunningham is the modern, more realistic equivalent of the legendary Robin-Gisbourne duel enacted by Flynn and Rathbone.)

Braveheart (Paramount, 1995)

Braveheart, the only theatrical motion picture based on the life of William Wallace, was the result of one man's inspiration. While on a Scottish holiday with his wife in 1983, Tennesseean Randall Wallace, a relatively obscure novelist and television producer, viewed a statue of the legendary warrior at Edinburgh Castle and, advised by a guard, became fascinated with studying the outlaw's exploits. After learning of the dearth of factual information about the subject, he sought out a 1721 book, *The Life of Sir William Wallace,* which he "read ... with trembling hands, a trembling heart."[18]

Having been a seminary student, he noticed the similarities between this book and the *New Testament*—that "the stories had the same kind of ring of truth in them"[19]—and was driven to write about his historical namesake:

> What William Wallace did can be inferred from the passion of his supporters and the hatred of his enemies. The great legends about him built a fire in my heart. His life communicated that you will prevail if you are faithful to what you believe in; and if those you love believe in you. Your body can be broken but not your spirit.[20]

After writing a full-length screenplay based on his research and impressions, Randall Wallace sent it to producer Alan Ladd, Jr., who at that time was head of MGM. Agreeing with Wallace's own casting suggestion, Ladd pitched the idea to Mel Gibson, who then was putting the finishing touches on his film *The Man Without a Face* (1993). Having no idea who William Wallace was, the star put the script aside and concentrated on his lead role in *Maverick,* directed by Richard Donner for Gibson's own Icon Productions and Warner Bros.

During the summer of 1993, Ladd left MGM to re-establish his own Ladd Company, taking *Braveheart* and one other project with him. When Gibson bowed out of starring in Terry Gilliam's proposed *A Tale*

of Two Cities, insisting that he direct the project, Ladd again approached
him about the Scottish epic. Having vowed never again to direct *and*
act in a film, Gibson wanted to helm *Braveheart* but *not* star in it.

In the meantime, Randall Wallace flew back to Scotland to attend
the Edinburgh Film Festival. Popping into Filmhouse, the headquarters
of the festival, located beneath the imposing Castle Rock along Loth-
ian Road, the author calmly imposed upon representatives of Scottish
Screen Locations, asking where an enterprising filmmaker might go
about making a Caledonian epic. They directed him to the imposing
sandstone Wallace Monument at Stirling, the site of the outlaw's legendary victory. After a local journalist interviewed him for a front-page
story in the newspaper *The Scotsman,* the Scottish people became interested in his project.

Unfortunately, local members of the press immediately thumbed
their noses at the thought of the American-Australian Mel Gibson interpreting their pseudo-Christ figure. They wanted Scotland's greatest
movie star, Sean Connery, to play the part, even though he was 30 years
older than Wallace was at the time of his execution. Mel was much too
short, they claimed, and Sean was only five inches shy of the medieval
monster's height. (Eventually, Connery was asked to portray Edward I,
but he declined, claiming that his commitment to another film, *Just
Cause*, prevented him from accepting the role.[21] However, interpreting
the "Hammer of the Scots" undoubtedly would *not* have endeared him
to his worshipful countrymen.)

"I couldn't wait to turn each page and was surprised at every turn,"
Mel Gibson admitted. "The screenplay had everything—heroic battles,
a powerful love story and the passion of one man's strength which fires
a whole country against its aggressors."[22] Reluctantly but ultimately
agreeing to star as well as direct, Gibson, during March 1994, began
scouting locations in Ireland and Scotland, where he visited the Glasgow headquarters of the current chieftain of the Wallace clan, Seoras,
who had definite ideas that added immeasurably to the spirit, if not
always the historical accuracy, of the script. Flying in the face of critics who have accused Gibson of selling *Braveheart* short by not hiring
a suitable Scot to play Wallace, he has revealed, "If possible I would
have cast Wallace [with an unfamiliar actor], but it just would have been
impossible to get the budget."[23]

Even with Gibson committed, the production team faced nearly as
many obstacles as William Wallace had during the bleak days of seven

centuries past. Ladd originally had estimated an MGM budget of $40 million. When Majestic Films, Icon's British financial backer, realized that Gibson's opus would cost far more, perhaps $70 million (an appalling outdistance of their previous Kevin Costner epic, *Dances With Wolves*, which made them treasures untold), the company beat the retreat. Undaunted, Gibson then contributed $15 million of his personal fortune to boost the budget to $55 million. In the end, *Braveheart* would cost just a wee $15 million more.

While the money men wrangled like the warriors who cast the lot of the British Islanders of the 1290s, Gibson's crew prepared meticulous research on the historical period. Costume designer Charles Knode designed more than 6,000 outfits, including the rugged tartan kilts worn by the Scottish commoners and the much more elegant apparel donned by the English court and the Scots nobles. While Knode based many of his designs on 13th-century carvings and tombstones, he also studied the holdings at London's Royal Armoury and the Tower of London, discovering two medieval shoulder pieces he then used to recreate the "Lion of Scotland" armor worn by Robert the Bruce.

The most lavish costumes were created for the members of Edward's court, who all wore velvet dyed by Mathilde Sandberg and fiberglass-resin "jewels" made by Martin Evans from designs by Knode. One of Knode's most stunning creations, the wedding gown worn by Princess Isabelle, was adorned with the arms of England and France—examples of which were found on a golden casket of Isabelle's now held in the British Museum.

On June 6, 1994, six weeks before the *Rob Roy* crew began filming in the same area, Gibson and his cohorts commenced shooting *Braveheart* in Glen Nevis, which became the Lowland village of Lanark. Working at the base of Ben Nevis, the cast and crew braved thunderstorms similar to those that occasionally would harry their *Rob Roy* counterparts the following month. Rain fell constantly, and the sun shone for only three days during their stay at the location. While the torrent was welcomed during the filming of a scene in which Wallace courts his love, Murron, out in the "fine Scottish weather," dry conditions were needed for the sequence in which they are secretly married in the Lanarkshire forest.

As part of the medieval village created by production designer Tom Sanders, the Sheriff of Lanark's impenetrable wooden stockade was based on an early English model, while the Scottish peasants' dwellings

Braveheart (1995). William Wallace (Mel Gibson) begins his courtship of Murron (Catherine McCormack) on horseback.

were recreations of earth homes viewed during a helicopter flight over the island of St. Kilda, a habitation abandoned during the 18th century. Constructed over a span of seven weeks, the homes featured three-foot plaster walls that were painted and "aged," and thatched roofs created with sod and seed that was sprouting thickly when filming began.

To recreate the realism of the village marketplace, raw meats and fish were hung on smoking racks, and animal bones and skins—staples used by the commoners of the period—were placed throughout the set. Sheep, pigs, dogs and cats were allowed to roam freely.

While the village scenes were filmed in Glen Nevis, the battle scenes, which required enormous preparation and ready access to equipment and supplies (including close proximity to a major airport), were conducted near Dublin, Ireland, where Gibson set up his headquarters for 15 weeks. For the battles of Stirling and Falkirk, he hired 1,700 Irish Army reserves to portray the infantry, archery and cavalry divisions of both the Scottish and English forces. While some of the footage was filmed on an outdoor location at Ardmore Studios (where most of the interior scenes were completed), shots requiring a large expanse of land were achieved at the Curragh and Ballymore Eustace, near the medieval castles of Trim and Dunsoghly.

The current members of Clan Wallace, including Seoras Wallace, joined the production team to act as advisors on historical and family matters, and even appeared in the battle scenes as extras in the Scottish army. Joining the 1,700 reserves, volunteers from across Ireland took part in the battles, waking at 4:00 each morning to undergo costuming, application of makeup and hairpieces, and weapons training before Gibson began to roll the cameras four hours later. Provided by armorer Simon Atherton, the weaponry included medieval war hammers, pikes, battle axes, spiked flails, modified farm implements, "knuckle dusters" made from deer antlers, and various types of swords. For Gibson, Atherton recreated Wallace's five-foot claymore, and the actor used 10 of them during production.

Veteran makeup artist Peter Frampton, who covered all the extras with dirt and grime, added an extra touch of medieval realism to the meticulous work of stunt coordinators Simon Crane and Mic Rodgers, sword master Nick Powell and horse master Tony Smart. He also painted some of the Scottish warriors' faces with "wode," a blue-and-white coloring (made of Fuller's earth and vegetable dye) that was used by the ancient Celts to frighten their enemies.

For the Battle of Stirling, Gibson, who choreographed the scene with Crane and Rodgers, assembled 3,000 extras and 150 horses to be ridden by the English cavalrymen. While Knode dressed the English, whom he wanted to look "like armadillos,"[24] in flax and chain mail custom-made in Italy, 3,000 meters of plaid created by Islay weaver Gordon Corvell were used to give the Scots an authentic period appearance. More than a thousand wigs and beards provided by hairdresser Paul Pattison added a final touch of realism.

To insure that none of the horses were injured, special effects supervisor Nick Allder designed two mechanical equines to be driven by nitrogen cylinders along 20-foot metal tracks. When the cylinders were fired, these "stunt horses" accelerated up to 30 miles per hour and then were stopped by a piston that sent them somersaulting over the defending

Scots' schiltroms. Allder also built an arrow launcher that used compressed air to send 360 rubber-tipped shafts into the sky in quick succession. To simulate the hails of arrows unleashed upon the Scots by Edward's army, Allder and his special effects crew produced a total of 10,000 shafts to be used in the launcher. For the Battle of Falkirk, Allder also placed steel tubing under the grass and pumped in propane that was ignited by the Scots' flaming arrows.

Originally a wooden fortress constructed by King John in 1210, Trim Castle was rebuilt in stone by William Peppard 10 years later, but now exists as a monumental ruin. Obtaining permission to build sets on the remains of the castle's 11-foot-thick walls, Sanders' crew became the first film production unit ever to do so. Construction of new plaster walls (molded from one of the actual castle walls), wooden buttresses and 30-foot, seven-ton wooden gates, as well as additional plastering and painting, continued for 12 weeks until medieval York had been satisfactorily resurrected. Behind the fortified wall now married to the remains of the castle, the crew built a set resembling a London square.

Sanders described a conservation technique used by his crew to preserve the integrity of the historic castle: "If anything was fixed to the real castle wall, we would first paint on a thin layer of latex rubber, which then peeled off when we came to strike the set. The old stone underneath was left untouched."[25]

After eight weeks of similar construction, Dunsoghly, which features Ireland's last surviving wooden castle roof, was transformed into the 14th-century version of Edinburgh Castle, including 30-foot battlements, a drawbridge, a great hall and several A-frame houses with pitched roofs. Further sets were built by Sanders in the ruins of Bective Abbey, which served as King Edward I's castle; at Coronation Plantation, where a second English stockade was constructed; in St. Nicholas Church at Dunsany Castle, which became Westminster Abbey; and at Blessington Lakes, where a 45-foot wooden tower was raised in seven-foot-deep water to provide a launch for Gibson in a scene showing Wallace's execution of Mornay and subsequent heroic escape. Back in Scotland, an interior scene set at Mornay's Castle was filmed in the Edinburgh Council chamber.

Cinematographer John Toll created a very realistic palette of colors, opening the film with misty, dour earth tones that immediately inform the viewer of its serious subject matter. In a scene based on the 1297 "Barns of Ayr" incident, young William (James Robinson) gets an

Prepared to decimate the English at Stirling, Wallace leads his men, including (left to right) Campbell (James Cosmo), Hamish (Brendan Gleeson) and Stephen (David O'Hara), into battle in *Braveheart*.

eye-opening taste of English justice as he, his father Malcolm (Sean Lawlor) and brother John (Sandy Nelson) discover their hanged countrymen who had been tricked with a promise of "negotiation."

Soon after, when Malcolm and John leave to fight the English, William, backgrounded by the mountains that surround his home, looks as if he is part of the glen as they ride off, leaving him alone and frightened. Later, when their comrades return, William, seeing neither of his relatives among them, turns his back as if it will help, but quickly learns that ignoring a problem solves nothing. One of the film's most poignant moments occurs after Malcolm and John are laid to rest, when young Murron (Mhairi Calvey) picks a thistle flower and hands it to William as a single tear falls from his right eye. (Later, when William courts Murron, he returns the now-dried flower, wrapped in a piece of cloth, a visual symbol of their love and, as a national emblem of Scotland, the conflict that is to come.)

Orphaned, William is taken under the wing of his Uncle Argyle Wallace (Brian Cox, finishing this brief role in time to play Killearn in *Rob Roy*), who, upon learning that his nephew cannot read Latin, replies,

"Well, that is something we shall have to remedy, isn't it?" Later, William repeats the line when he offers to teach the illiterate Murron to read (a link to the historical Wallace, who reputedly spoke several languages).

Gibson originally wanted to cast Cox (who earlier had played Wallace in a BBC-TV production) as Campbell, but the actor declined, believing that the *Rob Roy* character, being less clichéd than the *Braveheart* one, offered him a better opportunity. However, he agreed to portray Argyle, who exerts a positive influence over William, thus playing a significant role in the film.

As the *Braveheart* narrative shifts to King Edward's court in London, John Toll realistically depicts the authentic medieval interiors designed by supervising art director Dan Dorrance and his assistants. The cinematographer's brilliant use of color (capturing the lustrousness of the attire worn by Patrick McGoohan as Edward and Sophie Marceau as Princess Isabelle) shines through the low light levels used to recreate the poor illumination inherent in the often damp and cold stone castle rooms and halls of the Middle Ages.

Randall Wallace cleverly includes "historical explanations" throughout his screenplay, subtly and inobtrusively working them into the dialogue spoken by various characters (a standard element in period films, but rarely done well). Although Edward would not have to define *prima noctae*, or "first night," to his council, the presence of the French Princess Isabelle requires him to explain (both to her and the audience) the meaning of the chauvinistic practice that affords English nobles the right to have sex with a Scottish lass on her wedding night.

The screenwriter also explains the film's complicated political content by including a simple yet clever dramatic subplot involving Robert the Bruce's (Angus McFadyen) discussions and debates with his father (Ian Bannen), here depicted as a dying leper lodged in a turret of Edinburgh Castle. Although historically inaccurate, the characterization allowed Randall Wallace to dispense with a great deal of exposition and explanation that surely would have bogged down an already lengthy film.

When the adult Wallace returns to Scotland after years of traveling (including a trip to Rome) with Argyle, he is reunited with his boyhood friend, Hamish (Brendan Gleeson), with whom he had practiced the art of battle by throwing rocks at piles of animal bones. Now the two men heave much larger stones, resulting in William's besting of

Hamish by knocking him down with a rock to the forehead. Combining friendship with a "test of manhood," this scene is very similar to the legendary quarterstaff fight between Robin Hood and Little John. Soon after their friendly duel, the English arrive to put *prima noctae* into practice, thereby creating the ethnic and nationalistic conflict (much like the Saxon versus Norman motif) that eventually consumes Wallace.

Forced to court Murron (Catherine McCormack) in secret, tossing rocks (again) at her wooden shutter in the dead of night, he is startled by the bonny lass when she quietly sneaks up on him, an action that provides a stark counterpoint to the incredible military prowess he later demonstrates. Eloping, the couple is then married in a secret Celtic ceremony so that none of the English (depicted as pallid, debauched and arrogant ale quaffers) will find out. When Murron is murdered by the Magistrate (Malcolm Tierney), the film demonstrates its fidelity to historical fact, rather than adhering to the clichés of the adventure genre (in which the hero usually saves the distressed damsel); just before her throat is slashed, Murron desperately looks for deliverance (here Gibson includes a shot from her point of view), but Wallace, expecting her to meet him at an appointed spot, does not arrive. This tragic and powerful scene fuels the remainder of the film, which depicts Wallace's subsequent revenge that expands into a full-fledged national rebellion.

One of the most obvious Robin Hood–Wallace parallels, the name "Marion" worried Randall Wallace as he wrote the screenplay. Fearing that American audiences would confuse the historical Wallace with the legendary outlaw of Sherwood, he changed the leading lady's name to Elizabeth, a move that equally concerned the members of the Wallace Clan. Not wanting their hero's lover to share the same name as the English queen who executed Mary, Queen of Scots, Seoras Wallace suggested as a substitute the Caledonian equivalent "Murron."[26]

Unlike Michael Caton-Jones' unfortunate use of slow-motion in one obtrusive shot in *Rob Roy*, Gibson effectively uses slow-motion techniques to show details of battle and create suspense throughout *Braveheart*. This technique (similar to Kenneth Branagh's use of slow motion in depicting the Battle of Agincourt in *Henry V* [1989]) has the effect of briefly freezing history in time. In particular, slow motion plays a vital role in depicting the devastation inflicted on the English cavalry by Wallace's schiltroms, which the outlaw devises after gazing up at a group of tall trees.

The rapid editing techniques used in the battle scenes by Gibson and Stephen Rosenblum not only allowed them effectively to depict the utter confusion and calamity of medieval warfare but also to ensure the safety of both the men and horses. Remarkably realistic and shocking in their no-holds-barred brutality (some audience members actually walked out on the film during the initial 1995 release), these scenes, also featuring remarkable sound (particularly as the English heavy horses thunder toward the Scots), are the best of their kind.

But why did Gibson and Randall Wallace ignore the fact that the Scots' great monumental defeat of the English occurred at Stirling *Bridge*? Gibson admitted,

> To have a bridge, you've got to have something to put it over. We went throughout Scotland looking for the right location but when we found a body of water it wasn't horse-friendly. Plus, I discovered that using a bridge on camera involves a lot of mechanics to explain strategies and this is not really very cinematic. To have these two massive forces clashing had much more visual impact.[27]

When the savagely overworked Gibson barely staved off a nervous breakdown, first assistant director David Tomblin stepped in to helm the battle footage. And even as Tomblin called the shots, Gibson sometimes was unable to muster up enough energy to play his scenes; on one occasion, he neglected to report to the set during the filming of a major clash. Peter Mullan revealed:

> Nobody had thought to say to the great movie star, "Mel, you're on." He just didn't know and yet there were three and a half thousand of us all set to run two hundred yards in a shot that would probably cost at least a hundred thousand, just for the cameras and the time it would take for us all to go back to our first positions. It would have taken another two or three hours to do this damn thing again.[28]

While Gibson (an admitted homophobe) and Randall Wallace accurately depict the ineptitude of the foppish Prince Edward (Peter Hanly), who later would become the ineffectual King Edward II, they altered the behavior of Princess Isabelle to create an additional love interest for Wallace. Although some gay rights groups objected to the historical depiction of young Edward—in other words, the filmmakers did not bow to the practitioners of political correctness and update the character a mere 700 years—who makes telling glances at his friend Phillip

(Stephen Billington), their protests held no water. Later in the film, when the King pushes Phillip to his death, he does so because the lad's presumptuousness offends him, not out of vengeance against a homosexual relationship; after all, no such affair is depicted. This characterization of the Prince, who, as King, was buggered to death with a red-hot fire poker by Isabelle and her lover, Roger Mortimer, Earl of March ("perhaps the nastiest man ever to rule England"[29]) follows extant evidence. While Gibson and his cohorts could have played up his effeminacy, they instead chose a less flamboyant approach, depicting him as the coward he was.

Other characters are wholly fictitious, including Wallace's closest supporters: Hamish; Hamish's father, Campbell (James Cosmo); and Stephen (David O'Hara), a crazed Irish rogue who claims to speak personally with "the Almighty." "In order to find his equal, an Irishman is forced to talk to God," he boasts, constantly insisting that Ireland is "*my* island"; like Shakespeare's Falstaff, Stephen adds welcome humor to a very dour drama. Other brief comedy is provided by a Gibson in-joke, in which Wallace's entire force moons their English enemies prior to the Battle of Stirling. The effect of this act is at least two-fold: it refers to the fact that the Scots wear no undergarments beneath their kilts (the early Celts actually went into battle nude, with their bodies painted with substances such as wode, although the designs used by Gibson came much later), and answers critics who have derided Gibson for bearing his rear end in previous films. (An earlier shot shows the Scots waving their genitalia at the English.)

When not acting insane, Stephen often aids his commander, even saving his life at one point. In a scene depicting Wallace in a very Robin Hood–like act, Stephen impales with a short-sword an infiltrator who attempts to kill William as the outlaw creeps up on a deer with his bow and arrow. A short time later, Wallace experiences a dream—in which a hooded monkish figure (the spirit of Murron) warns him of impending danger—that would not be out of place in a Robin Hood ballad.

Often the film depicts the legends about Wallace's career rather than the (perhaps less interesting and certainly less dramatic) facts, including the long-held notion that Robert the Bruce turned traitor at Falkirk. Appearing in the classic guise of a "mysterious knight" during the battle, he is un-helmeted by Wallace after Mornay (Alun Armstrong) and Lochlan (John Murtagh) turn tail and abandon the Scots infantry on the field. Although this event did not actually occur, it

provides a strong analogy for the endless political wrangling that hin-
dered Scottish independence until Bruce's lengthy campaign, solidified
with the Battle of Bannockburn in 1314, achieved success for the Scots.
The in-fighting between the Scots nobles and their support for various
adherents to the throne, including Balliol (Bernard Horsfall), is depicted
in several scenes, in which Wallace is continually disgusted by their
inability to unite against the English. Bruce, however, agrees to "unite
the clans" just before he turns coat at Falkirk. Just before Wallace is
tricked and captured late in the film, Bruce again agrees to aid the outlaw but is prevented from doing so by several unscrupulous traitors who
have been paid off by Longshanks.

After the tragic debacle at Falkirk, the film depicts Wallace's "years
in the wilderness," during which he executes the two traitors, Mornay
and Lochlan, and becomes a legend in his own lifetime. The scene
depicting the murder of Mornay is truly nightmarish, showing the
terrified traitor awakening from a premonitory dream only to have his
head crushed by an enormous flail swung by the outlaw, who, on horseback, has smashed through the wall and thundered into his remote hide-
away. A true masterwork of suspense, the scene shows Mornay, realizing
he has suffered a nightmare about Wallace's revenge, sighing in relief
a split second before the outlaw breaks in to bludgeon him. Wallace then
disposes of Lochlan, whose bloody corpse drops through a roof and
onto a table where Bruce and other nobles are discussing "who might
be next."

In a beautifully edited montage sequence, the outlaw is depicted
sprinting up a Highland mountainside as various Scots commoners tell
exaggerated tales of him personally annihilating "fifty men, fifty, if it
was one ... a hundred men ... with his own sword, cut through them
like *Moses through the Red Sea*." As Wallace reaches the peak of the
mountain, the scene concludes with a breathtaking juxtaposition of a
tight close-up of Gibson's striking face and a 180-degree panoramic
shot of the ethereal Highlands flawlessly executed by Toll.

The fictitious "relationship" between Wallace and Isabelle, who
attempts to aid the outlaw on several occasions, has a very Robin-and-
Marian essence, but, of course, the affair cannot culminate with a happy
ending. The depiction of Prince Edward's ineffectual, cowardly nature
reinforces Isabelle's "need for love" (as addressed in a scene between the
princess and her servant and confidant, the promiscuous Nicolette [Jeanne
Marine]), making her resulting fascination with Wallace believable. The

illness and death of King Edward is also altered and tied in with the Isabelle-Wallace affair. Rather than contracting a respiratory ailment and dying while fighting Bruce in the later wars, here the monarch, worn out by his all-consuming hatred for Wallace, falls fatally ill during the capture and "trial" of the outlaw: Isabelle, claiming to Edward that she carries the baby of a man "not of the royal line," then tells Wallace's jailer that "the King will be dead in a month."

Traditionalist historians, particularly the eminent James Mackay ("It got very little right"[30]), heavily criticized *Braveheart*'s cinematic revisionism (a tendency unforgivable when depicting modern history, such as in the content of Oliver Stone's *JFK*, but unavoidable and even necessary in a visualization of the 13th century). In his admirable study of Gibson's films, Brian Pendreigh writes:

> A feature film is not a history lesson; it needs a more formal narrative structure, it needs focus in terms of character and motivation and it does not normally allow for discussion of three or four different theories. Given the criticism of films dealing with much more recent history ... *Braveheart* is remarkable not for how much it gets wrong, but how much it gets right.[31]

For example, Randall Wallace did not concoct the tryst between William and Isabelle, but dramatized it from the poetry of Blind Harry, who hinted that such an affair (between the outlaw and Princess "Marguerite") did occur. Pendreigh notes, "It may be rubbish, but at least it is indigenous Scottish rubbish, and not simply Hollywood invention, as has been suggested."[32]

The sentencing and execution closely adheres to the facts. Being drawn to the torture platform in a cart, Wallace, his arms tied to a wooden beam behind him, is depicted as a Christ figure (though Gibson chose not to include the laurel leaves that were placed on the historical outlaw's head). After the gathered populace (except for his disguised adherents) taunt him and throw food and rubbish in his face, the executioner proceeds to hang him, rack him and finally (off camera) disembowel him. Gibson *could* have shown far more if he really had wanted to be accurate, but he tactfully chose to depict only enough to suggest Wallace's ultimate fate. Again, slow motion is incorporated effectively, as the headsman's ax finally falls (after Wallace shouts, "Freedom!" as one last act of defiance) and a wisp of the outlaw's hair falls from his face to suggest the decapitation. The powerful scene

concludes with a final slow motion, low-angle shot of Murron's piece of cloth falling from his dying hand. It is an unforgettable scene (and one that is difficult to watch for some viewers).

Pendreigh supports Gibson's approach of depicting "just enough":

[A]s the ordeal comes to an end, [Gibson] cross-cuts between a whole series of different faces, all showing different emotions, not all of them present at the scene but all of them aware of it. There is King Edward on his deathbed, his son, his daughter-in-law Isabelle with a tear falling from her eye, two of Wallace's men in the crowd, Bruce far away in Scotland, and even the ghost of Murron. And just when we think that Wallace might beg for mercy he summons up a hidden reserve of courage and energy and yells out the single, final word "Freedom."[33]

To provide a more positive ending and proof that "Braveheart's" sacrifice did not go unrewarded, Gibson and Randall Wallace included the Battle of Bannockburn as an epilogue, making it look as if it happened immediately after Wallace's execution in 1305. As Bruce and his army (including Hamish and Stephen) take the field supposedly to pay homage to the English, the new Scottish King, wearing steel armor decorated with the insignia of William the Lion and carrying the cloth so prized by Wallace, instead rouses his troops to fight. Paraphrasing Robert Burns' national anthem, "Scots Wha Hae Wi' Wallace Bled," written nearly 500 years later, Bruce exhorts, "You have bled with Wallace. Now bleed with me!" Carrying Wallace's formidable claymore, Hamish throws it into the air. After the sword spirals through the blue, it then skewers the ground and stands with the hilt upright, flexing like a waving crucifix as Gibson's voice-over (which includes the actual date of the battle) declares the outcome on that historic day:

In the year of our Lord 1314, patriots of Scotland, starving and outnumbered, charged the fields of Bannockburn. They fought like warrior-poets. They fought like Scotsmen. And won their freedom.

Prior to the release of *Braveheart*, hardly anyone outside Scotland, excluding scholars, students of history, and those who had read Jane Porter's *The Scottish Chiefs*, were aware of the significance of William

Opposite: **Wallace bids adieu to the sumptuous Princess Isabelle (Sophie Marceau) after their romantic tryst in *Braveheart*.**

Wallace. And certainly only a handful could ever have noticed any similarities between his life and the legendary depictions of Robin Hood. Incredibly, the Academy of Motion Picture Arts and Sciences, a body that arguably rarely selects the best or most deserving films to receive its heralded Oscars but often (as sometimes admitted by its own members) bows to the political winds blown by award nominees, bestowed both the Best Director award on Mel Gibson and the Best Picture statuette on the production itself, acts hardly anyone would have predicted before *Braveheart*—after all, an adventure film directed by box-office favorite "Mad Mel"—was released. It is a remarkable film about a towering man, excellent in every department, including the beautiful musical score by James Horner, who created a sweeping main theme reminiscent of the classic epic compositions of Miklos Rozsa (*Ben Hur*, *El-Cid* and many others) while also including a healthy dose of ethnic elements, particularly well-integrated bagpipes, in many scenes.

The performances are uniformly first-rate, particularly those of the superb supporting cast. Brendan Gleeson, David O'Hara and the always magnificent James Cosmo (who also appears in period roles in TNT's excellent *Treasure Island* [1990] and the latest television adaptation of *Ivanhoe* [1997], co-produced by the BBC and the A&E cable network) are splendid as Wallace's top men, and are matched on the opposing side by Martin Murphy and Gerald McSorley as the pompous, overconfident English commanders, Lords Talmadge and Cheltham, who support McGoohan's recalcitrant and iniquitous Longshanks, a characterization closely based on the real Edward I's deeds and physical appearance. As the elder Robert Bruce (referred to only as "the Leper" in the credits), Ian Bannen gives one of his trademark icy performances, but here, as required by the role, is positively repugnant. As the two women in Wallace's life, Sophie Marceau is perfectly cast as Isabelle, and Catherine McCormack leaves an indelible impression as the beautiful, resourceful and tragic Murron.

Those who are quick to criticize Mel Gibson for his past swaggering hero roles should leave former impressions behind when viewing *Braveheart* and instead concentrate on *this* performance, probably a character more difficult to play than Hamlet because Wallace actually existed, a phenomenal human being hailed by many over the past seven centuries as the most important player on the stage of Scottish history. The trademark Gibson charm (such as seen in his *Maverick* characterization) is certainly present, but there are precious few of the tongue-in-cheek heroics found in films such as the hugely popular *Lethal Weapon* series or other films of their ilk. He plays Wallace as a slightly larger-than-life warrior who, at times, does exhibit qualities of the "mindless barbarian" (as he is called by Isabelle when she attempts to impress Longshanks after he has ordered her to offer the outlaw a royal bribe), but also demonstrates a caring, gentle, passionate and intelligent side. There are many moments of quiet understatement in his performance (he actually looks like a Native American warrior of the Plains during a tender scene set in Isabelle's field tent), and his accent is quite excellent; even legions of Scots thought so.

Gibson, notorious in Hollywood circles as an unrepentant right-wing hardliner, revealed that he had intended to make no specific political statement with *Braveheart*. But the film made a statement nonetheless. Perhaps the very contradiction in Gibson's *oeuvre* is the key. Although the man himself is unremittingly conservative, his artistic message is one of freedom, of individual expression in the face of oppression: how can we, as a people, merge order and individuality and make it work?

During the making of *Braveheart*, Gibson mucked about with the common folk, wanting to lend a tinge of realism to the proceedings. His wife and children visited him on location, and each day he joined the cast and crew in the catering tents to wait for his meals. Whenever a supporting player, extra or technician broke off conversation to account for his dominating presence, he became visibly uncomfortable.[34] The only nocturnal refuge he experienced were the tents set up by the Wallace Clan and a surprise birthday party thrown for Randall Wallace in Dublin, where Gibson briefly escaped his 20-hour workdays. Seoras Wallace recalled, "He was really worn out, but he just fought, fought, fought. We saw him on the set when he was really, really ill. The main thing that brought us all down was fatigue."[35]

During the initial release of *Braveheart* in Scotland, the Scottish Nationalist Party set up recruiting stations in theater lobbies, taking advantage of the film's powerful depiction of Wallace's quest for freedom. Two years later, on September 12, 1997, in a move encouraged by British Prime Minister Tony Blair, the Scots made their first real bid for independence since Bonnie Prince Charlie's army was decimated on the bloody battlefield of Culloden in April 1746. Inspired by colorful political posters bearing Gibson's photograph and the rallying cry of "Freedom!" voters throughout the country discussed what came to be known as "the *Braveheart* ticket" and then elected the right to establish their own parliament for the first time in three centuries.

To commemorate the impact of the film, Tom Church, a stonemason from Brechin, fashioned a 13-foot statue of Wallace, wearing his claymore and holding a targe featuring his sobriquet "Braveheart," standing atop a slab sculpted with the word "FREEDOM" in large, block letters. Intentionally, Wallace looks conspicuously like Mel Gibson.

Commenting on the fact that his screenplay actually helped to bring about political change in old Caledonia, Randall Wallace said, "People tell me, 'You wrote this movie, and now Scotland is free.' I'm not looking to be involved in a political situation. [The Scots] are extremely motivated by this movie."[36]

Regardless of the writer's intention not to get politically involved, he nonetheless wrote a very political film whose popularity had a real affect on audiences who saw it. His depiction of this Scottish Robin Hood added impetus to a movement similar to that which the historical Wallace inspired in his countrymen 700 years ago. But while Wallace's men were forced to use violence in those savagely brutal times, the Scots of 1997 were able to initiate change at the ballot box. Only time will tell if Scotland again will be truly free of English rule, but the fact remains that *Braveheart*, embodying the Robin Hood motif of the lone outlaw leading his dispossessed comrades to freedom from tyranny, may be the only motion picture ever to accomplish such a feat. William Wallace may or may not have been the real Robin Hood, but *Braveheart*, the film depicting his exploits, has, in a tangible way, brought the outlaw's spirit to bear on modern society.

Sixteen

Wither the Greenwood?

Although Rob Roy MacGregor and William Wallace have graced theaters since 1993, Robin Hood's only visual incarnations have occurred on the small screen, primarily in the BBC-A&E three-part miniseries *Ivanhoe* (1997) and a ludicrously anachronistic series, *The New Adventures of Robin Hood*, produced by Turner Network Television.

Ivanhoe, scripted by Deborah Cook and directed by Stuart Orme, expands upon Scott's already overlong novel, dedicating half its 300-minute running time to fleshing out the motivations of various characters, particularly Prince John (Ralph Brown) and his aide, Fitzurse (Ronald Pickup), and Cedric (James Cosmo) and those within his Saxon sphere. The first 100-minute episode drags on interminably before the tournament at Ashby begins, and then the visual technique completely negates the historical authenticity of the combat. In typical television style, an overabundance of close-ups, quick montage editing and obtrusive slow-motion effects do not allow the viewer to see much dueling or jousting. The siege of Torquilstone is not a siege at all: consisting primarily of poorly edited infantry assaults, it embarrassingly pales in comparison to its counterparts in MGM's 1952 masterpiece and the 1982 television version.

The Semitic subplot is very well handled, and David Horovitch and Susan Lynch are excellent as Isaac and Rebecca. Deborah Cook's teleplay does contain a fair degree of historical revisionism, including Ivanhoe's (Stephen Waddington) lamenting of King Richard's (Rory Edwards) behavior at Acre and Queen Eleanor's "scolding" of her two sons, whom she blames equally for creating the turmoil between the Normans and Saxons. Although the focus on character motivation unnecessarily extends the film's length, this element allows modern viewers to understand better some of the complicated issues of the era, even if they are combined with fiction and legend.

Stuart Orme admirably depicts the outlaws of Sherwood very realistically, as they are dressed drably and covered with dirt and grime throughout. Interestingly, the Merry Men, including Little John (David J. Nicholls) and Friar Tuck (Ron Donachie), actually are more visible than (the fully bearded) Robin of Locksley (Aden Gillett), and they play their military role as written by Scott. (Robin's most daring act is his kicking of Richard the Lionheart into a stream; at this point, not knowing the king's true identity, he is disgusted by his drunkenness [and that of Tuck, who had provided the wine for a previous political discussion].) In fact, this *Ivanhoe* was the first to feature each of the major events created by Scott, including all the various tournaments: the jousting, the hand-to-hand combat and the archery contest. The script and actor Rory Edwards also place great emphasis on King Richard's battle prowess, often showing him in the very thick of it.

The cast is the miniseries' greatest asset and makes the five-hour experience more than tolerable. *Braveheart* veterans James Cosmo and Jimmy Chisholm (as Wamba) are superb, as are Ralph Brown and Christopher Lee, who was cast perfectly as Beaumanoir, the Grand Master of the Knights Templar. Who better to say (when referring to Rebecca), "Bring the witch forward" than this legendary veteran of horror films? His best role in decades, Beaumanoir demonstrates how an actor of Lee's caliber can inject life into a tedious proceeding; nearly four hours into the production, he lends it the dramatic power it could use in its earlier scenes.

The New Adventures of Robin Hood, filmed on location in Czechoslovakia and relying on popular fantasy elements, is another exponent of the tongue-in-cheek 1990s action genre that includes *Hercules: The Legendary Journeys*, *Zena: Warrior Princess*, *The New Adventures of Sinbad* and *The New Adventures of Tarzan*, all of which have little in common with their characters' original literary and historical sources. Another similar, short-lived program, *Roar*, "inspired" by *Braveheart* and set in "5th-century Ireland," was broadcast on the Fox network in 1997. All of the shows feature outlandish plots, ahistorical content, ludicrous dialogue, stilted performances and weapons far too modern for their time periods. *The New Adventures of Robin Hood*, integrating such fantasy elements as sorcery and dragons, is just another generic action potboiler and, as far as its content is concerned, is far worse than the low-budget Richard Greene series and the Hammer Z-films of the 1950s and '60s.

Unlike most motion pictures adapted from the literary works of specific authors, the films based on the vast and varied legends of Robin Hood have maintained a reasonable degree of consistency over a span of 85 years. For instance, while there are only a tiny handful of fine films based on the oft-lensed works of Robert Louis Stevenson, a very few quality Edgar Allan Poe thrillers, and only one faithful feature-film adaptation of a Sir Arthur Conan Doyle story, the cinema of the English outlaw and his Scottish counterparts boasts some true masterpieces (*The Adventures of Robin Hood* [1938], *Ivanhoe* [1952], *Braveheart* [1995]), several superior offerings (*The Story of Robin Hood* [1952], *Robin Hood* [1991], *Rob Roy* [1995]), and a very good television adaptation of *Ivanhoe* (1982). However deviant, there are also a unique, highly entertaining satire (*Robin and the Seven Hoods* [1964]), an enjoyable children's feature cartoon (*Robin Hood* [1973]), and the absurd sequence from *Time Bandits* (1981). And while *Robin Hood* (1922), *Rob Roy: The Highland Rogue* (1954), *Robin and Marian* (1976) and *Ivanhoe* (1997) are fraught with problems, they are not productions without merit. Of course, there are truly dreadful films as well, particularly the turgid Hammer programmers and *Robin Hood: Men in Tights* (1993). But the film that justifiably receives the "black arrow award" as the most abysmal excuse for a Sherwood outlaw epic is *Robin Hood: Prince of Thieves* (1991), a travesty that literally robbed the poor filmgoer to give to the rich filmmaker.

More than six decades have passed since the definitive incarnation of the Sherwood rebel gloriously cut a dashing swath across the silver screen. Yet, for better or worse, spurred on by a legend that will not die, his various forms have made a cinematic comeback now and then. And it is certain that filmgoers have not seen the last of Sir Robin of Locksley, Robert Fitzooth, Robert Hode, or simply Robin Hood. (Whether or not Wallace or Rob Roy will return is another matter.) Somewhere, down the greenwood path, a filmmaker wanting to produce an action epic again will turn to this most durable of English legends. But before the arrows fly, let us hope that historically accurate art direction, costumes and weaponry will be accompanied by equally adept actors interpreting a superior script.

Films About the English Robin Hood

The following listing includes silent films and major English-language sound films produced for theatrical release and television broadcast from 1908 through 1997.

Silent Films

Robin Hood (1908)

Credits: *a Kalem production; running length:* 1 reel.

Robin Hood and His Merry Men (1908)

Credits: *director:* Percy Stow; *screenplay:* Langford Reed; *running length:* 1 reel.

Robin Hood Outlawed (1912)

Credits: *director:* Charles Raymond; *screenplay:* Harold Brett; *running length:* 3 reels.

Cast: A. Brian Plant (Robin Hood), Ivy Martinek (Maid Marian), George Foley (Friar Tuck), Edward Durrant (Will Scarlett), Jack Houghton (Sir Hubert de Boissy), J. Leonard (Abbot of Ramsey), Harry Lorraine (Little John).

Robin Hood (1913)

Credits: *director:* Theodore Marston; *running length:* 4 reels.

Cast: William Russell, Gerda Holmes, James Cruze, William Garwood.

Ivanhoe (1913)

Credits: *director and screenplay:* Herbert Brenon; based on the novel by Sir Walter Scott; *directors of photography:* E. G. Palmer, S. P. Kinder; an Independent Moving Picture (IMP) production; running length: 4 reels.

Cast: King Baggot (Ivanhoe), Leah Baird (Rebecca), Evelyn Hope (Lady Rowena), Arthur Scott-Craven (King Richard), W. Thomas (Robin Hood),

W. Calvert (Gurth), Mr. Norman, Wallace Bosco (Cedric), George Courtenay (Prince John), Wallace Widdescombe (Sir Brian), Jack Bates (Sir Reginald), A. J. Charlwood (Athelstane), Herbert Brenon (Isaac), H. Holles (Friar Tuck), Helen Downing, W. Thomas.

Ivanhoe (1913) [U. S. title: *Rebecca the Jewess*]

Credits: *director and screenplay:* Leedham Bantock; based on a play by Walter and Frederick Melville adapted from the novel by Sir Walter Scott; a Zenith–Big A production; *running length:* 6 reels.

Cast: Lauderdale Maitland (Ivanhoe), Edith Bracewell (Rebecca), Nancy Bevington (Lady Rowena), Hubert Carter (Isaac), Henry Lonsdale (Sir Brian), Austin Milroy (Front de Boeuf).

Robin Hood (1922)

Credits: *director:* Allan Dwan; *producer:* Douglas Fairbanks; *screenplay:* Lotta Woods; based on a story by Elton Thomas (Douglas Fairbanks); *director of photography:* Arthur Edeson; *editor:* William Nolan; *art directors:* Wilfred Buckland, Irvin J. Martin, Edward M. Langley; *costumes:* Mitchell Leisen; *special effects:* Paul Eagler; a Douglas Fairbanks production; released by United Artists Pictures; *running length:* 11 reels.

Cast: Douglas Fairbanks (The Earl of Huntington/Robin Hood), Wallace Beery (Richard the Lion-Hearted), Sam De Grasse (Prince John), Enid Bennett (Lady Marian Fitzwalter), Paul Dickey (Sir Guy of Gisbourne), William Lowery (The High Sheriff of Nottingham), Roy Coulson (The King's Jester), Billie Bennett (Lady Marian's Serving Woman), Merrill McCormick, Wilson Benge (Henchmen to Prince John), Willard Louis (Friar Tuck), Alan Hale (Little John), Maine Geary (Will Scarlett), Lloyd Talman (Alan-a-Dale), Rita Gillman.

Robin Hood, Jr. (1923)

Credits: *director:* Clarence Bricker; *running length:* 4 reels.
Cast: Frankie Lee, Peggy Cartwright, Stanley Bingham, Ashley Cooper.

Robin Hood's Men (1924) [part II of *Fights Through the Ages*]

Credits: a Regent Films production.
Cast: Gerald Ames (Robin Hood).

Sound Films

The Adventures of Robin Hood (May 1938)

Credits: *directors:* Michael Curtiz and William Keighley; *executive producer:* Hal B. Wallis; *associate producer:* Henry Blanke; *screenplay:* Norman Reilly Raine and Seton I. Miller; *musical score:* Erich Wolfgang Korngold; *orchestrations:* Hugo Friedhofer, Milan Roder; *musical director:* Leo F. Forbstein; *dialogue director:* Irving Rapper; *second unit director:* B. Reeves Eason; *directors of photography (Technicolor):* Tony Gaudio, ASC, and Sol Polito, ASC; *editor:* Ralph Dawson; *art director:* Carl Jules Weyl; *costumes:* Milo Anderson; *makeup artist:* Perc Westmore; *sound:* C. A. Riggs; *Technicolor representative:* W. Howard Greene; *Technicolor*

color director: Natalie Kalmus; *associate:* Morgan Padelford; *technical adviser:* Louis Van Den Ecker; *unit production manager:* Al Alleborn; *archery supervisor:* Howard Hill; *fencing master:* Fred Cavens; *assistant directors:* Lee Katz, Jack Sullivan; *stuntman:* Buster Wiles; released by Warner Bros. Pictures; *running time:* 102 minutes.

Cast: Errol Flynn (Robin Hood), Olivia de Havilland (Maid Marian), Basil Rathbone (Sir Guy of Gisbourne), Claude Rains (Prince John), Patric Knowles (Will Scarlet), Eugene Pallete (Friar Tuck), Alan Hale (Little John), Melville Cooper (High Sheriff of Nottingham), Ian Hunter (King Richard the Lion-Heart), Una O'Connor (Bess), Herbert Mundin (Much the Miller's Son), Montagu Love (Bishop of the Black Canons), Leonard Willey (Sir Essex), Robert Noble (Sir Ralf), Kenneth Hunter (Sir Mortimer), Robert Warwick (Sir Geoffrey), Colin Kenny (Sir Baldwin), Lester Matthews (Sir Ivor), Harry Cording (Dickon Malbete), Howard Hill (Captain of Archers), Ivan Simpson (Proprietor of Kent Road Tavern), Charles McNaughton (Crippen), Lionel Belmore (Humility Prin), Austin Fairman (Sir Nigel), Reginald Sheffield (Herald at Archery Tournament), Wilfred Lucas (Archery Official), Holmes Herbert (Archery Referee), James Baker (Phillip of Arras).

The Bandit of Sherwood Forest (1946)

Credits: *directors:* George Sherman and Henry Levin; *producers:* Leonard S. Picker and Clifford Sanforth; *screenplay:* Wilfred H. Pettitt and Melvin Levy; *based on the novel: The Son of Robin Hood* by Paul A. Castleton; *directors of photography (Technicolor):* Tony Gaudio, William Snyder, George Meehan, Jr.; *editor:* Richard Fantl; *musical score:* Hugo Friedhofer; *art directors:* Stephen Gooson, Rudolph Sternad; released by Columbia Pictures; *running time:* 85 minutes.

Cast: Cornel Wilde (Robert of Nottingham), Anita Louise (Lady Catherine Maitland), Jill Esmond (The Queen Mother), Edgar Buchanan (Friar Tuck), Henry Daniell (The Regent), George Macready (Fitz-Herbert), Russell Hicks (Robin Hood), John Abbott (Will Scarlet), Lloyd Corrigan (Sheriff of Nottingham), Eva Moore (Mother Meg), Ray Teal (Little John), Leslie Denison (Allan-a-Dale), Ian Wolfe (Lord Mortimer), Maurice R. Tauzin (The King).

The Prince of Thieves (January 5, 1948)

Credits: *director:* Howard Bretherton; *producer:* Sam Katzman; *screenplay:* Maurice Tombragel and Charles H. Schneer; based on the novel by Alexandre Dumas; *director of photography (Cinecolor):* Fred H. Jackman, Jr.; *editor:* James Sweeney; *musical direction:* Mischa Bakaleinikoff; *art director:* Paul Palmentola; released by Columbia Pictures; *running time:* 72 minutes.

Cast: Jon Hall (Robin Hood), Patricia Morison (Lady Marian), Adele Jergens (Lady Christabel), Alan Mowbray (The Friar), Michael Duane (Sir Allan Claire), H. B. Warner (Gilbert Head), Lowell Gilmore (Sir Phillip), Gavin Muir (Baron Tristram), Robin Raymond (Maude), Lewis L. Russell (Sir Fitz-Alwin), Walter Sande (Little John), Syd Saylor (Will Scarlet), I. Stanford Jolley (Bowman), Fredric Santley (Lindsay), Belle Mitchell (Margaret Head).

Rogues of Sherwood Forest (June 1950)

Credits: *director:* Gordon Douglas; *producer:* Fred M. Packard; *screenplay:* George Bruce; based on a story by Ralph Bettinson; *director of photography (Technicolor):* Charles Lawton, Jr.; *editor:* Gene Havlick; *musical score:* Heinz

Roemheld, Arthur Morton; *musical direction:* Morris Stoloff; *art director:* Harold
MacArthur; released by Columbia Pictures; previewed June 15, 1950; *running time:*
80 minutes.

Cast: John Derek (Robin, Earl of Huntington), Diana Lynn (Lady Marianne),
George Macready (King John), Alan Hale (Little John), Paul Cavanagh (Sir Giles),
Lowell Gilmore (Count of Flanders), Billy House (Friar Tuck), Lester Matthews
(Alan-A-Dale), William ["Billy"] Bevan (Will Scarlet), Wilton Graff (Baron
Fitzwalter), Donald Randolph (Archbishop Stephen Langton), John Dehner (Sir
Baldric), Gavin Muir (Baron Alfred), Tim Huntley (Baron Chandos), Paul Collins
(Arthur), Campbell Copelin, James Logan (Officers), Valentine Perkins (Milk Maid),
Gilliam Blake (Lady in Waiting), Pat Aherne (Trooper), Olaf Hytten (Charcoal
Burner), Symona Boniface (Charcoal Burner's Wife), Paul Bradley (Court Official),
Matthew Boulton (Abbot), Nelson Leigh (Merton), Colin Keith Johnson (Munster),
Byron Poindexter (Man).

Tales of Robin Hood (January 2, 1952)

Credits: *director:* James Tinling; *producer:* Hal Roach, Jr.; *screenplay:* Leroy
H. Zehren; *director of photography:* George Robinson; *editor:* Richard Currier;
musical score: Leon Klatzkin; *art director:* McClure Capps; released by Lippert
Pictures; *running time:* 61 minutes.

Cast: Robert Clarke (Robin Hood), Mary Hatcher (Maid Marian), Paul
Cavanagh (Sir Guy), Wade Crosby (Little John), Whit Bissell (Will Stutely), Ben
Welden (Friar Tuck), Robert Bice (Will Scarlet), Keith Richards (Sir Alan), Bruce
Lester (Alan-A-Dale), Tiny Stowe (Sheriff of Nottingham), Lester Matthews (Sir
Fitzwalter), John Vosper (Earl of Chester), Norman Bishop (Much), Margia Dean
(Betty), Lorin Raker (Landlord), George Slocum (Captain of the Guards), John
Doucette (Wilfred), John Harmon, Matt HcHugh, David Stollery.

Ivanhoe (June 1952)

Credits: *director:* Richard Thorpe; *producer:* Pandro S. Berman; *screenplay:*
Noel Langley; based on the novel by Sir Walter Scott; *director of photography
(Technicolor):* Freddie A. Young; *editor:* Frank Clarke; *musical score:* Miklos Rozsa;
art director: Alfred Junge; *costumes:* Roger Furse; *special effects:* Tom Howard;
released by Metro-Goldwyn-Mayer Pictures; London preview at the Metro Theatre,
June 4, 1952; *running time:* 106 minutes.

Cast: Robert Taylor (Ivanhoe), Elizabeth Taylor (Rebecca), Joan Fontaine
(Rowena), George Sanders (De Bois-Guilbert), Emlyn Williams (Wamba), Robert
Douglas (Sir Hugh De Bracy), Finlay Currie (Cedric), Felix Aylmer (Isaac), Fran-
cis De Wolff (Front De Boeuf), Guy Rolfe (Prince John), Norman Wooland (King
Richard), Basil Sydney (Waldemar Fitzurse), Harold Warrender (Locksley), Patrick
Holt (Philip De Malvoisin), Roderick Lovell (Ralph de Vipont), Sebastian Cabot
(Clerk of Copmanhurst), John Ruddock (Hundebert), Michael Brennan (Baldwin),
Megs Jenkins (Servant to Isaac), Valentine Dyall (Norman Guard), Lionel Harris
(Roger of Bermondsley), Carl Jaffe (Austrian Monk).

The Story of Robin Hood and His Merrie Men (July 1952)

Credits: *director:* Ken Annakin; *producer:* Perce Pearce; *screenplay:* Lawrence
E. Watkin; *director of photography (Technicolor):* Guy Green; *editor:* Gordon
Pilkington, B.S.C.; *musical score:* Clifton Parker; *musical direction:* Muir Matheson;

music performed by the Royal Philharmonic Orchestra; *art directors:* Carmen Dillon, Arthur Lawson; *production manager:* Douglas Peirce; *unit manager:* Anthony Nelson-Keys; *assistant director:* Peter Bolton; *matte artist:* Peter Ellenshaw; *camera operator:* Dave Harcourt; *Technicolor consultant:* Joan Bridge; *location directors:* Alex Bryce, Basil Keys; *location cameramen:* Geoffrey Unsworth, Bob Walker; *makeup:* Geoffrey Rodway; *hairstylist:* Vivienne Walker; *sound director:* C. C. Stevens; *sound editor:* Wyn Ryder; a Walt Disney production; released by RKO Pictures; *running time:* 84 minutes.

Cast: Richard Todd (Robin Hood), Joan Rice (Maid Marian), Peter Finch (Sheriff of Nottingham), James Hayter (Friar Tuck), James Robertson Justice (Little John), Martita Hunt (Queen Eleanor), Hubert Gregg (Prince John), Bill Owen (Stutely), Reginald Tate (Hugh Fitzooth), Elton Haytes (Allan-a-Dale), Antony Eustrel (Archbishop of Canterbury), Patrick Barr (King Richard), Anthony Forwood (Will Scarlett), Hal Osmond (Midge the Miller), Michael Hordern (Scathelock), Clement McCallin (Earl of Huntingdon), Louise Hampton (Tyb), Archie Duncan (Red Gill), Julian Somers (Posse Leader), Bill Travers (Posse Man), David Davies (Forester), Ivan Craig, Ewen Solon, John Stamp, John Brooking, John Martin, Geoffrey Lumsden, Larry Mooney, John French, Nigel Neilson, Charles Perry, Richard Graydon, Jack Taylor (The Merrie Men).

Men of Sherwood Forest (1957)

Credits: *director:* Val Guest; *producer:* Michael Carreras; *screenplay:* Allen MacKinnon; *director of photography (Eastmancolor):* Jimmy Harvey; a Hammer Films production; released by Astor Pictures; *running time:* 77 minutes.

Cast: Don Taylor (Robin Hood), Reginald Beckwith (Friar Tuck), Eileen Moore (Lady Alys), David King-Wood (Sir Guy Belton), Patrick Holt (King Richard), John Van Eyssen (Will Scarlett), Douglas Wilmer (Sir Nigel Saltire), Harold Lang (Hubert), Leslie Linder (Little John), Vera Pearce (Elvira), John Kerr (Brian of Eskdale), John Stuart (Moraine), Raymond Rollett (Abbot of St. Jude), Leonard Sachs (Sheriff of Nottingham), Bernard Bresslaw (Outlaw), Ballard Berkeley (Walter), Wensley Pithey (Hugo), Toke Townley, Jackie Lane, Tom Bowman, Edward Hardwicke, Michael Godfrey, Robert Hunter, Dennis Wyndham, Peter Arne, Jack McNaughton.

Son of Robin Hood (June 1959)

Credits: *director and producer:* George Sherman; *screenplay:* George W. George and George Slavin; *director of photography (Cinemascope):* Arthur Grant; *editor:* Alan Osbiston; *musical score:* Leighton Lucas; *art director:* Norman Arnold; an Argo production; released by Twentieth Century-Fox Pictures; previewed June 16, 1959; *running time:* 81 minutes.

Cast: Al Hedison (Jamie), June Laverick (Deering Hood), David Farrar (Des Roches), Marius Goring (Chester), Philip Friend (Dorchester), Delphi Lawrence (Sylvia), George Coulouris (Alan Adale), George Woodbridge (Little John), Humphrey Lestocq (Blunt), Noel Hood (Prioress), Shelagh Fraser (Constance), Jack Lambert (Will Scarlet), Maya Koumani (Lady in Waiting), Oliver Johnston, Russell Napier, Alastair Hunter, Robert Bruce, Jack Taylor, Christine Halward, Richard Walters, Doreen Dawne.

Sword of Sherwood Forest (January 1961)

Credits: *director:* Terence Fisher; *producers:* Sidney Cole and Richard Greene; *screenplay:* Alan Hackney; *director of photography (Megascope and Eastmancolor):* Ken Hodges; *editor:* Lee Doig; *musical score:* Alun Hoddinott; *songs:* Stanley Black; *vocalist:* Dennis Lotis; *art director:* John Stoll; *costumes:* John McCorry; *makeup:* Gerry Fletcher; *sound:* John Mitchell, Harry Tate; *assistant director:* Bob Porter; *technical advisers:* Ivor Collin, Patrick Crean, Jack Cooper; a Hammer-Yeoman production; released by Columbia Pictures; previewed January 5, 1961; *running time:* 80 minutes.

Cast: Richard Greene (Robin Hood), Peter Cushing (Sheriff of Nottingham), Niall MacGinnis (Friar Tuck), Sarah Branch (Maid Marian Fitzwalter), Richard Pasco (Earl of Newark), Nigel Green (Little John), Jack Gwillim (Hubert Walter, Archbishop of Canterbury), Vanda Godsell (Prioress), Dennis Lotis (Alan A'Dale), Desmond Llewelyn (Wounded Traveler), Edwin Richfield (Sheriff's Lieutenant), Brian Rawlinson (1st Falconer), Patrick Craen (Ollerton), Oliver Reed (Melton), Derren Nesbitt (Martin), Reginald Hearne (1st Man of Arms), Jack Cooper (Master of Archery), Adam Keane (Retford), Charles Lamb (Old Bowyer), Aiden Grennell (1st Veteran Outlaw), James Neylin (Roger), Barry De Boulay (Officer), John Hoey (Old Jack), Anew McMaster (Judge), John Franklin (Archbishop's Secretary), Maureen Halligan (Portress).

Robin and the Seven Hoods (June 18, 1964)

Credits: *director:* Gordon Douglas; *producer:* Frank Sinatra; *screenplay:* David R. Schwartz; *director of photography (Panavision and Technicolor):* William H. Daniels; *editor:* Sam O'Steen; *musical score and direction:* Nelson Riddle; *songs:* Sammy Cahn and James Van Heusen; *art director:* LeRoy Deane; *set designer:* Raphael Bretton; *costumes:* Don Feld; *choreography:* Jack Baker; *makeup:* Gordon Bau; *assistant director:* David Salven; a Sinatra Production; released by Warner Bros. Pictures; *running time:* 123 minutes.

Cast: Frank Sinatra (Robbo), Dean Martin (Little John), Sammy Davis, Jr. (Will), Bing Crosby (Allen A. Dale), Peter Falk (Guy Gisborne), Barbara Rush (Marian), Edward G. Robinson (Big Jim), Victor Buono (Sheriff Potts), Barry Kelley (Police Chief), Hank Henry (Six Seconds), Robert Carricart (Blue Jaw), Allen Jenkins (Vermin), Jack LaRue (Tomatoes), Hans Conried (Mr. Ricks), Sig Rumann (Hammacher), Robert Foulk (Sheriff Glick), Sonny King, Phil Crosby, Richard Bakalyan (Robbo's Hoods), Phil Arnold (Hatrack), Harry Swoger (Soup Meat), Joseph Ruskin (Tick), Bernard Fein (Charlie Bananas), Carol Hill (Cocktail Waitress), Diane Sayer ("Booze" Witness), William Zuckert, Richard Simmons (Prosecutors), Milton Rudin (Judge), Maurice Manson (Dignitary), Chris Hughes (Jud), Harry Wilson, Joe Brooks, Richard Sinatra, Roger Creed (Gisborne's Hoods), Carolyn Morin (House Guard), Aldo Silvani (Guard), Joe Gray, John Delgado, Boyd "Red" Morgan, John Pedrini, Al Wyatt, Tony Randall (Hoods), Eddie Ness, Frank Scannell (Lawyers), Thom Conroy, Joey Jackson (Butlers), Linda Brent (Woman Derelict), Jerry Davis, Manuel Padilla, Mark Sherwood (Boys), Ron Dayton (Man), Larry Mann (Workman).

A Challenge for Robin Hood (July 1968)

Credits: *director:* C. M. Pennington-Richards; *producer:* Clifford Parkes; *screenplay:* Peter Bryan; *director of photography (DeLuxe Color):* Arthur Grant,

B.S.C.; *supervising editor:* James Needs; *editor:* Chris Barnes; *musical score:* Gary Hughes; *musical supervisor:* Philip Martell; *production manager:* Bryan Coates; *assistant director:* Ray Corbett; *camera operator:* Moray Grant; *sound mixer:* George Stephenson; *sound recordist:* Laurie Barnett; *sound editor:* Jack T. Knight; *continuity:* Elizabeth Wilcox; *makeup:* Michael Morris; *hairstylist:* Bill Griffiths; *wardrobe mistress:* Dulcie Midwinter; *casting:* Irene Lamb; *special effects:* Bowie Films, Ltd.; *fight arranger:* Peter Diamond; a Seven Arts–Hammer Films production; released by 20th Century–Fox Pictures; previewed July 25, 1968; *running time:* 96 minutes.

Cast: Barrie Ingham (Robin), James Hayter (Friar Tuck), Leon Greene (Little John), Peter Blythe (Roger de Courtenay), Gay Hamilton (Maid Marian), Jenny Till ("Lady Marian"), John Arnatt (Sheriff of Nottingham), Eric Flynn (Alan-a-Dale), John Gugolka (Stephen), Reg Lye (Much), William Squire (Sir John), Donald Pickering (Sir Jamyl de Penitone), Eric Woolfe (Henry de Courtenay), Douglas Mitchell (Will Scarlet), John Harvey (Wallace), John Graham (Austin), Arthur Hewlett (Edwin), Alfie Bass (Pie Merchant), Norman Mitchell (Dray Driver).

Robin Hood (1973)

Credits: *director and producer:* Wolfgang Reitherman; *screenplay:* Larry Clemmons; based on characters and story by Ken Anderson; *editors:* Tom Acosta, Jim Meltor; *art director:* Don Griffith; *directing animators:* Milt Kahl, Frank Thomas, Ollie Johnston, John Lounsberry; *character animators:* Hal King, Art Stevens, Cliff Norberg, Burny Mattison, Eric Larson, Don Bluth, Dale Baer, Fred Hellmich; *musical score:* George Bruns; *songs:* "Whistle Stop," "Oo-de-Lolly," "Not in Nottingham" by Roger Miller (sung by Roger Miller), "Love" by Floyd Huddleston and George Bruns (sung by Nancy Adams), "The Phony King of England" by Johnny Mercer (sung by Phil Harris); released by Walt Disney–Buena Vista Pictures; *running time:* 83 minutes.

Cast: voices of Roger Miller (Allan-a-Dale), Brian Bedford (Robin Hood), Monica Evans (Maid Marian), Phil Harris (Little John), Andy Devine (Friar Tuck), Carole Shelley (Lady Kluck), Peter Ustinov (Prince John), Terry-Thomas (Sir Hiss), Pat Buttram (Sheriff), George Lindsay (Trigger), Ken Curtis (Nutsy).

Robin and Marian (1976)

Credits: *director:* Richard Lester; *producer:* Denis O'Dell; *executive producer:* Richard Shepherd; *screenplay:* James Goldman; *director of photography (Panavision and Technicolor):* David Watkin; *editor:* John Victor Smith; *musical score:* John Barry; *production designer:* Michael Stringer; *costume designer:* Yvonne Blake; *production supervisors:* Barry Melrose, Roberto Roberts; *art director:* Gil Perondo; *2nd unit photography:* Paul Wilson; *production manager:* Apolinar Rabinal; *assistant director:* Jose Lopez Rodero; *camera operator:* Jim Turrell; *unit managers:* Dusty Symonds, Juan Clemente; *construction manager:* Francisco Prosper; *sound editors:* Don Sharpe, Paul Smith; *sound recordists:* Roy Charman, Gerry Humphreys; *music editor:* Michael Clifford; *assistant editor:* Peter Boyle; *continuity:* Ann Skinner; *casting:* Mary Selway; *unit publicist:* Nat Weiss; *still photographers:* Iain Coates, Frederico Grau; *special effects:* Eddie Fowlie; *property master:* Julian Mateos; *assistant art director:* Tony Reading; *gaffer:* Miguel Sancho; *makeup:* Jose Antonio Sanchez; *fight arrangers:* William Hobbs, Ian McKay; *stunt arrangers:* Miguel Pedregosa, Joaquin Parra; *production services:* Merry Band

Associates; a Rastar Pictures production; released by Columbia Pictures; *running* time: 106 minutes.
      Cast: Sean Connery (Robin Hood), Audrey Hepburn (Maid Marian), Robert Shaw (Sheriff of Nottingham), Richard Harris (King Richard the Lionheart), Nicol Williamson (Little John), Denholm Elliott (Will Scarlet), Kenneth Haigh (Sir Ranulf), Ronnie Barker (Friar Tuck), Ian Holm (King John), Bill Maynard (Mercadier), Esmond Knight (Old Defender), Veronica Quilligan (Sister Mary), Peter Butterworth (Surgeon), John Barrett (Jack), Kenneth Cranham (Jack's Apprentice), Victoria Merida Roja (Queen Isabella), Monserrat Julio (1st Sister), Victoria Hernandez Sanguino (2nd Sister), Margarita Minguillon (3rd Sister).

Time Bandits (1981)

      Credits: *director and producer:* Terry Gilliam; *executive producers:* George Harrison and Denis O'Brien; *screenplay:* Terry Gilliam and Michael Palin; *director of photography (Technicolor):* Peter Biziou; *editor:* Julian Doyle; *musical score:* Mike Moran; *songs:* George Harrison; *production designer:* Millie Burns; *art director:* Norman Garwood; a Handmade Films production; released by Paramount Pictures; *running time:* 110 minutes.
      Cast: John Cleese (Robin Hood), Sean Connery (King Agamemnon), Shelley Duvall (Pansy), Katherine Helmond (Mrs. Ogre), Ian Holm (Napoleon), Michael Palin (Vincent), Ralph Richardson (Supreme Being), Peter Vaughan (Ogre), David Warner (The Evil One), Craig Warnock (Kevin), David Rappaport (Randall), Kenny Baker (Fidgit), Malcolm Dixon (Strutter), Mike Edmonds (Og), Jack Purvis (Wally), Tiny Ross (Vermin), David Baker (Kevin's Father), Sheila Fearn (Kevin's Mother), Jim Broadbent (Compere), John Young (Reginald), Myrtle Devenish (Beryl), Brian Bowes (Stunt Knight/Hussar), Leon Lissek (1st Refugee), Terence Baylor (Lucien), Preston Lockwood (Neguy), Charles McKeown (Theater Manager), David Leland (Puppeteer), John Hughman (The Great Rumbozo), Derrick O'Connor (Robber Leader), Peter Jonfield (Arm Wrestler), Derek Deadman (Robert), Jerold Wells (Benson), Roger Frost (Cartwright), Martin Carroll (Baxi Brazilla III), Marcus Powell (Horse Flesh), Winston Dennis (Bull-Headed Warrior), Del Baker (Greek Fighting Warrior), Juliette James (Greek Queen), Ian Muir (Giant), Mark Holmes (Troll Father), Andrew MacLachlan (Fireman), Chris Grant (Voice of TV Announcer), Tony Jay (Voice of Supreme Being), Edwin Finn (Supreme Being's Face), Neil McCarthy (2nd Robber), Declan Mulholland (3rd Robber), Frances De La Tour (Salvation Army Major).

Ivanhoe (February 23, 1982) [television film]

      Credits: *director:* Douglas Camfield; *producer:* Norman Rosemont; *teleplay:* John Gay; based on the novel by Sir Walter Scott; *director of photography:* John Coquillon; *musical score:* Allyn Ferguson; a Rosemont Production for Columbia Pictures Television; broadcast by CBS Television; *running time:* 142 minutes.
      Cast: James Mason (Isaac of York), Anthony Andrews (Ivanhoe), Olivia Hussey (Rebecca), Lysette Anthony (Rowena), Sam Neill (Brian de Bois-Gilbert), Michael Hordern (Cedric the Saxon), John Rhys-Davies (Reginald Front-de Beouf), Ronald Pickup (Prince John), Stuart Wilson (Maurice de Bracy), David Robb (Locksley), Michael Gothard (Athelstane), Julian Glover (King Richard), Tony Haygarth (Friar Tuck).

Robin Hood: Prince of Thieves (1991)

Credits: *director:* Kevin Reynolds; *executive producer:* James G. Robinson; *producers:* John Watson, Pen Densham, and Richard B. Lewis; *executive co-producers:* David Nicksay and Gary Barber; *co-producer:* Michael J. Kagan; *screenplay:* Pen Densham and John Watson; *story:* Pen Densham; *musical score:* Michael Kamen; *director of photography:* Douglas Milsome, BSC; *production designer:* John Graysmark; *set decorator:* Peter Young; *editor:* Peter Boyle; *costume designer:* John Bloomfield; *casting directors:* Noel Davis, Jeremy Zimmerman (UK), Ilene Starger (USA); *special effects supervisor:* John Evans; *stunt coordinator:* Paul Weston; *still photographer:* David James; *special publicity:* Ronni Chasen; *second unit directors:* Mark Illsey, Max J. Kleve; *production supervisor:* Malcolm Christopher; *archery expert:* Gabe Cronnelly; *stunt double:* Simon Crane; a Morgan Creek Productions, Inc., production; released by Warner Bros., Inc.; *running time:* 143 minutes.

Cast: Kevin Costner (Robin of Locksley), Morgan Freeman (Azeem), Christian Slater (Will Scarlet), Alan Rickman (Sheriff of Nottingham), Mary Elizabeth Mastrantonio (Marian), Geraldine McEwan (Mortianna), Michael McShane (Friar Tuck), Brian Blessed (Lord Locksley), Michael Wincott (Guy of Gisborne), Nick Brimble (John Little), Soo Drouet (Fanny), Daniel Newman (Wulf), Daniel Peacock (Bull), Walter Sparrow (Duncan), Harold Innocent (Bishop of Hereford), Jack Wild (Much), Michael Goldie (Kenneth of Cowfall), Liam Halligan (Peter Dubois).

Robin Hood (1991)

Credits: *director:* John Irvin; *producers:* Sarah Radclyffe and Tim Bevan; *executive producer:* John McTiernan; *associate producer:* Chris Thompson; *screenplay:* Sam Resnick and John McGrath; *story:* Sam Resnick; *director of photography:* Jason Lehel; *editor:* Peter Tanner; *production designer:* Austen Spriggs; *musical score:* Geoffrey Burgon; *costume designer:* Emma Porteous; *casting:* Susie Figgis; *a Working Title production;* released by 20th Century–Fox Pictures (Europe); broadcast on the Fox television network (United States); *running time:* 104 minutes.

Cast: Patrick Bergin (Robin Hood), Uma Thurman (Maid Marian), Jurgen Prochnow (Sir Miles Falconet), Edward Fox (Prince John), Jeroen Krabbe (Baron Daguerre), Daniel Webb (Much the Miller), Conrad Asquith (Lodwick), Barry Stanton (Miter), Owen Teale (Will Scarlet), Phelim McDermott (Jester), Carolyn Backhouse (Nicole), David Morrissey (Little John), Caspar De La Mare (Sam Timmons), Cecily Hobbs (Mabel), Gabrielle Reidy (Lily), Stephen Pallister (Jack Runnell), Kevin Pallister (Charlie Runnell), Alex Norton (Harry), Jeff Nuttall (Friar Tuck), Richard Moore (Abbot), Jonathan Cullen (Gerald of Tewksbury), Anthony O'Donnell (Emlyn), Gabrielle Lloyd (Gammer Tanzie), Josh Moran (Castle Guard), Stan Pinton (Bearded Mason) .

Robin Hood: Men In Tights (1993)

Credits: *director and producer:* Mel Brooks; *screenplay:* Mel Brooks and J. David Shapiro; based on a story by J. David Shapiro and Evan Chandler; *director of photography:* Michael O'Shea; *editor:* Stephen E. Rivkin; *musical score:* Hummie Mann; *production designer:* Roy Forge Smith; *art director:* Stephen Myles Berger; *set designers:* Ronald R. Reiss, Bruce Robert Hill, Gary A. Lee; *costumes:*

Dodie Shepard; *choreography:* Cindy Montoya-Picker; a Brooksfilms, Ltd., production; released by Gaumont-Fox; *running time:* 102 minutes.

Cast: Cary Elwes (Robin Hood), Richard Lewis (Prince John), Roger Rees (Sheriff of Rottingham), Amy Yasbeck (Maid Marian), Mark Blankfield (Blinkin), Dave Chapelle (Ahchoo), Isaac Hayes (Asneeze), Megan Cavanagh (Broomhilde), Eric Allan Kramer (Little John), Matthew Poretta (Will Scarlet O'Hara), Tracey Ullman (Latrine), Patrick Stewart (King Richard), Dom DeLuise (Don Giovanni), Dick Van Patten (Abbot), Robert Ridgely (Hangman), Mel Brooks (Rabbi Tuckman), Steve Tancora (Filthy Luca), Joe Dimmick (Dirty Ezio), Avery Schreiber (Tax Assessor), Chuck McCann (Villager), Brian George (Dungeon Maitre d'), Zito Kazann (Head Saracen Guard), Richard Assad (Assistant Saracen Guard), Herman Poppe (Sheriff's Guard), Clive Revill (Fire Marshall), Joe Baker (Angry Villager), Carol Arthur (Complaining Villager), Kelly Jones (Buxom Lass), Clement Von Franckenstein (Royal Announcer), Rudy DeLuca (Party Guest), Ronny Graham (Villager).

Ivanhoe (1997) [3-episode television miniseries]

Credits: *director:* Stuart Orme; *producer:* Jeremy Gwilt; *executive producer:* Chris Parr; *associate producer:* Kevan Van Thompson; *teleplay:* Deborah Cook; based on the novel by Sir Walter Scott; *musical score:* Colin Towns; *production designer:* Michael Trevor; *designer:* Adele Marolf; *director of photography:* Clive Tickner, B.S.C.; *film editor:* David Yardley; *casting adviser:* Anne Henderson; *second-unit director and stunt co-ordinator:* Gareth Milne; *horse master:* Steve Dent; *sword master:* Nick Powell; *stunt performers:* Joss Gower, Nick Hobbs, Nrinder Dhudwar, Tom Lucy; *historical adviser:* Christopher Gravett; *Judaica adviser:* Lewis Grinert; *medieval food stylist:* Colin Capon; *makeup and hair design:* Jill Hagger; *makeup artists:* Anna Lubbock, Sian Turner, Elaine Davis, Sue Beswick; *costume design:* Joan Wadge; *costume design assistants:* Theresa Hughes, Jane Clive; *dressers:* Donna Nicholls, David Wootton, Ray Greenhill; *camera operator:* Jeremy Gee; *focus puller:* Jonathan Sykes; *clapper/loader:* Chris Bain; *grip:* Alan Rank; *lighting gaffer:* Michael Hand; *best boy:* John Walker; *electricians:* Chris Polden, Mick Casserly, Martin Bloye; *rigger:* Graham Baker; *sound recordist:* Tony Jackson; *boom operator:* Peter Murphy; *painters:* Harry Hull, Tony Lenman; *carpenters:* John Gibson, Robert Sansom, Steve Protheroe; *properties master:* Kevin Hegarty; *armourer:* Rob Partridge; *standby props:* Dave Rogers, Rob Sellers, Roy Murray, Tony Minnie, Kipling Walter; *art directors:* Becky Harvey, Madelaine Leech; *matte artist:* Jim McCarthy; *properties buyer:* Dave Morris; *construction manager:* John Thorpe; *publicist:* Alan Ayres; *stills photographer:* Mark Bourdillon; *graphic designer:* Linda Sherwood-Pace; *visual effects designer:* Chris Lawson; *visual effects assistant:* Russell Pritchet; *assistant editor:* Alistair Grimshaw; *dialogue editor:* Bernard O'Reilly; *telecine colourist:* Nigel Shaw; *on-line editor:* Gary Brown; *dubbing editor:* Paul Davies; *dubbing mixer:* Tim Alban; *first assistant director:* Chris Le Grys; *location managers:* Vanessa de Souza, Lucy Nightingale; *script supervisor:* Caroline Sax; *second assistant directors:* Charlie Leech, Hilary Barrett; *third assistant director:* Helen Plunkett; *production co-ordinator:* Claudine Sturdy; *production secretary:* Kay Sherwood; *production accountant:* David Jones; *assistant accountants:* Julia Lloyd, Derek Donohoe; *script editor:* David Crane; a British Broadcasting Corporation (BBC) and Arts and Entertainment (A&E) Network production; broadcast by the A&E cable network; *executive in charge for A&E:* Delia Fine; *running time:* 300 minutes.

Cast: Ronald Pickup (Fitzurse), Ralph Brown (Prince John), Valentine Pelka

(Maurice de Bracy), Rory Edwards (King Richard), Aden Gillett (Robin of Locksley), Jimmy Chisholm (Wamba), David J. Nicholls (Little John), Susan Lynch (Rebecca), Stephen Waddington (Ivanhoe), Ciaran Hinds (Brian de Bois Gilbert), Christopher Lee (Beaumanoir), David Horovitch (Isaac), Trevor Cooper (Gurth), Sian Phillips (Queen Eleanor), Victoria Smurfit (Rowena), James Cosmo (Cedric), Chris Walker (Athelstane), Ron Donachie (Friar Tuck), David Barrass (Hubert), Peter Needham (Abbot), Renny Krupinski (Bardon), Jack Klaff (Malvoisin), Simon Donald (Louis Winklebrand), Peter Guinness (Montfitchet), Martin Walsh (Young Guard), Ewan Marshall (Higg), Rosalind Knight (Edith), Chris Barnes (Priest), Cynthia Grenville (Elgitha), Ken Kitson (Henry Bohun).

Films About the
"Scottish Robin Hoods"

This listing includes major theatrical releases, *not* "documentary" video releases placed on the market since the 1995 popularity of the theatrical films *Rob Roy* and *Braveheart*.

Rob Roy (1911)

Credits: *director:* Arthur Vivian; *producer:* James Bowie; based on the novel by Sir Walter Scott; filmed entirely on location in Scotland; a United Films production; *running length:* 6 reels.

Cast: John Clyde (Rob Roy MacGregor), Theo Henries (Helen MacGregor), Durward Lely (Francis Osbaldistone), W. G. Robb (The Bailie), George Hunter (Dougal Craitur).

Rob Roy (1922)

Credits: *director:* W. P. Kellino; based on a story by Alicia Ramsey; a Gaumont-Westminster production; *running length:* 6 reels.

Cast: David Hawthorne (Rob Roy MacGregor), Gladys Jennings (Helen Campbell), Sir Simeon Stuart (Duke of Montrose), Wallace Bosco (James Grahame), Alec Hunter (The Dougal Creatur), Tom Morris (Sandy the Biter), Eva Llewellyn (Mother MacGregor), Roy Kellino (Ronald MacGregor).

Rob Roy, The Highland Rogue (February 27, 1954)

Credits: *director:* Harold French; *producer:* Perce Pearce; *screenplay:* Lawrence E. Watkin; *director of photography:* Guy Green, B.S.C.; *editor:* Geoffrey Foot; *musical score:* Cedric Thorpe Davie; *musical direction:* Muir Mathieson; *costumes:* Phyllis Dalton; *production manager:* Douglas Peirce; *assistant director:* Gordon Scott; *matte artist:* Peter Ellenshaw; *Technicolor consultant:* Joan Bridge; *production designer:* Carmen Dillon; *location director:* Alex Bryce; a Walt Disney production; released by RKO-Radio Pictures; *running time:* 85 minutes.

Cast: Richard Todd (Rob Roy MacGregor), Glynis Johns (Helen Mary MacGregor), James Robertson Justice (Duke of Argyll), Michael Gough (Duke of Montrose), Finlay Currie (Hamish MacPherson), Jean Taylor-Smith (Lady Glengyll), Geoffrey Keen (Killearn), Archie Duncan (Dougal MacGregor), Russell Waters

(Hugh MacGregor), Marjorie Fielding (Maggie MacPherson), Eric Pohlmann (King
George I), Ina de la Haye (Countess von Pahlen), Michael Goodliffe (Robert Wal-
pole), Martin Boddey (General Cadogan), Ewen Solon (Major General Wightman),
James Sutherland (Torcal), Malcolm Keen (Duke of Marlborough).

Rob Roy (April 1995)

Credits: *director:* Michael Caton-Jones; *producers:* Peter Broughan and
Richard Jackson; *screenplay:* Alan Sharp; *director of photography:* Karl Walter
Lindenlaub, BVK; *editor:* Peter Honess, A.C.E.; *costume designer:* Sandy Powell;
musical score: Carter Burwell; orchestrated by Sonny Kompanek; *conductors:*
Carter Burwell and Sonny Kompanek; *musicians:* Davy Spillane (uilleann pipes and
low whistle), Capercaille, The Musicians of Swanne Alley, The Chieftains; *vocal-
ist:* Karen Matheson; *music consultant:* Dublin: Bill Whelan; *scoring mixer:* Mike
Farrow; *music recordist:* Geoff Foster; *music contractor:* Tonia Davall; *casting:*
Susie Figgis; *first assistant director:* Bill Westley; *second assistant directors:* Adam
Goodman, Sean Clayton, Guy Heeley, John Withers; *location manager:* Keith
Hatcher; *unit manager:* Paul Frift; *assistant location managers:* Janet Riddoch,
Brian Horsburgh; *art directors:* John Ralph, Alan Tomkins; *set decorator:* Ann
Mollo; *assistant art director:* Frederic Evard; *camera operator:* Mike Roberts; *"A"
camera first assistant:* Simon Hume; *second assistant:* Paddy Kiely; *loader:* Bar-
ney Davis; *"B" camera operator:* Peter Cavaciuti; *first assistant:* Angus Hudson;
still photographer: Tom Collins; *video assist:* Lester Dunton; *script supervisor:*
Anne Coulter; *production coordinator:* Joyce Turner; *chief lighting technician:*
Eddie Knight; *assistant lighting technician:* Dave Ridout; *key grip:* Colin Manning;
second company grip: Nick Pearson; *crane operator:* Keith Manning; *costume
supervisor:* Clare Spragge; *set costumers:* Nigel Egerton, Mandy Bryan, Nick
Heather; *assistant costume designer:* Frank Gardiner; *chief makeup designer:* Morag
Ross; *makeup artist to Miss Lange:* Dorothy Pearl; *makeup artists:* Miri Ben-
Shlomo, Sallie Jaye; *chief hairdresser:* Jan Archibald; *hairdresser to Miss Lange:*
Toni-Ann Walker; *hairdressers:* Eithne Fennell, Barbara Taylor; *property master:*
Charles Torbett; *assistant property masters:* Philip "Maxie" MacDonald, Bradley
Torbett, Jason Torbett; *chargehand dressing propman:* Les Benson; *dressing prop-
men:* John Hogan, Dave Midson; *drapes master:* Eddie Rees; *production buyer:*
David Lusby; *construction coordinator:* Harry Metcalfe; *construction buyer:* Brian
Windus; *H.O.D. carpenter:* Bob Eames; *H.O.D. rigger:* Kenny Richards; *H.O.D.
painter:* Derrick Smith; *lead set designer:* Toad Tozer; *set designer:* Poppy Luard;
storyboard artist: Keith Crossley; *special effects coordinator:* Ulrich Nefzer; *special effects crew:* Michael Luppino, Gerd Feuchter, Markus Geiger, Erno Bajus,
Simon Baker; *armourers:* Tony O'Connor, Dale Clarke; *transportation coordinator:* Gerry Gore; *unit publicist:* Quentin Donoghue; *assistant production coordinators:* Lesley Keane, Winnie Wishart, Kirsten Wing, Emma Cullen; *location
assistant:* Sarah Jane Kerr; *production accountant:* Michele Tandy; *assistant
accountants:* Samantha Glen, Sarah Booth, Rajeshree Patel; *dialect coach:* Elizabeth Smith; *choreographer:* Gillian Barton; *assistant to the director:* Beverly Caton-
Jones; *casting assistant:* Romany Turner; *extra casting:* Anne Campbell; *assistant
to the producers:* Bettina Lyster; *production sound recordist:* David John; *boom
operator:* Peter Murphy; *sound maintenance:* Paul Cridlin; *first assistant director:*
Beth Jochem Besterveld; *assistant editors:* Wayne Smith, Gabrielle Smith, Ben
Yates; *lightworks assistant:* Elizabeth Sherry; *supervising sound editor:* Richard
King; *re-recording masters:* Chris Jenkins, Mark Smith, Adam Jenkins; *sound*

effects editors: Patricio A. Libenson, David F. Van Slyke; *assistant sound editors:* Catherine Calleson, Mark Rathaus, Susan Demsky; *supervising ADR editor:* Campbell Askew; *ADR editor:* Cliff Latimer; *ADR assistant:* Graham Sutton; *dialogue editors:* Jim Matheny, Sukey Fontelieu; *foley editors:* Mark Pappas, Don Sylvestor, Nash Michael; *sound effects recordist:* Eric Potter; *foley artists:* Gary Hecker, Daniel O'Connell; *foley mixers:* Charlene Richards, Greg Steele, Kevin Taylor, David Novack; *music editor:* Adam Smalley; *assistant music editor:* Paisley Pappe; *fights:* William Hobbs; **second unit**: *second unit director:* Vic Armstrong; *director of photography:* Jim Devis; *camera operator:* Malcolm Mackintosh; *first assistant cameraman:* Simon Mills; *horse master:* Wendy Armstrong; *head groom:* Bruce Armstrong; *grooms:* Jeni Dodd, Sean Jones, Angel Louis Gomez, Mark MacLean; *dog trainer:* Gilly Raddings; *animal prosthetics:* John Humphries; *stunt coordinator:* Vic Armstrong; *stunt players:* Jorge Casares, Mark Stewart, Sylwester Zawadski, Nick Gillard, Mark Southworth, Seon Rogers, Dickey Beer, Terry Plummer, Trevor Steedman, Broncho McLaughlin, Gerard Naprous; *title design:* Ian Murray; *titles and opticals:* Howard Anderson Company; *negative cutter:* Gary Burritt; *color timer:* Phil Hetos; *DTS consultant:* Jeff Levison; *cameras and anamorphic lenses:* Joe Dunton and Company; re-recorded at Todd-AO Studios; music recorded at Air Studios, Lyndhurst, London; *lighting:* Lee Lighting, Ltd.; *catering:* Location Caterers, Ltd., London; filmed entirely on location in Scotland; developed with the support of The Scottish Film Production Fund, The European Script Fund and British Screen Finance, Ltd., London; released by United Artists; *running time:* 139 minutes.

Cast: Liam Neeson (Rob Roy), Jessica Lange (Mary), John Hurt (Montrose), Tim Roth (Cunningham), Eric Stoltz (McDonald), Andrew Keir (Argyll), Brian Cox (Killearn), Brian McCardie (Alasdair), Gilbert Martin (Guthrie), Vicki Masson (Betty), Gilly Gilchrist (Iain), Jason Flemyng (Gregor), Ewan Stewart (Coll), David Hayman (Sibbald), Brian McArthur (Ranald), David Palmer (Duncan), Myra McFadyen (Tinker Woman), Karen Matheson (Ceilidh Singer), Shirley Henderson (Morag), John Murtagh (Referee), Bill Gardiner (Tavern Lad), Valentine Nwanze (Servant Boy), Richard Bonehill (Guthrie's Opponent).

Braveheart (May 1995)

Credits: *director:* Mel Gibson; *producers:* Mel Gibson, Alan Ladd, Jr., and Bruce Davey; *executive producer:* Stephen McEveety; *screenplay:* Randall Wallace; *director of photography:* John Toll, ASC; *production designer:* Tom Sanders; *editor:* Steven Rosenblum; *musical score:* James Horner; *orchestrations:* James Horner; performed by The London Symphony Orchestra: Tony Hinnegan (kena and whistle), James Horner (keyboards), Eric Rigler (uilleann pipes), Mike Taylor (bodhran and whistle), Ian Underwood (synth programming); *music editor:* Jim Henrikson; *assistant music editor:* Christine Cholvin; *recorder and mixer:* Shawn Murphy, EMI Abbey Road, London; ADR recorded at De Lane Lea; *sound facilities:* Todd-AO; *costume designer:* Charles Knode; *casting:* Patsy Pollock; *associate producers:* Dean Lopata, Elizabeth Robinson; *production and financial controller:* Paul Tucker; *second unit directors:* Mic Rodgers, Matt Earl Beesley; *first assistant director:* David Tomblin; *production supervisor:* Ted Morley; *production manager:* Mary Alleguen; *unit manager:* Kevin De La Noy; *second assistant directors:* Patrick Kinney, David Carrigan, Paul Gray, Kate Hazell; *stunt coordinators:* Simon Crane, Mic Rodgers; *stuntmen:* Gary Powell, Graeme Crowther, David Cronnelly, Gabe Cronnelly, Dominic Hewitt, Donal O'Farrell,

Jamie Edgell, Mark Southworth, Paul Jennings, Sean McCabe, Brian Bowes, Stuart Clark, Tom Delmar, Steve Griffin, Paul Heasman, Mark Henson, Tim Lawrence, Alan Walsh, Terry Forrestal, Pater Pedrero, Phil Lonergan, Luis Gutierez Santos, Julian Spencer, Tom Struthers; *sword master:* Nick Powell; *horse master:* Tony Smart; *supervising art director:* Dan Dorrance; *art directors:* Nathan Crowley, Ken Court, John Lucas, Ned McLoughlin: *assistant art directors:* Clare Langan, Anna Rackard, Padraig O'Neill, Brenda Rankin; *storyboard artist:* Dan Sweetman; *production illustrator:* Neil Ross; *draughtsman:* Ken Ferguson; *art department coordinator:* Lisa Parker; *still photographer:* Andrew Cooper; *"A" camera operator:* John Clothier; *"B" camera operator/Steadicam:* Klemens Becker; *focus puller ("A" camera):* Graham Hall; *focus puller ("B" camera)/Steadicam assistant:* Sascha Mieke; *clapper loader ("A" camera):* Adam Biddle; *clapper loader ("B" camera):* Shaun Evans; *projection and display services:* Eric Bastin; *key grip:* Bobby Huber; *"A" camera grip:* John Murphy; *grips:* Robbie Reilly, Terry Mulligan, Philip Murphy; *camera crane:* David Rist; *gaffers:* Jim Planette, Louis Conroy, Chuck Finch; *best boys:* Noel Cullen, Billy Merrell; *electricians:* Garret Baldwin, Gerard Donnelly, David Durnay, James McGuire, Ricky Pattenden, Brian Sheridan, Anthony Swan, Stephen Finch, Mark Evans, Toby Tyler; *genny operator:* Alan Grosch; *video assist:* Bill Dowling, Ray McHugh; *property master:* Terry Wells; *sculptor:* Eddie Butler; *property buyer:* Belinda Edwards; *chargehand prop storeman:* Bob Douglas; *standby chargehand props:* Mickey Pugh; *chargehand propman:* John Graham; *standby propman:* Micky Woolfson; *propmen:* Terry Wells, Jr., Jake Wells, Noel Walsh, Cos Egan; *assistant props:* Tony Nicholson, Jr.; *chargehand dressing propman:* Mike Fowlie; *dressing props:* Triona Coen, John Wells, Daren Reynolds; *supervising draper:* Graham Caulfield; *drapes:* Jimmy Kavanagh; *chief special effects:* Nick Allder; *special effects senior technicians:* Graham Longhurst, Gerry Johnston, Robert Bromley, Neil Swan, Peter Arnold, Steve Crawley; *costume design assistant:* Justine Luxton; *wardrobe master:* David Whiteing; *wardrobe mistress:* Allison Wyldeck; *wardrobe supervisor:* Rhona McGuirke; *set supervisor:* Gabriel O'Brien; *costume assistant:* Al Barnett; *costume painting and dyeing:* Mathilde Sandberg; *costumers:* Russell Barnett, Frances Hill, Penny McVitie, Michael Barber; *milliner:* Sean Barett; *jewelry:* Martin Adams; *shoes:* Elizabeth Stuart-Smith; *costumiers:* Angels & Bermans, Academy Costumes, Royal National Theater Hire, Royal Shakespeare Company Costume Hire, Farani, Tirelli Costumi Roma—Italy, G.P.II, E. Rancati; *chief makeup artist:* Peter Frampton; *Mr. Gibson's makeup artist:* Lois Burwell; *Mr. Gibson's hairstylist:* Sue Love; *makeup artists:* Amanda Knight, Beryl Lerman; *crowd makeup supervisor:* Jennifer Hegarty; *chief hairdresser:* Paul Pattison; *hairdressers:* Francesca Crowder, Eileen Doyle, Barry Richardson, Annie Townsend; *armourer/gunsmith:* Simon Atherton; *assistant to Mr. Ladd:* Anne Farnsworth; *assistant to Mr. Davey:* Bonnie F. Watkins; *assistants to producers:* Samantha Thomas, Robert "Trenchy Ol' Boy" Trench; *production coordinators:* Fiona Traynor, Marilyn Clarke; *production secretaries:* Liz Kenny, Clare Scully, Claire Higgins; *production assistants:* Adam Green, Tasmia Power, Daisy Cummins, Glenn Delaney, Anna Dolan, Barbara Mulcahy, Amma Angel, David Flynn, Romek Delmata, Graeme Bird, Maria O'Connor, Geraldine Daly, Clodagh Tierney, Melanie Gore Grimes, Alex Gladstone, Donna Stewart; *assistant accountants:* Lyndy Noakes, Jane Trower, Kathy Ewings, Sarah Millar; *payroll:* Bernie McEnroe; *cashier:* Paul Delaney; *accounts assistant:* Sheila Farrell; *casting associates:* Julia Duff, Jina Jay, Leo Davis; *extras casting coordinators:* Manus Hingerty, Anne Campbell; *location managers:* Paul Shersby, John McDonnell, Dougal Cousins, Grania O'Shannon, Frances Byrne; *assistant location managers:* Andrew Hegarty, Christian

McWilliams; *script supervisor:* Sally Jones; *additional script supervisor:* Anna Worley; *trainee script supervisor:* Kate Pakenham; *sound mixer:* Brian Simmons; *boom operator:* Gerry Bates; *sound maintenance:* John Pitt; *dialect coach:* Julia Wilson Dixon; *sound assistant:* Barry O'Sullivan; **second unit**: *first assistant director:* Kieron Phillips; *second assistant director:* Trevor Puckle; *third assistant directors:* Peter Agnew, Paul Barnes, Charlotte Somers; *directors of photography:* Eddie Collins, John Clothier, Raymond Stella; *makeup supervisor:* Maire O'Sullivan; *hair supervisor:* Anne Dunne; *focus pullers:* Alan Butler, Ken Byrne, Ciaran Kavanagh; *clapper loaders:* John Conroy, Jo Gibney, Stewart Whelan; *grips:* Luke Quigley, Philip Kenyon, Jimmy O'Meara, John Dunne; *standby stagehand:* Gerry Quigley; *additional film editor:* Victor Dubois; *first assistant film editor:* Cynthia E. Thornton; *assistant lightworks editors:* Sheila MacDowell, William Yeh; *assistant film editors:* Paul Martinez, Paula Greatbatch; *apprentice film editors:* Laura Steiger, Pablo Prietto; *assistant film editors (location unit):* Matthew Tucker, Ben Yeates, Paul Topping; *sound editing:* Soundelux; *supervising sound editors:* Per Hallberg, Lon Bender, MPSE; *first assistant sound editor:* Karen M. Baker; *ADR supervisor:* Joe Mayer; *foley supervisor:* Craig S. Jaeger; *sound effects editors:* Peter Michael Sullivan, Christopher Assells, Randy Kelley, Joseph Phillips, Jeff Largent, Jay B. Richardson, Nigel Holland, Scott Martin Gershin, MPSE, Chris Hogan, Peter J. Lehman, Craig Harris, Dan Rich, Richard Dwan, Jr., Sarah Rothenberg Goldsmith, Mark LaPointe, Robert Heffernan, Beth Bergeron, Mary Ruth Smith, Lou Kleinman, Phil Hess, Stuart Copley, Hector Gik, Kim Waugh; *assistant sound editors:* Horace Manzanares, Judson Leach, Timothy Groseclose, Elizabeth Tobin Kurtz; *foley artists:* John Roesch, Hilda Hodges; *re-recording mixers:* Andy Nelson, Scott Millan, Anna Behlmer; *publicist:* Rogers & Cowan; *production publicist:* Corbett & Keene; *unit publicist:* Jennifer Collen-Smith; *marketing consultant:* Peter Graves; *chiropractor:* Dr. Robert Norett; *unit nurse:* Claire Litchfield; *construction manager:* Terry Apsley; *construction manager (Irish unit):* Russ Bailey; *assistant construction manager:* John New; *construction buyer:* Michael King; *master painter:* Owen Murnane; *chargehand painter:* Bobby Richardson; *supervising painter:* Douglas Regan; *head of department painter:* Adrian Start; *head of department plasterer:* Ken Barley; *head of department stagehand:* Kenneth Stachini; *head of department rigger:* Ron Newvell; *transportation coordinator:* Willie Fonfe; *transport liaison:* Brian Baverstock; *transport captain:* Gerry Fearon; *producers' transportation:* Fred Chiverton, Peter Devlin, Bob "Heart Attack" Lilley; *catering:* First Unit Caterers, Fitzers; *opticals:* Pacific Title; *color timer:* Terry Hagar; *negative cutter:* Garry Burritt; *main and end titles:* R/Greenberg Associates West, Inc.; *title designer:* Kyle Cooper; *digital visual effects and computer generated imagery:* R/Greenberg Associates West, Inc.; *visual effects executive producer:* Tricia Ashford; *visual effects supervisor:* Michael Fink; *visual effects producer:* Steven T. Puri; *digital artists:* Laurel Klick, Amie Slate, Chris Sjoholm, Larry Weiss, Kirk Cadrette, Andrew Rosen, Marsha Gray Carrington, Tim Guyer, Robert Scifo; *additional compositioning:* Computer Film Company, Stuart McAra, Janet Vale; *motion control systems:* Peerless Camera Co., Ltd., London; *motion control supervisor:* Kent Houston; *cameras and anamorphic lenses:* Panavision UK; *color:* Rank Film Laboratories, Ltd.; *prints:* DeLuxe; *lighting equipment:* Lee Lighting, Ltd.; *legal services:* Sinclair Tenenbaum Olesiuk and Co., Inc.; *banking services:* City National Bank, The Mitsubishi Trust and Banking Corporation, Los Angeles Agency, The Daiwa Bank, Ltd.; *completion guaranty:* International Film Guarantors, Inc.; filmed at Ardmore Film Studios and on location in Scotland and Ireland; an Icon Production; released by Paramount Pictures; *running time:* 177 minutes.

Cast: Mel Gibson (William Wallace), Sophie Marceau (Princess Isabelle), Patrick McGoohan (King Edward I), Catherine McCormack (Murron), Brendan Gleeson (Hamish), James Cosmo (Campbell), David O'Hara (Stephen), Angus McFadyen (Robert the Bruce), Peter Hanly (Prince Edward), Ian Bannen (Leper), James Robinson (Young William), Sean Lawlor (Malcolm Wallace), Sandy Nelson (John Wallace), Sean McGinley (MacClannough), Alan Tall (Elder Stewart), Andrew Weir (Young Hamish), Gerda Stevenson (Mother MacClannough), Ralph Riachi (Priest No. 1), Mhairi Calvey (Young Murron), Brian Cox (Argyle Wallace), Stephen Billington (Phillip), Barry McGovern (King's Advisor No. 2), John Kavanagh (Craig), Alun Armstrong (Mornay), Tommy Flanagan (Morrison), Julie Austin (Mrs. Morrison), Alex Norton (Bride's Father), Joanne Bett (Toothless Girl), Rupert Vansittart (Lord Bottoms), Malcolm Tierney (Magistrate), William Masson (Corporal), Dean Lopata (Madbaker/Flagman), Tam White (MacGregor), Donal Gibson (Stewart), Jeanne Marine (Nicolette), Martin Dunne (Lord Dolecroft), Fred Chiverton (Leper's Caretaker), Jimmy Chisholm (Faudron), David McKay (Young Soldier), Peter Mullan (Veteran), Martin Murphy (Lord Talmadge), Gerard McSorley (Cheltham), Bernard Horsfall (Balliol), Richard Leaf (Governor of York), Daniel Coli (York Captain), Niall O'Brien (English General No. 2), Liam Carney (Sean), Bill Murdoch (Villager), Phil Kelly (Farmer), Martin Dempsey (Drinker No. 1), Jimmy Keogh (Drinker No. 2), Joe Savino (Chief Assassin), David Gant (Royal Magistrate), Mal Whyte (Jailor), Paul Tucker (English Commander).

Appendix C

Robin Hood Westerns

Lady Robin Hood (August 14, 1925)

Credits: *director:* Ralph Ince; *screenplay:* Fred Myton; based on a story by Clifford Howard and Burke Jenkins; *director of photography:* Silvano Balboni; *assistant director:* Pandro S. Berman; an R. C. Pictures Corporation production; released by F.B.O.; *running time:* 65 minutes.

Cast: Evelyn Brent (Senorita Catalina/La Ortiga), Robert Ellis (Hugh Winthrop), Boris Karloff (Cabraza), William Humphrey (Governor), D'Arcy Corrigan (Padre), Robert Cauterio (Raimundo).

Robin Hood of El Dorado (1936)

Credits: *director:* William A. Wellman; *producer:* John W. Considine, Jr.; *screenplay:* William A. Wellman, Joseph Calleia and Melvin Levy; based on the novel by Walter Noble Burns; *director of photography:* Chester Lyons; *editor:* Robert H. Kern; *musical score:* Herbert Stothart; *costumes:* Dolly Tree; released by MGM; *running time:* 86 minutes.

Cast: Warner Baxter (Joaquin Marrieta), Ann Loring (Juanita de la Cuesta), Bruce Cabot (Bill Warren), Margo (Rosita Murrieta), J. Carroll Naish (Three-Fingered Jack), Soledad Jimenez (Madre Murrieta), Eric Linden (Johnnie Warren), Edgar Kennedy (Sheriff Judd), Charles Trowbridge (Ramon de la Cuesta), Harvey Stephens (Captain Osborne), Ralph Remley (Judge Perkins), George Regas (Tomas), Francis MacDonald (Pedro the Spy), Kay Hughes (Louise), Paul Hurst (Wilson), Boothe Howard (Tabbard), Harry Woods (Pete).

Robin Hood of the Pecos (1936)

Credits: *director and producer:* Joseph Kane; *screenplay:* Olive Cooper; based on a story by Hal Long; *director of photography:* Jack Marta; *editor:* Charles Craft; *musical director:* Cy Feuer; *songs:* Peter Tinturin and Eddie Cherkose; released by Republic Pictures; *running time:* 59 minutes.

Cast: Roy Rogers (Vance Corgin), George ["Gabby"] Hayes ("Gabby" Hornaday), Marjorie Reynolds [Peg Riley] (Jeanie Grayson), Cy Kendall (Ballard), Leigh Whipper (Kezeye), Sally Payne (Belle Starr), Eddie Acuff (Sam Starr), Robert Strange (Cravens), William Haade (Captain Morgan), Jay Novello (Stacy), Roscoe Ates (Guffy), Jim Corey, Chick Hannon, Trigger the Horse.

Robin Hood of the Range (1943)

Credits: *director:* William Burke; *producer:* Jack Fier; *screenplay:* Betty Burbridge; *director of photography:* Benjamin Kline; *editor:* Jerome Thoms; *art director:* Lionel Banks; *songs:* Gene Autry, Jimmy Wakely, Dick Heinhart and Johnny Bond; released by Columbia Pictures; *running time:* 57 minutes.

Cast: Charles Starrett (Steve Marlowe), Arthur Hunnicutt (Arkansas), Kay Harris (Julie Marlowe), Kenneth MacDonald (Henry Marlowe), Douglass Drake (Ned Harding), Hal Price (Sheriff), Edward Piel, Sr. (Grady), Frank LaRue (Carter), Bud Osbourne (Thompson), Stanley Brown (Santana), Frank McCarroll, Ray Jones, Johnny Bond, Merrill McCormack, The Jimmy Wakely Trio.

Trail of Robin Hood (1950)

Credits: *director:* William Witney; *producer:* Edward J. White; *screenplay:* Gerald Geraghty; *director of photography:* John McBurnie; *editor:* Tony Martinelli; *musical score:* Nathan Scott; *songs:* Jack Elliott and Foy Willing; *art director:* Frank Arrigo; *set decoration:* John McCarthy, Jr., and James Redd; *costumes:* Adele Palmer; *special effects:* Howard Lydecker and Theodore Lydecker; released by Republic Pictures; *running time:* 67 minutes.

Cast: Roy Rogers (Himself), Penny Edwards (Toby Aldridge), Gordon Jones (Splinters McGonigle, Blacksmith), Jack Holt (Himself), Emory Parnell (J. Corwin Aldridge), Clifton Young (Mitch McCall, Foreman), James Magill (Murtagh), Carol Nugent (Sis McGonigle), Edward Cassidy (Sheriff Duffy), Rex Allen, Allan ["Rocky"] Lane, Monte Hale, William Farnum, Tom Tyler, Ray ["Crash"] Corrigan, Kermit Maynard, Tom Keene, George Chesebro, Foy Willing and the Riders of the Purple Sage (Guest Stars), Trigger the Horse.

Chapter Notes

Chapter One

1. John Gillingham, *Richard the Lionheart* (New York: Times Books, 1978), p. 278.
2. J. C. Holt, *Robin Hood* (London: Thames and Hudson, 1982), p. 54.
3. Holt, p. 37.
4. Gillingham, p. 4.
5. Gillingham, p. 7.
6. Holt, p. 40.

Chapter Two

1. James Mackay, *William Wallace: Brave Heart* (Edinburgh: Mainstream, 1995), p. 265.
2. Maurice Keen, *The Outlaws of Medieval Legend* (New York: Dorset, 1989), p. 64.
3. J. C. Holt, *Robin Hood* (London: Thames and Hudson, 1982), p. 7.
4. Holt, p. 41.
5. Keen, pp. 74-75.
6. R. James Goldstein, *The Matter of Scotland: Historical Narrative in Medieval Scotland* (Lincoln: University of Nebraska Press, 1993), p. 215.
7. Stevenson, Joseph, ed., *Documents Illustrative of Sir William Wallace, his Life and Times* (Edinburgh, 1841) Cottonian MS, *Wallace Papers*, p. 8.
8. Keen, p. 65.
9. Mackay, p. 267.
10. Jim Bradbury, *The Medieval Archer* (Woodbridge, Suffolk: Boydell, 1985), pp. 68-69.
11. Bradbury, p. 69.

Chapter Three

1. J. C. Holt, *Robin Hood* (London: Thames and Hudson, 1982), p. 51.
2. Holt, p. 51.

3. Maurice Keen, *The Outlaws of Medieval Legend* (New York: Dorset, 1989), p. 191.

4. Stephen Knight, *Robin Hood: A Complete Study of the English Outlaw* (Oxford: Blackwell, 1994), p. 51.

5. Knight, p. 168.

6. Keen, p. 191.

7. Knight, p. 26.

8. Knight, p. 26.

Chapter Four

1. Stephen Knight, *Robin Hood: A Complete Study of the English Outlaw* (Oxford: Blackwell, 1994), p. 1.

2. Knight, p. 15.

3. J. C. Holt, *Robin Hood* (London: Thames and Hudson, 1982), p. 16.

4. Holt, p. 16.

5. Holt, p. 36.

6. Knight, p. 95.

7. Knight, p. 143.

8. Holt, p. 174.

Chapter Five

1. W. H. Murray, *Rob Roy MacGregor: His Life and Times* (Edinburgh: Canongate, 1995), p. 156.

2. Murray, p. 162.

3. Murray, p. 221.

4. Murray, p. 222.

5. Murray, p. 254.

6. Murray, p. 205.

Chapter Six

1. Stephen Knight, *Robin Hood: A Complete Study of the English Outlaw* (Oxford: Blackwell, 1994), p. 176.

2. Edgar Johnson, *Sir Walter Scott: The Great Unknown* (New York: MacMillan, 1970), p. 744.

3. Johnson, p. 746.

Chapter Seven

1. *Variety*, 22 August 1913.

Chapter Eight

1. Ralph Hancock and Letitia Fairbanks, *Douglas Fairbanks: The Fourth Musketeer* (New York: Henry Holt, 1953), p. 191.
2. Booton Herndon, *Mary Pickford and Douglas Fairbanks* (New York: W. W. Norton, 1977).
3. Charles Chaplin, *My Autobiography* (New York: Simon & Schuster, 1964).

Chapter Nine

1. Rudy Behlmer, *The Adventures of Robin Hood* (Madison: University of Wisconsin Press, 1979), p. 23.
2. Behlmer, p. 23.
3. Behlmer, p. 24.
4. Buster Wiles, *My Days with Errol Flynn* (Santa Monica: Roundtable, 1988), pp. 73-74.
5. Tony Thomas, *Errol Flynn: The Spy Who Never Was* (Secaucus: Citadel Press, 1990), pp. 173-174.
6. Behlmer, p.31.
7. Wiles, pp. 76-77.
8. Behlmer, p. 32.
9. Behlmer, pp. 34-35.
10. Rudy Behlmer, *Erich Wolfgang Korngold Society Newsletter*, No. 6 (January 1984), p. 14.
11. Stephen Knight, *Robin Hood: A Complete Study of the English Outlaw* (Oxford: Blackwell, 1994*)*, p. 228.
12. Wiles, p. 77.

Chapter Ten

1. *Variety*, 16 February 1946.
2. *Variety*, 5 January 1948.
3. Jay Robert Nash and Stanley Ralph Ross, *The Motion Picture Guide* (Chicago: Cinebooks, 1986), p. 1437.
4. *Motion Picture Guide*, p. 1437.
5. Richard VanDerBeets, *George Sanders: An Exhausted Life* (New York: Madison Books, 1990) pp. 82, 134.
6. VanDerBeets p. 108.
7. VanDerBeets p. 149.
8. Leonard Maltin, *The Disney Films* (New York: Crown, 1973), pp. 105-06.

Chapter Eleven

1. *Variety*, 11 January 1961.
2. *Variety*, 25 July 1962.
3. *Variety*, 25 July 1962.

Chapter Twelve

1. Nancy Sinatra, *Frank Sinatra: An American Legend* (Santa Monica: General, 1995), p. 178.
2. Bill Zehme, *The Way You Wear Your Hat: Frank Sinatra and the Lost Art of Livin'* (New York: HarperCollins, 1997), p. 188.
3. *Variety*, 24 June 1964.

Chapter Thirteen

1. Andrew Yule, *Sean Connery: From 007 to Hollywood Icon* (New York: Donald I. Fine, 1992), p. 157.
2. Yule, p. 162.
3. Yule, p. 162.
4. Yule, p. 162.
5. Kim ("Howard") Johnson, *Life Before and After Monty Python: The Solo Flights of the Flying Circus* (New York: St. Martin's, 1993), p. 164.

Chapter Fourteen

1. Todd Keith, *Kevin Costner: The Unauthorized Biography* (Netley, South Australia: Wilkinson, 1991).
2. Garth Pearce, *Robin Hood: Prince of Thieves: The Official Movie Book* (New York: Mallard, 1991), pp. 21-22.
3. Pearce, p. 23.
4. Pearce, p. 7.
5. Pearce, p. 26.
6. Pearce, p. 27.
7. Pearce, p. 61.
8. Pearce, p. 59.
9. Pearce, p. 61.
10. Pearce, p. 64.
11. Pearce, p. 64.
12. Pearce, pp. 72, 76.
13. Pearce, p. 78.
14. David Denby, *New York*, 24 June 1991, p. 47.
15. David Sterritt, *Christian Science Monitor*, 14 June 1991, p. 14.
16. Marcia Magill, *Films in Review*, August 1991, p. 252.
17. Kenneth Turan, *Los Angeles Times*, 14 August 1991, Calendar, p. 1.
18. Denby, p. 47.
19. Jami Bernard, *New York Post*, 14 June 1991, p. 35.
20. Jack Mathews, *Newsday*, 14 June 1991, Part II, p. 63.
21. Richard Corliss, *Time*, 24 June 1991, p. 58.
22. J. Hoberman, *Village Voice*, 25 June 1991, p. 53.
23. Turan, p. 1.
24. Adrian Wright, *Kevin Costner: A Life on Film* (London: Robert Hale, 1992), p. 149.

Chapter Fifteen

1. *Rob Roy* pressbook (United Artists, 1995), p. 2.
2. *Rob Roy* pressbook, p. 3.
3. *Rob Roy* pressbook, p. 3.
4. *Rob Roy* CD-ROM (MGM Interactive, 1995).
5. *Rob Roy* pressbook, p. 5.
6. *Rob Roy* pressbook, p. 5.
7. *Rob Roy* CD-ROM.
8. *Rob Roy* CD-ROM.
9. *Rob Roy* CD-ROM.
10. *Rob Roy* pressbook, p. 7.
11. *Rob Roy* pressbook, pp. 7-8.
12. *Rob Roy* CD-ROM.
13. *Rob Roy* CD-ROM; *Rob Roy* pressbook, pp. 11-12.
14. *Rob Roy* pressbook, p. 14.
15. *Rob Roy* pressbook, p. 15.
16. *Rob Roy* CD-ROM.
17. *Rob Roy* press kit, Gannett syndicated review.
18. *Braveheart* CD-ROM (Midisoft Corporation, 1995).
19. *Braveheart* CD-ROM.
20. *Braveheart* pressbook (Paramount Pictures, 1995), p. 5.
21. Brian Pendreigh, *Mel Gibson and His Movies* (London: Bloomsbury, 1997), p. 193.
22. *Braveheart* pressbook, p. 5.
23. Pendreigh, p. 193.
24. *Braveheart* pressbook, p. 14.
25. *Braveheart* pressbook, p. 11.
26. Pendreigh, p. 184.
27. Pendreigh, p. 207.
28. Pendreigh, p. 208.
29. Desmond Seward, *The Hundred Years War: The English in France, 1337–1453* (New York: Atheneum, 1978), p. 20.
30. Pendreigh, p. 215.
31. Pendreigh, p. 216.
32. Pendreigh, p. 217.
33. Pendreigh, p. 214.
34. Pendreigh, p. 205.
35. Pendreigh, p. 211.
36. *Entertainment Weekly*, 3 October 1997, p. 10.

Bibliography

Primary Sources

Autobiographies and Memoirs

Chaplin, Charles. *My Autobiography*. New York: Simon & Schuster, 1964.

Wiles, Buster. *My Days With Errol Flynn*. Santa Monica: Roundtable, 1988.

Screenplays

The Adventures of Robin Hood. Madison: University of Wisconsin Press, 1979.

Pressbooks, Presskits and Program Books

Braveheart presskit. Paramount Pictures, 1995.

A Challenge for Robin Hood pressbook. 20th Century-Fox Pictures, 1968.

Pearce, Garth. *Robin Hood: Prince of Thieves: The Official Movie Book*. New York: Mallard, 1991.

Rob Roy presskit. United Artists Pictures, 1995.

Robin and Marian pressbook. Columbia Pictures, 1976.

CD-ROMs

Braveheart CD-ROM. Midisoft Corporation, 1995.

Rob Roy CD-ROM. MGM Interactive, 1995.

Newspapers and Trade Papers

Christian Science Monitor, 14 June 1991.

Los Angeles Times, 14 August 1991.

New York, 24 June 1991.

New York Post, 14 June 1991.

Newsday, 14 June 1991.

Time, 24 June 1991.

Variety, 1913–1995.

Village Voice, 25 June 1991.

Secondary Sources

Books About the Robin Hood Legends

Holt, J. C. *Robin Hood*. London: Thames and Hudson, 1982.

Keen, Maurice. *The Outlaws of Medieval Legend*. New York: Dorset, 1989.

Knight, Stephen. *Robin Hood: A Complete Study of the English Outlaw*. Oxford: Blackwell, 1994.

Phillips, Graham, and Martin Keatman. *Robin Hood: The Man Behind the Myth*.
    London: Michael O'Mara, 1995.

BOOKS ABOUT ENGLISH HISTORY

Barlow, Frank, ed. and trans. *The Life of King Edward who rests at Westminster*.
    (*Vita Edwardi*.) Oxford: Clarendon, 1992.
Gillingham, John. *Richard the Lionheart*. New York: Times, 1978.
Goodman, Anthony. *The Wars of the Roses*. New York: Dorset, 1981.
Howarth, David. *1066: The Year of the Conquest*. New York: Barnes and Noble, 1993.
Seward, Desmond. *The Hundred Years War: The English in France, 1337–1453*.
    New York: Atheneum, 1978.
Somerset Fry, Plantagenet. *The Kings and Queens of England and Scotland*. New
    York: Grove, 1990.
Swanton, Michael, trans. *The Lives of the Last Englishmen*. London: Garland, 1984.
Treece, Henry. *The Crusades*. New York: Barnes and Noble, 1994.
Wilson, Derek. *The Tower: The Tumultuous History of the Tower of London from
    1078*. New York: Charles Scribner's Sons, 1979.

BOOKS ABOUT SCOTTISH HISTORY

Duncan, A. A. M. *Scotland: The Making of the Kingdom*. Edinburgh: Mercat,
    1992.
Fry, Peter, and Fiona Somerset Fry. *The History of Scotland*. New York: Barnes and
    Noble, 1995.
Goldstein, R. James. *The Matter of Scotland: Historical Narrative in Medieval
    Scotland*. Lincoln: University of Nebraska Press, 1993.
Gray, D. J. *William Wallace: The King's Enemy*. London: Robert Hale, Ltd., 1991.
Keay, John, and Julia Keay. *Collins Encyclopedia of Scotland*. London: HarperCol-
    lins, 1994.
Lindsay, Maurice. *Burns: The Man, His Work, the Legend*. London: Granada, 1971.
Mackay, James. *William Wallace: Brave Heart*. Edinburgh: Mainstream, 1995.
Murray, W. H. *Rob Roy MacGregor: His Life and Times*. Edinburgh: Canongate,
    1995.
Nicholson, Ranald. *Scotland: The Later Middle Ages*. Edinburgh: Mercat, 1993.
Prebble, John. *The Lion in the North: A Personal View of Scotland's History*. New
    York: Coward, McCann and Geohagan, 1971.
Scott, Ronald McNair. *Robert the Bruce: King of Scots*. New York: Peter Bedrick,
    1989.
Tranter, Nigel. *Rob Roy MacGregor*. Moffat, Scotland: Lochar, 1991.

BOOKS ABOUT THE HISTORY OF ARCHERY IN THE BRITISH ISLES

Bradbury, Jim. *The Medieval Archer*. Woodbridge, Suffolk: Boydell, 1985.
Featherstone, Donald. *The History of the English Longbow*. New York: Barnes and
    Noble, 1995.

LITERARY EDITIONS

Byers, George F., ed. *The Valiant Scot by J. W.: A Critical Edition.* New York: Garland, 1980.
Porter, Jane. *The Scottish Chiefs.* New York: Charles Scribner's Sons, 1949.
Pyle, Howard. *The Merry Adventures of Robin Hood of Great Renown in Nottinghamshire.* New York: Dover, 1968.
Rhead, Louis. *Robin Hood.* New York: Random House, 1988.

BIOGRAPHIES

Hancock, Ralph, and Letitia Fairbanks. *Douglas Fairbanks: The Fourth Musketeer.* New York: Henry Holt, 1953.
Herndon, Booton. *Mary Pickford and Douglas Fairbanks.* New York: W. W. Norton, 1977.
Johnson, Edgar. *Sir Walter Scott: The Great Unknown.* New York: MacMillan, 1970.
Keith, Todd. *Kevin Costner: The Unauthorized Biography.* Netley, South Australia: Wilkinson, 1991.
Pendreigh, Brian. *Mel Gibson and His Movies.* London: Bloomsbury, 1997.
Sinatra, Nancy. *Frank Sinatra: An American Legend.* Santa Monica: General, 1995.
Thomas, Tony. *Errol Flynn: The Spy Who Never Was.* Secaucus: Citadel Press, 1990.
Wright, Adrian. *Kevin Costner: A Life on Film.* London: Robert Hale, 1992.
Yule, Andrew. *Sean Connery: From 007 to Hollywood Icon.* New York: Donald I. Fine, 1992.
Zehme, Bill. *The Way You Wear Your Hat: Frank Sinatra and the Lost Art of Livin'.* New York: HarperCollins, 1997.

BOOKS ABOUT AMERICAN AND BRITISH CINEMA

Johnson, Kim ("Howard"). *Life Before and After Monty Python: The Solo Flights of the Flying Circus.* New York: St. Martin's, 1993.
Maltin, Leonard. *The Disney Films.* New York: Crown, 1973.
Nash, J. Robert, and Stanley Ralph Ross. *The Motion Picture Guide.* Chicago: Cinebooks, 1986.
Tibbetts, John C., and James M. Welsh. *His Majesty the American: The Cinema of Douglas Fairbanks, Sr.* New York: A. S. Barnes, 1977.

BOOKS ABOUT FILM ADAPTATIONS OF LITERATURE

Nollen, Scott Allen. *Robert Louis Stevenson: Life, Literature, and the Silver Screen.* Jefferson, North Carolina: McFarland, 1994.
Nollen, Scott Allen. *Sir Arthur Conan Doyle at the Cinema.* Jefferson, North Carolina: McFarland, 1996.

PERIODICALS

Behlmer, Rudy. *Erich Wolfgang Korngold Society Newsletter*, No. 6 (January 1984).
Entertainment Weekly, 3 October 1997.
Films in Review, August 1991.

Index

Numbers in **boldface** indicate photographs or illustrations.

253